● The Best of L.A.

● **BY THE STAFF OF THE** *L.A.WEEKLY*

The
BEST
Of
LA

■ EDITED BY MARY BETH CRAIN

Chronicle Books • San Francisco

Printed in the United States of America.

**Library of Congress Cataloging in
Publication Data**
Main entry under title:
L.A. weekly's Best of L.A.
    1. Los Angeles (Calif.)—Description—
Guide-books. I. Crain, Mary Beth.
II. L.A. weekly. III. Title: L.A. weekly's
Best of L.A. IV. Title: Best of L.A.
F869.L83L15 1984   917.94″940453
84-3139
ISBN 0-87701-306-3

Composition: Accent & Alphabet

Chronicle Books
870 Market Street
San Francisco, CA 94102

Table of Contents

About the Editor:

Mary Beth Crain is a freelance writer currently working as the Associate Entertainment Editor for the *L.A. Weekly.* She has written for numerous major publications, among them the *Los Angeles Times, Chicago Sun-Times, Los Angeles Herald-Examiner, Detroit Free Press, Playgirl Magazine, American Film Magazine,* and others.

Contributors:

Judith Auberjonois, Bill Bentley, Jeff Berry, Anne Braff, Janet Cunningham, Jodi H. Curlee, Reggie Daniel, Brad Dunning, Laura Escovar, Jerry Frankel, Pleasant Gehman, Kathy McGuire, Judy Raphael, Jed Rasula, Don Ray, Bruce D. Rhodewalt, Manette Beth Rosen, Bob Sawyer, Pat Smith, Zan Stewart, John Sutton-Smith, Phil Tracy, Julie Wheelock.

Authors of Special Sections:

Mary Katherine Aldin is the *L.A. Weekly*'s rhythm and blues columnist and is the host of several music programs on local radio.

Margaret Bach is a former editor of *L.A. Architect.*

Sharon Bell is the Calendar assistant at the *L.A. Weekly.*

John Chase is the author of the book *Exterior Decor.*

Joie Davidow is the Entertainment and Style Editor of the *L.A. Weekly.*

Ken Dickmann is a freelance writer for the *L.A. Weekly.*

Hunter Drohojowska is the *L.A. Weekly*'s Art Editor.

Ann Edelman is the former Associate Calendar Editor of the *L.A. Weekly.*

Michael Fatula is a freelance writer for the *L.A. Weekly.*

Alice Fisher is a reference librarian at Santa Monica Public Library.

Anne Haskins is the *L.A. Weekly*'s dance columnist.

Steve Holley is a writer and active member of the Los Angeles gay community.

Christi Kissell is the editor of the *Community Resources Directory.*

Sharon McDonald is a freelance writer and syndicated columnist in the gay press.

Jude McGee writes many of the *L.A. Weekly* Shopping Guides.

Kathi Norklun is the former Associate Art Editor of the *L.A. Weekly.*

Carolyn Reuben is the *L.A. Weekly*'s Health Editor.

Les Paul Robley is a freelance writer for the *L.A. Weekly.*

In Memoriam?

THE BIGGEST NUT ON A SKATEBOARD

There used to be a marvelous crack-pot in Westwood, who skateboarded through the Village — dressed in track shorts, feathers, and beads — using ski poles. But he was nothing compared to L.A.'s Skateboard Lunatic. *He* used to slide down the notoriously steep hill of La Cienega Boulevard from Sunset to Santa Monica boulevards. To live, he had to brave the incredible, San Francisco–like La Cienega grade, make green lights at two major intersections, and come to a complete stop at one of the busiest streets in the city. Once he made it on a single *roller* skate. The Biggest Nut on a Skateboard has not been seen since the summer of 1980.

Introduction

The L.A. Weekly's Best of L.A. can perhaps best be described as one large multisensory mood piece—an attempt to simulate, through words and pictures, the actual experience of encountering one of the world's great and insane urban centers.

Because of its distinctive peculiarity, L.A., in many ways, defies classification. Boston has its history, New York its urbanity, San Francisco its fantasy, Cleveland its reality. These are the good children, the ones that can at least be defined, comprehended, cataloged.

L.A., by comparison, is the class delinquent. Like a huge, ungainly Gulliver among its smaller, more proper peers, our city sits, or rather sprawls, in its geographical seat, unable to be disciplined, let alone reasoned with.

L.A. is the one that wears the "I Hate All Your Friends" T-shirt, dyes its flattop a flaming shade of beet, puts its Niked feet up on the desk, and cracks everybody up. Yes, L.A.'s got its problems, but its personality rather makes up for them. Rude, engaging, beautiful, ugly, smart, vacuous, predictable, mysterious—this is not, in short, a common city. Neither is it an easy city to get to know. But perhaps the following pages will make this task a bit less intimidating.

By way of a disclaimer: this book is not the gospel. There's always room for disagreement, after all, and besides, we would have needed several hundred more people, pages, and years to cover everything in this monster metropolis. By the same token, although we've done our best to give you The Best in terms of accuracy, inevitable changes may have occurred during the time lag between galleys and printing. In general, however, most of this material is (A) authentic and (B) current, and for those few places or individuals that have changed addresses, phone numbers, or identities, well—just have yourself a ball with L.A.'s dozen or so phone directories, or simply dial 411, where a helpful operator will be standing by to tell you to use your phone book whenever possible.

Before I sign off and your tour begins, let's offer special thanks to your tour guides: the contributors, listed on the following page, and the entire staff of the L.A. Weekly, in particular: the stoic art editor, Cindy Roberts, and her assistants, Judy Aakhus and Annie Jackson; the indefatigable typesetting team, headed by Liz Weston; the ad staff; the production staff; and last, but assuredly not least, managing editor Phil Tracy and editor-in-chief Jay Levin, without whose confidence, coaching, and ridiculous optimism this project would still be the figment of someone's imagination.

—Mary Beth Crain, Editor

1.

CITY LIFE

Welcome to L.A.

BEST PLACES TO WATCH THE SUNSET

1. Take a nice drive north on the Pacific Coast Highway and turn right (if you turn left, it's good-bye) on Topanga Canyon Boulevard. Keep driving and you'll gradually notice that the higher you go the better the view. Take one of the winding small roads to the right and about half an hour later you should be somewhere near the clouds, at which point you'll be able to see the city, the ocean, the mountains all at once, in a panorama resembling one of those ancient Japanese silkscreens with the weird, everything-piled-on-top-of-everything perspective. As an added bonus, get out of the car and breathe deeply. The funny smell is fresh air. This is also close to the best view in L.A., which is owned by aging Zen hippie Lewis Beach Marvin III, heir to the Green Stamp fortune. He's got the highest spot on the mountain (identifiable by the antenna) and the closer you get to it, the better the chance you'll have the second best view. Truly breathtaking.

2. Going north on Pacific Coast Highway in Malibu, take a right on Corral Canyon Road (beyond Malibu Canyon Road). Climb all the way to the top, where the road dead ends. A trail to the right leads to some huge boulders, which you may scale without too much effort, from which you get virtually a 360-degree panorama —to the east, the west San Fernando Valley, to the west and south, the Pacific, and mountains everywhere else. What makes this view of a good sunset something more than your average spectacular Malibu beach sunset are (1) it is blessedly quiet up here, and (2) the command of so broad a view makes for a great variety in the play of light on the various types of terrain.

BEST PLACE TO SEE DISNEYLAND FIREWORKS FOR FREE

Every night of the summer at nine o'clock sharp Disneyland conducts its "Fantasy in the Sky" fireworks show, a display *so* big, and *so* dependable, that folks all over Orange County go outside at the appointed time to watch, just as if it were the six o'clock news. But here's a tip: any time you want, you can see this for absolutely nothing—and from a better vantage point than those folks who paid to get into the park. Just take the Santa Ana Freeway south and get off at the Ball Road exit. Continue straight across Ball onto Global Way, then make a left and immediately park in the little dusty parking lot. The fireworks are ignited about 100 feet to the south, in the employee parking lot. This is the closest you can get to them without getting a pyrotechnician's license or breaking a law.

BEST ETHNICALLY MIXED NEIGHBORHOOD

Wilshire District between Vermont and Western. Do you harbor a secret desire to have a Japanese driving instructor? Have you been searching for a Cuban grocery store? Are you curious about the ritual at a Korean Christian Church? All of these experiences and more are available in this part of the Wilshire District, where in the same apartment building you might have a chatty neighbor from Belfast and a gregarious couple from Amsterdam. A few intersections in another direction, black professionals are buying up condominiums. And if you want to know if money is in *your* future, you can seek out the Gypsy fortune teller with the sign in her window. Mexican-American men gather around cars (operable and otherwise) and exchange the day's news, while the women shop at the local market, which is owned and operated by a large and amicable tribe of Armenians. Old Jewish women compare aches and pains at the bus stop as they head west to Fairfax, while a Korean bartender opens his doors for the day and drills himself on basic Spanish. There's even a pleasant sprinkling of white-bread Americans on the streets. If America is a melting pot, the flame is at its highest here. A great place to visit or in which to live.

MOST INTERESTING WALK

Downtown L.A. Only in L.A., where people still learn to walk, even though, thank God, they don't have to, can you find a four-block urban walking tour that encompasses not one inch of sidewalk. Le Corbusier would have been proud. Start in the vast lobby of the Security Pacific Bank Building on Hope Street at the top of Bunker Hill, and take the sky ramp to the World Trade Center, walking through its long lobby to yet another sky ramp, this one leading to the antiseptic cavern of the Bonaventure Hotel. From that lobby, take the curving staircase to level three and a third ramp, over Fifth Street, then down a steep escalator into the dungeonlike shopping mall under the Arco Towers. Here you might want to surface in the south tower lobby for a look at the mammoth art deco elevator doors, a reminder of the splendor of the old building destroyed on this site. Conclude your walking tour by taking the Sixth Street escalator up to the street, where you'll have to walk on real sidewalks if you want to continue anywhere.

BEST NEIGHBORHOOD IN WHICH TO DROWN IN HOLLYWOOD NOSTALGIA

Whitley Heights Rudolph Valentino used to thrill the ladies as he walked around the streets of Whitley Heights. He also loved to tinker with his collection of old cars, which he kept in Francis X. Bushman's several garages. Valentino and Bushman's houses are long since gone, but many of the imposing Mediterranean homes of their day still stand on the hill that rises above Franklin and Highland avenues in Hollywood. Built by developer Hobart J. Whitley in the '20s and '30s and modeled after Italian villas, each was unique, and all were ingeniously designed to fit into the hillside. The exteriors have stone lions and stone pillars, tiled staircases, courtyards with fountains, turrets, towers, balconies, and gardens lush with magnolia and oleander. Inside are carved fireplaces, high-ceiling rooms trimmed with ornate painted designs, rotundas, and circular staircases. Among the famous residents were Marie Dressler, Marion Davies, Beulah Bondi, Katharine Cornell, Ethel Barrymore, and Gloria Swanson. (William Faulkner wrote screenplays here, and Richard Barthelmess and Norma Talmadge had a hot love affair.) Now Whitley Heights is a National Historical Landmark and it's well worth a hike around the steep, hilly streets to admire it. North of Franklin Ave. and east of Highland Ave., Hollywood.

BEST PLACE TO SEE A VALLEY GIRL

The Sherman Oaks Galleria "On Ventura, there she goes, She's just bought some bitchin' clothes." The Sherman Oaks Galleria jumped from the obscurity of being just another chic suburban shopping mall when Moon Unit Zappa extolled its virtues in the now famous Valley girl song. The Galleria's got some really awesome clothing stores, super novelty shops, tubular theaters, and dynamite eateries, for sure. But they're not easy to find. The floors are designated by colors rather than numbers, presumably because Valley girls can't count. Noo biggie. It's more fun watching the girls than shopping. But beware, Valley girls and their mothers look just alike, right down to the miniskirt and pedicure. The mothers, however, are the ones with the little surgical scars behind their ears. At the intersection of Sepulveda and Ventura blvds., Sherman Oaks (not quite in Encino, Moon Unit).

BOY–WATCH
GIRL–WATCH

ABC Entertainment Center and Plaza
In *chic alors* Century City, you can park yourself in the plaza at lunchtime or 5 P.M. and watch these two austere towers empty out hundreds of professional/secretarial young things. Here hot men in hot suits mingle with women sporting trendy sheers and tousled tresses. The Look is the thing, and if you just want to observe the sexes at their most fashionable, sensual best, this is the place. If, however, you're into a little less style and a little more skin, try:

Main Street in Venice, U.S.A. This is where you'll see legs. Hairy ones, smooth ones, slim ones, cellulitic ones —everybody's got their track shorts on and their sweatsuits off on funky, classy Main Street. Tall, statuesque blondes on the existential quest for the right look to bring their life together trip along in athletic style next to furry-chested jocks and slim, trim beachies. On a Saturday or Sunday, you'll see them all.

MOST UNRESTRAINED NEIGHBORHOOD ART

St. Elmo's Village is a monument to man's individuality and creativity. A cross between the Watts Towers and Grandma Prisbrey's Bottle Village, the cluster of bungalows that was once squalid housing for migrant farm workers has been transformed into a primitive, psychedelic-jungle plea for peace and brotherhood. There are sculptures made from discarded trash, and all the courtyards and driveways have been wildly painted. (If you've seen the Famous Amos parking lot on Sunset, you're familiar with the artist's work.) Wisely declared a cultural landmark, the site is often used for community gatherings and as a children's art center. 4830 St. Elmo Dr., Los Angeles (take La Brea south past Venice Blvd., then go east on St. Elmo Dr.).

BEST NEON SIGN

Felix On a crisp, clear night, as you're headed east on the Santa Monica Freeway going onto the Harbor Freeway, keep your eyes peeled for one of L.A.'s oldest and most illustrious keepers of the light, Felix the Cat, who, in giant neon form, watches over all of us from his perch atop Felix Chevrolet. Felix dates from 1921, which makes him eligible for status as an historical figure of sorts, and, frankly, the Washington Monument and the Statue of Liberty literally pale before him. It's truly a mystical and thrilling experience to see him twinkling all in blue, red, and green, his bright cat eyes blazing and blinking over the city. 3330 S. Jefferson Blvd. (at Figueroa St.), downtown.

BEST LOVERS' SPOTS

When romance comes to mind, one's thoughts naturally revert to real cities like San Francisco or New York. Or to mythical cities, like Shangri-la or Daytona Beach. Believe it or not, though, L.A. has its share of sites conducive to the budding and flowering of the delicate bloom of love, a few of which are:

The Four Oaks Cafe You don't need to fly to Vienna to find an intimate haunt with a string quartet, and an occasional harp or sobbing guitar. The Four Oaks has everything you'll need in the way of a tender rendevous, with its dim but not murky candlelight, quiet elegance, and thoroughly professional host-owner Jack Allen, who will be happy to escort you to your very own corner table and will throw you out if you ask for catsup. 2181 Beverly Glen, Bel Air; 474-9317.

The Huntington Gardens Not on a weekend, of course, when everybody and his great-aunt from Oshkosh come to ooh and ah over some of the most spectacular grounds and gardens in the U.S. But try this place, just the two of you, on a deserted weekday morning or afternoon. You can take your pick of benches or paths in the renowned Cactus Garden; you can lie together near the stream in the Zen Garden; you can take turns reading the Bard's winsome quotes in the Shakespeare Garden, or you can just plain walk off into one of the myriad forests or glens and never come back. In case you get hungry, though, there's a lovely little outdoor-indoor restaurant just past the Rose Garden, where you can moon over yogurt or a can of V8. 1151 Oxford Rd., San Marino.

Temescal Canyon We hate to give this place away, but here goes: take the Pacific Coast Highway to Temescal Canyon Boulevard, turn right, and go up on Temescal north of Sunset. You can park near the YMCA and then head on into a truly glorious hiking and/or cuddling paradise, complete with babbling brooks, mountaintop views, tangled brush, and, for the herb freak, a host of naturally sprouting varieties. Beware of warm weekends, when city dwellers and ghetto blasters tend to make a mockery of all that is sweet. But for a weekday or night trysting ground, it's a classic.

The Bel Air Hotel If you're in the bucks, or having a heavy affair and want to indulge, this is the place to disappear into an elegant, gracious, and artful Other World. Serene and lovely, with a quiet turn-of-the-century elegance and superb room service, you can move your nitrous tank into a suite and party to your and your lover's hearts' content, with nary a murmur from the very discreet staff. If you can't afford the room fee, you can still walk around on the grounds and hold hands and, if you can't resist, slip into the foliage for a quick one while the gray-haired darlings toddle on by. Watch for the hotel turnoff sign on Sunset Boulevard in Bel Air.

The Inn of the Seventh Ray Situated high up in the hills of scenic Topanga Canyon, The Inn of the Seventh Ray is one of the most beautiful outdoor-indoor places at which to meet, eat, stroll, etc. The simple, rustic facade in no way prepares one for what lies inside—tables with linen cloths and candles flickering in the night air situated right beside a running stream, while music by Beethoven or Pachelbel assails one's ears and an excellent display of dinner items and wines assails one's palate. Eat late and go for an after-dark wander along surrounding canyon paths. 128 Old Topanga (corner of Topanga and Old Topanga Canyon blvds.), Topanga Canyon; 455-1331.

Paradise Cove—The Sandcastle This well-known restaurant that graces the entrance to infamous Paradise Cove may be a Howard Johnson's cleverly disguised as a Cape Cod cottage, but nobody can fake the gorgeous surroundings. While the food is unspectacular, many pre-mad-affair dinners have been had here, followed by a moonlight stroll and whatever else on the beach. If your table's by the window, you can clasp hands and watch the sunset. 28128 Pacific Coast Hwy., Malibu; 457-2503.

BEST LOVERS' BAR

Zindabad Pub A plush little East Indian—style hideway for nurturing a budding romance or adding fuel to a flourishing one. The ambience is discreet, from pierced-brass lanterns to pillowy corners. Drinks are generous and service is quiet. If the nuzzling gets too heavy, the bartender steps in, but discreetly. All the world loves a lover, especially at the Zindabad Pub. Beverly-Wilshire Hotel, 9500 Wilshire Blvd., Beverly Hills; 275-4282.

BEST PUBLIC NECKING PLACES

Any departure gate at LAX Just saunter up and get lost in the crowd of fond farewells. It doesn't matter that you're not going anywhere. Everyone is too busy weeping and kissing to notice.

The exterior glass elevator at the Bonaventure Hotel.

The Haunted Mansion at Disneyland for necrophiliactic fellow travelers.

The top deck of the Catalina Ferry for best bussing on a boat.

The back seat of a parked car on Mulholland Drive. Just be sure you've got the emergency brake on. The earth won't move, but your car might.

The Santa Monica Pier merry-go-round. Hint: don't eat corn dogs first.

UCLA's Franklin Murphy Sculpture Garden. There are plenty of secluded spots in the foliage, but beware of tenured profs looking down from Bunche Hall.

The Norton Simon Museum of Art in Pasadena. Not only is this one hell of an art museum, but it's also erotically romantic, what with all those sensuous outdoor sculptures lining a pristine pool and overlooking some of the finest mountain scenery around. Go there on a weekday afternoon and neck away, or if you must neck in public on a crowded weekend, just take a pose as Rodin's "Lovers Embracing." So what if Rodin never did a "Lovers Embracing"? You know that people'll believe anything in L.A.

The benches at Palisades Park, Santa Monica. Great view of the ocean and the mountains, and the only people to witness your sin will be joggers, who'll be moving too fast to harrass you, derelicts, who'll be moving too slowly to harass you, and senior citizens, who might shake an occasional cane at you. Big deal.

The escalator at the Beverly Center. The answer to everyone's most sadistic public-necking fantasies. There you are, going full steam ahead, while everybody else is forced to participate as captive audience. For a real rousing finale, try causing a pile up at the eighth floor.

BEST BACKGAMMON CLUB

Cavendish Club Serious backgammon players will find the liveliest game in town at the Cavendish Club, a newly renovated membership club tucked speakeasy style on the second floor of a Sunset Strip high rise. As you enter the smoke-filled premises, you'll hear the friendly greeting *salam-alek* ("hello" in Farsi) from a coterie of Iranian emigres, not tired, not poor, not humble, but yearning to roll well. You are also more than likely to meet some bridge and backgammon champs and a celeb or two. Rubber, bridge, gin, even an occasional game of pinochle or chess provides some time diversion for the rare devotee who feels backgammoned out. Members may bring guests; nonmembers may play on the two tournament nights. On Tuesday, it's an intermediate tournament at 8:15 P.M. ($25); on Thursday, there's an open tournament at 8 P.M. ($50). A bonus: good, home-cooked food at reasonable prices. 9255 W. Sunset Blvd., West Hollywood; 540-1333.

BEST WEIRD PLACES TO VISIT

Opinions in this category vary, depending on what drug you're on or what may be your particular perversions. One person, for instance, thought churches were weird; another's favorite weird spot was the Akron on a Sunday afternoon. Needless to say, these suggestions were not ventured from Orange County. Personal idiosyncrasies aside, we think the following places are definitely weird.

The Breathing Bush So what's the big deal; Moses knew a burning one. Only his, as far as we know, didn't happen to be in L.A. Seriously folks, there is a Breathing Bush; whether it heaves, pants, or merely inhales and exhales normally can be answered only by those who have actually seen it. This phenomenon has been reported by local high schoolers in the Burbank area, but as far as the exact location goes, you'll have to ask a Valley girl. All we know is that it's somewhere on Glen Oaks Boulevard.

Pyramid Birds There can't be anywhere else quite like Pyramid Birds, or Parrotdise, as it is otherwise known. As a members-only establishment devoted to feather flappers of all colors and creeds, Pyramid is unsurpassed in bird service. There's the beauty salon, which provides shampoos, blow drying, and manicures;

the Parritz Hotel, with private perches and meals; a bird maternity ward and, of course, Parrotdise Charm School, where your fresh-mouthed pet can learn to speak elegantly and keep his beak to himself. A must for a weird afternoon. 1407 W. Magnolia Blvd., Burbank; 843-5505.

The Union Bank "Historical" Museum As a bewildering phenomenon of the late 20th century, banks have been jumping with studied abandon into the realm of Culture. First came art, then sculpture, and now there are museums, the strangest of which belongs to the downtown Union Bank. First of all, it's almost never open. Second, when it *is* open, it offers for your viewing pleasure such curious items as replicas of the pens used to sign the Declaration of Independence and a large collection of malachite. There is probably also a globe that came along with a complete set of the *World Book Encyclopedia*. Very weird. Mon.–Fri., noon–2 P.M.. Main Plaza, Union Bank Building and Figueroa, downtown; 236-7386.

The Olympic Auditorium Strangest crowd in L.A., bar none. On fight nights, it's an assemblage of Fellini, Buñuel, the racetrack on a Tuesday afternoon, the barrio, and Damon Runyon without a bath. Forget the grime of the old auditorium. Forget the gym lighting. Forget the stench of antiseptic beer piss. This is Real Life in all its glory. And it's safer than you think. And twice as dangerous. 1801 S. Grand Ave., downtown; call 749-5171 for programs.

The Merle Norman Tower of Beauty This strange, windowless building rises mysteriously out of the arid plains of Sylmar. It has, however, nothing to do with cosmetics or facials; within its walls lies Merle

Norman's tribute to all that is beautiful. The Tower of Beauty is actually a hodgepodge museum of things like antique cars, nickelodeons, and other wonderful but thoroughly idiosyncratic items, all jumbled together under the same benevolent roof. Here Rudy Vallee's private touring car shares equal time with Franz Josef of Austria's own Steinway grand. One of the highlights of the place is the strangely lit dining room at one end of the second floor, with antique furnishings and cherubs sailing about on the ceiling. Another is the nickelodeon room, with some real ancient beauties. A visitor best described the Tower of Beauty as Las Vegas's version of The Louvre. Mon.–Fri., 8:30 A.M.–4 P.M.; tours Tues.–Sat., 10 A.M.–1:30 P.M.; call 367-1085 for advance reservations. 15180 Bledsoe, Sylmar.

The Old Zoo There is hardly a more depressing outing than a trip to the L.A. Zoo, where poor misplaced animals swelter under unrelenting heat and smog. Much more interesting are the ruins of the old zoo, nestled in a small canyon just past a bunch of park vehicles and heavy equipment. Here you can swing like monkeys in deserted and mangled cages and follow narrow, dark, winding stone-lined passages deep underground, coming up into cool, stone-moat-surrounded caves that once harbored bears and elephants. There is an eerie and very cinematic feel to this area, which is located behind the high fenches right across from the Griffith Park merry-go-round and accessible through a small tunnel that runs under the roadway. Griffith Park Dr. (across from merry-go-round), Los Feliz.

Forest Lawn Why drive around for hours looking at houses where the "stars" live when you can see the graves where the bodies lie rotting? For instance, at Forest Lawn, that Disneyland of cemeteries, lie the remains of such notables as Walt Disney, Clark Gable, Theda Bara, Jean Harlow, Errol Flynn, Spencer Tracy, and many more. But the resting places themselves are just a small part of Forest Lawn's exciting "attractions," such as Babyland, where your entrance automatically trips a tape playing lullabies; the famous *Smiling Jesus* statue; a huge re-creation of the Last Supper in stained glass; a monstrous mural of the crucifixion; and some of the most stupendously tacky "artistic" reproductions on the planet. 1712 S. Glendale Ave., Glendale; 254-3131.

2380 Laurel Canyon Boulevard Here you'll find a grandiose, weed-covered romantic stairway that leads to nothing. All that is left of a never-finished mansion that was being built by Harry Houdini is meandering paths, stairs, stone benches, and a garage and servant's quarters. There are numerous tales of hauntings on these grounds and a recent trip there at 4 A.M. found a group of hippies sitting around an open fire chanting the "a-weem-a-wek" chorus from "The Lion Sleeps Tonight."

BEST RESTROOM

Los Angeles Theater For some reason, the male half of the species could not come up with a winner in this category, so honors go to the ladies, and in particular, to the Los Angeles Theater. The building itself shouldn't be missed; it's an exuberant sort of French Renaissance explosion built in 1931 (Charlie Chaplin's *City Lights* premiered there). To find the ladies' room, simply descend a wide, carpeted double stairway and there it is, just off the palatial wood-paneled ballroom. You will enter an arched doorway into a spacious oval foyer, where 13 — yes, 13 — graceful carved mahogany dressing tables with mirrors are set into the wall. Ceiling and walls are ornamented with rococo painted plaster designs, and a fabulous chandelier lights it all. The toilet booths, which, sadly, have seen better days, were a wonder in their time, as each is made from a different kind of marble. Eat your hearts out, guys. 615 S. Broadway, downtown.

BEST FREE ORGAN CONCERTS

First Congregational Church Despite whatever else you may have heard, the largest organ in L.A. is in the First Congregational Church—and they know how to use it. Every Tuesday and Thursday at noon, the Skinner-Schlicker organ, under the confident control of resident organist Lloyd Holzgraf, shivers timbers from chancel to narthex in half-hour free concerts. Until the music begins, the great gothic sanctuary, with its nave of midnight-blue stained glass and cool stone, might lead you to assume that the sounds will be dignified and subdued. Propulsive baroque fugues appear, however, side by side with 20th-century fanfares and ferocious romantic pieces that would scare Lon Chaney. Not counting the percussive attachments—yes, those are real bells—the organ has 11,848 pipes, from piccolo size to giant brass monsters 36 feet tall and as big around as an elephant's forearm. Those are the ones you *don't* hear, the 16 Hz chest rattlers that'll have you on your knees in a second, praying for mercy. Which, of course, is precisely what a good church organ is for. Sixth St. and Commonwealth Ave., downtown.

BEST PLACES TO EAVESDROP

The elevators in the Criminal Courts Building, which are crowded and move slowly, allowing time to hear lots of intriguing buzz. Also piquant is the freight elevator, which moves faster and is used by lawyers and DAs in a hurry.

Any DMV or Post Office Good for mass hostility, rage, and hysteria, or individual breakdowns.

Movie lines at the revival houses. Forget Westwood; the conversations are as interchangeable as the people and movies.

That old EDer's standby, the Hollywood Unemployment Office, is better than ever.

The Fairfax and downtown city bus runs. Tons of outspoken ethnicity of the most picturesque flavor.

Rodeo Drive and the curbside at Chasen's Restaurant (Beverly Hills). Best spots for tourists ear-hungry for celebs.

Any beach on Ocean Front Walk in Venice, especially the ones nearest the Israel Levin Center, where juniors sass seniors and vice versa.

Small claims court for drama and traffic court for whoppers.

Large brokerage houses, where the regulars gather to watch the tape. Tall tales by small investors of high finance.

The bathrooms at Filmex Highbrow film analysis and unpressured relief.

BEST WAY TO WATCH THE SKY

The L.A. Astronomical Society In the midst of smog, noise, and general world madness, it's comforting to know that above us the universe goes right on doing its dark, cold, starry things. Keeping tabs on these celestial events, the L.A. Astronomical Society holds monthly meetings, arranges for star treks to nearby observatories, and operates an information service for schools and local organizations. Prospective members are welcome. Meetings are the second Monday of every month, except July and August, at 7:45 P.M. at either the Griffith Park Observatory or the Department of Water and Power. 833-NOVA; July and August, call 834-4383.

BEST STREET MUSICIAN

The Androgynous Drummer Most often found on weekends north of Windward Avenue on Ocean Front, this percussionist's kit consists of an empty Sparklettes bottle, a large plastic bucket, several pots and pans, and a shattered cymbal that sounds like a schizophrenic fire bell. What saves the drummer from complete cacophony is a pair of wrists that is a study in elegance. They flick the sticks with the ease and speed of a professional performer. The player, who couldn't be older than a midteen, is clearly marching to the beat of a different drummer way beyond the rudimentary, somewhere off in the spheres.

BEST LEGENDARY FEMALE FLASHER

She does not wear a trench coat. L.A.'s female flasher is a voluptuous blonde who strolls Santa Monica Boulevard between Fairfax and La Cienega on hot summer afternoons in a frilly white housecoat. She prefers the north side of the street—the tanning side. With a smile of purest innocence, she engages the attention of young male passersby. The moment they look up from their bus schedules or newspapers to return her smile, she throws open her housecoat, flashing lewdly at her victim. To date, none have screamed or called the police.

BEST PLACE IN WHICH TO SLIP BACKWARD INTO ANOTHER ERA

Bullock's Wilshire Built in 1929, Bullock's Wilshire is an architectural triumph, with its handsome vertical lines, its art deco ornamentation, and its distinctive green copper tower rising above Wilshire Boulevard. Patrons drive through ornate gates to the parking lot, then enter the store through a glass-walled port cochere,
glancing in passing, of course, at the famous transportation mural on the ceiling. Inside is a fantasy land of marble, wood paneling, and art deco design. Everyone seems polite and decorous, and the service makes one feel like an old-time aristocrat. Particularly famed is the spacious fifth-floor tearoom, a peaceful retreat of soft carpets, gold-framed mirrors, chandeliers, and fabric-decorated walls. Soft salon music plays in the background, while Umberto, the maitre d' who has presided there for over 25 years, ushers well-coiffed ladies to their tables. An hour or two spent in Bullock's is balm for the soul. 3050 Wilshire Blvd., Los Angeles.

BEST EMPTY SWIMMING POOL

In Hollywood at the very top of Fuller Avenue, north of Franklin, stand the sagging iron gates of the old Huntington Hartford estate. Enter if you dare; the entire canyon was originally sown with rare tropical plants from around the world, and their dying and choking remains make for an eerie setting. The main house is gone; only a surreal series of steps leading nowhere remains. An out-of-control cactus garden is still a sight to behold; it's so large and cavelike you can walk inside it. But the real payoff comes when you follow the road all the way to the top of the hill, past the old tennis court. Perched on a cliff, with a panoramic view of the L.A. basin from downtown to the sea, is a deserted swimming pool and a crumbling rock pool house (once occupied by Errol Flynn)—a sad, extravagant reminder of past glory and opulent Hollywood life-style.

BEST NEARBY TOWN IN WHICH TO SPEND A DAY ON FOOT

San Pedro Founded as a fishing town, San Pedro has old houses with porches and cupolas, a wonderful ethnic mix and a great view of the harbor, of the bridge, and of numerous ships. Stoned or straight, it's a pleasant outing. If you're feeling touristy, check out the Cabrillo Marine Museum to learn about food chains and who eats what. Outside is a whale skeleton and a sign that says Please Touch. Nearby is a wide, sandy strand for swimming. And there are several good restaurants. Coming back, you might stop at the Banning House in Wilmington. Built by railroad and ship magnate Phineas Banning, this is a huge, handsome Greek Revival building dating from 1864. Cabrillo Marine Museum, 3720 Stephen White Dr., San Pedro. Banning House, 401 E. M St., Wilmington.

BEST PLACE TO MAKE YOU FEEL BETTER ABOUT WHERE YOU ALREADY LIVE

The long, dark, littered tunnel under the Sixth Street Bridge leading down to the concrete-lined Los Angeles River bed. It's an area of desolate train tracks, old warehouses, and burnt-out Amtrak cars now inhabited by pigeons. Overhead the sky is a maze of power lines and WPA bridges. For warped and twisted beauty, this place can't be beat.

BEST WALKING TOURS OF L.A.

The Conservancy Tours "Sooo big." Such is the universal complaint about this town, if you can call it a town; or this city, if you can call it a city. Sprawling, ungainly, diverse, perverse, it's tough to have a sense of continuity in a place where antique sites are bulldozed in favor of condos and life without wheels is unthinkable. There are, however, a few places in L.A. that you can explore on foot. The Los Angeles Conservancy, for instance, offers several enchanting glimpses of the quainter side of the roaring metropolis. Dedicated to the preservation of historic buildings, The Conservancy has two main tours, one of Pershing Square and architectural monuments such as the old Biltmore and the Bradbury, and another of the Broadway theater district's classic old movie palaces. Get your culture and your workout all in one. Los Angeles Conservancy Tours, leaving every Saturday at 10 A.M. from the Subway Terminal Bldg., 417 S. Hill St.; for reservations (required), call 623-CITY.

Round Town Tours The emphasis here is on ethnic culture, with some of the popular jaunts being to neighborhoods like Little Tokyo, Little Armenia, and, of course, the Chinatown Adventure, an in-depth tour of L.A.'s version of Hong Kong, Peking et al. Stops at such native haunts as Argentine delis, Indian spice stores, and, for the masochists, the flower market at *dawn* followed by a peek at the nearby Japanese Gardens, make this a varied (to say the least) experience. If you can't make it to the Orient or Athens this year, Round Town Tours are the next best thing. Call 836-7559 for information and reservations.

BEST PRIVATE LANDSCAPING

Mr. George Wagner's House In Los Angeles, where you are not allowed to have leaves on the sidewalk, suntans and automobiles dominate the culture, even the horticulture. Starting in the late '20s, architectural styles were influenced by the view from the car. The linear city of Wilshire Boulevard, from the Wilshire District west, is the best example. Landscape architecture seems to have followed the same trend. Most of the marvelous landscaping in L.A. is seen in motion or from a distance. An obsession with suntanning brings about the second most influential aspect of landscape style, shade avoidance. Combine the "driving eye" with shade avoidance and you basically have the "Los Angeles Landscaping Style."

To see a treasure of private landscaping, check out 307 South McCadden (near Beverly) in West Hollywood. Even throughout Beverly Hills, Bel Air, and Brentwood, where money and maintenance can create an appearance, you may never find a more charming and well-designed yard. The landscaper and contractor was the owner, Mr. George Wagner, and you must see his handiwork to appreciate it.

BEST COMMERCIAL LANDSCAPING

The Wells Fargo Bank Building, still under construction downtown, was designed by Bob Carter. At the corner of Fifth and Flower, the bank sits in a stark concrete piazza set in a palm grove containing about 30 matching 30-foot date palms. It is these trees that make the site outstanding. When agriculture was domesticated thousands of years ago, one of the earliest styles to be used in public grounds and palaces was the palm grove, some containing hundreds of palms. This demonstrated order and power and provided shady areas, like a controlled oasis.

The Wells Fargo installation is young, though the palms are quite mature. For purposes of handling and survival, a huge amount of the fronds have been removed. So, be patient. The site will not be fully actualized for about a year, when the palms will become comfortable and full.

BEST PAINTED CEILING

Union Station This classic train station gives a better reason to "neck crane" than any other place in town. A rich and glorious scene hovers above your upturned eyes as you wait for Amtrak. The predominant material is 1930s acoustical tile, in shades of brown, rust, and green, with travertine and Belgian black marble tile wainscoting along the lower walls. At night, Spanish-style fixtures ten feet in diameter illuminate the whole panorama in a glow worthy of the Sistine Chapel. 800 N. Alameda, Los Angeles.

BEST GOLD–INLAID HARDWARE STORE

Andrew's Hardware has got to have the most outrageously gaudy, gorgeous, and unusual building of any hardware store (or any other kind of store) in L.A. Gold inlays and Egyptian motifs crown the walls, making this the best place to pretend you're inside a pyramid. It's for your shopping pleasure, though many folks go simply to gawk. 1660 W. Seventh St., downtown.

BEST PLACE TO FLY A KITE

Take Mulholland Drive west all the way past the San Diego Freeway until it turns into a gravel road. Make a left (the only marker is a simple street corner pole marking the 17100 block) and follow the bumpy road about a quarter mile until you see a squat concrete pumping station. Follow the path up to the second hill, where there's a breathtaking view of the Valley and downtown L.A. (gray miniature buildings peeking through the brown smog), and to the west, the sea and Catalina. The whole area is part of the undeveloped Santa Monica Mountains State Park and the county keeps all these hills mowed for a firebreak. In the spring, the place bears an uncanny resemblance to an alpine meadow, and you half expect to see Julie Andrews, arms open wide, racing toward you. There's a constant breeze, even on what seems like the calmest day, and plenty of wildlife. A haven for misanthropes.

BEST PLACE TO IMAGINE YOU'RE LIVING IN THE FIFTIES

Johnnie's Actually, there's still a wealth of these places in L.A. (The Flying Saucer, Tiny Naylor's, and Ship's Coffee Shop, to name just a few), but a classic has to be Johnnie's, in Culver "The Town That Time Forgot" City. The main attractions here are the individual jukeboxes that sit at every table and on the counters. This is one of the only places that still has these relics. There are other period accoutrements like neon ceiling fans, metal patio-table umbrellas, and gleaming stainless-steel kitchen appliances. But somebody's got to get rid of those hanging macrame plant holders. Sepulveda Blvd. at Washington, Culver City; 397-6654.

BEST BUILDING INSCRIPTION

Seemingly mocking the bus passengers below are the immortal words above the entrance to the modest building at 439 South Hill: "Wealth means power, it means leisure, it means liberty."

BEST SHIPWRECK

Star of Scotland   At various times a warship, a bordello, a gambling ship, and finally a fishing barge, the *Star of Scotland* now lies in 70 feet of water in Santa Monica Bay, providing a lush but rusty home for myriad undersea creatures. She was built as a Q-ship for the U.S. Navy in 1917 to resemble a harmless merchant ship; then, when German U-boats surfaced and demanded surrender, false bulwarks would fall away to reveal hidden guns.

She survived the war and for a while was employed in the mundane task of conveying tourists and produce along the west coast of South America. In the early '30s she became a floating bordello anchored off Ensenada. Another change of owner found her three miles offshore from Santa Monica accommodating a brisk traffic of dabblers in craps, roulette, poker, and slots. The ship was last employed as a fishing barge and party boat and sank in a storm in 1942. Today she can be found 1.7 miles off the north end of Santa Monica breakwater on a bearing of 210 degrees.

BEST BANK GLADE

Security Pacific Bank   Every once in a while a public building exhibiting good taste and creativity pops up, and in the realm of bank landscaping it would be hard to find a more beautiful concept than the plaza outside the Security Pacific on South Hope. From the inside of the bank, workers and patrons can behold, through long glass windows, a great pool surrounded by ivy beds and trees with drooping foliage. Several waterfalls cascade into the pool, which is bordered by a ledge that must make an unbeatable lunch spot. What a place to serve your nine-to-five time. 333 S. Hope, downtown.

Architecture: From the Sublime to the Serendipitous

by John Chase

BEST STUCCO BOX—APARTMENT HOUSE

Bahamas Apartments There must be no doubt in anyone's mind that we are once again in the 1950s. Now that Chevy Bel Airs and wire-basket chairs are the last collectibles, why not go back to the source? The stucco box-apartment house is the offspring of the '50s love for splashy expressionistic modernism married to ruthlessly pragmatic building and development practices. The Pico Boulevard facade of the Bahamas is a billboard of alternating rectangular projections and voids, giving a curiously monumental scale. 1206 Pico Blvd., Santa Monica.

BEST DROP—DEAD ELEGANCE

Case Study House No. 21 (Pierre Koenig, 1958) The Case Study House program was an attempt by John Entenenza's *Arts and Architecture* magazine to popularize and develop the modern house in Southern California. It is uncertain how much the program modified the local public's unquestionable thirst for schlockola (H. L. Mencken was right), but it did leave us with a series of exemplary buildings. House No. 21, the Bailey House, is a smart little steel-and-glass pavilion set adrift on a reflecting pool. Less than this wouldn't have been more. 9036 Wonderland Park Ave., Laurel Canyon.

BEST CIVIC MONUMENT

Pasadena City Hall (John Bakewell, Jr. and Arthur Brown, Jr., 1925–27) In Los Angeles, the town that civic virtue forgot, where everyman's Datsun is a castle on wheels, and to hell with the rest, there are precious few acknowledgments of the collective public aspects of life. Pasadena City Hall is one of these acknowledgments. That it has managed to survive with much of its power intact, despite the repeated efforts of the good city fathers to transform their town into a bloated replica of Glendale, is a testament to design. Its architects, Bakewell and Brown, are also responsible for the San Francisco City Hall. San Francisco's may be grander in the strictly formal sense, but our building is far more pleasant. The palm-decked courtyard and the open belvederelike tower integrate the Southern California climate and landscape into the building. 100 N. Garfield, Pasadena.

BEST LITTLE BUILDING IN LOS ANGELES

Fellowship Park Pavilion (Harwell Hamilton Harris, 1935) A building as unobtrusive as a good waiter, so discreet that it allows one to relax and take in the surroundings. The surroundings here are worth taking in, a lush canyon lost in the hills of Elysian Heights. This is a beautifully made wooden pavilion that could be furnished well with just a few bamboo shades and tatami mats because of its simplicity. 2311 Fellowship Park Way, Echo Park.

BEST FUTURISTIC FANTASY

Union 76 Gas Station A Tom Wolfe fave, this must be the station where the Jetsons fuel up. Shaped like a concave croissant, it throbs with the excitement of Los Angeles's modern-consumer golden age of the '50s and '60s, when the only mobility was upward, gas was cheap, and there was always room for another subdivision in the Valley. Corner of Little Santa Monica Blvd. and Crescent Dr., Beverly Hills.

BEST ICONOCLASTIC BUILDING

Frank O. Gehry House (Frank O. Gehry & Associates, 1978) To the uninitiated, Gehry's house looks like a bunkhouse for the Plasmatics—a collision of chainlink fence, plywood, and corrugated metal set off against the banal domesticity of the original 1920s house. Upon closer examination, however, it becomes readily apparent that this is not just another ugly face, for its appearance is an exposition of the building process raised to the level of art. 1902 22nd St., Santa Monica.

BEST REPRESENTATIVE OF THE SOUTHERN CALIFORNIA GOOD LIFE

Lee Burns House The Burns house is a sybaritic personal paradise, an example of a building fitted to its client, its site, and its period with supernatural adroitness and sensitivity. Each room takes on an identity beyond the usual definition. The tall living room holds a huge organ, the angled stairway corridor is lined with bookcases, a bed becomes a balcony projecting out over the den, and the bathrooms are so spacious, light, and airy that you could happily live in them. 230 Amalfi Dr., Pacific Palisades.

BEST CONSTRUCTIVIST SCULPTURE

Adolphe Tischler House (P. M. Schindler, 1949–50) In the period from World War II to his death in 1953, Schindler employed forms that had complex and ambiguous connotations of flimsiness and impermanence, and he used prosaic elements in extraordinary ways. The Tischler house is composed like a pile of pickup sticks left by a furious child. 175 Greenfield Ave., Westwood.

BEST BAD BUILDING

11111 Building (Rubenstein and Swed, 1982) Can you imagine? The architects responsible for this horror actually located their offices there. You'd think they would be hiding out under an assumed name in Needles. Like the absentminded authors who change the prior history of their characters from chapter to chapter, Rubenstein and Swed seem to have forgotten about the existence of the other parts as they worked on each new section of the building. Cheeks of mirror glass are slapped next to jowls of stucco. Even that jelly-beanlike finish that the Shah-ette slapped on her infamous Sunset Boulevard remodel shows up here. A slightly more coherent version of the "stucco box meets the curtain wall and neither of them gets along with the other" school is the building by Johannes Van Tilburg and Associates kitty-corner from the 11111 building. Personally, as far as stucco-and-curtain-wall mixers go, we'll take the little Rayco Tires building that faces the 11111 on Olympic. 11111 Olympic Blvd., West Los Angeles.

BEST MONUMENT TO DEATH

Calvary Cemetery Mausoleum Could the building where the Barrymores are memorialized be anything but the best? Calvary's mausoleum has a marble-and-art-glass interior that merits superlative status. Don't be surprised if you think the set from D. W. Griffith's *Intolerance* was spirited away to East Los Angeles when you see this building for the first time. Lillian Gish would have looked wonderful fleeing down the outrageously grandiose steps. 4210 E. Whittier Blvd., East Los Angeles.

BEST FIFTEEN L.A. LANDMARKS

by Margaret Bach

1. Bradbury Building (George H. Wyman, 1893) An inspiration. L.A.'s most extraordinary interior space—a luminous skylit court with open balconies and stairwells, intricate ironwork, warm tones of marble, oak, and brick—superbly proportioned, at once intimate and monumental. The Bonaventure should be so lucky. 304 S. Broadway, downtown.

2. Gamble House (Charles and Henry Greene, 1908) The California bungalow *par excellence* by the architects whose work inspired a whole generation of vernacular Los Angeles homes. 4 Westmoreland Pl., Pasadena.

3. Hollywood Sign (1923, reconstructed 1978) A massive hillside advertisement for the Hollywoodland subdivision became, with the dropping of "land" in 1945, one of L.A.'s most enduring and beloved self-referential landmarks. An early — and inadvertent — example of reuse.

4. Ennis House (Frank Lloyd Wright, 1920) The Ennis house is perhaps the most dramatic and fully realized of Wright's L.A. work of the 1920s. It perches on its hillside like a centuries-old presence, acknowledging its counterpart to the south, Wright's Hollyhock House. 2607 Glendower, Los Feliz.

5. Los Angeles Central Library (Bertram G. Goodhue, 1925) Probably Los Angeles's finest public building, Bertram Goodhue's last and most provocative work offers a rich integration of architecture, art theme, and siting (the latter seriously marred by the 1969 removal of the west gardens for parking). It is a building to be read, like a book. 630 W. Fifth St., downtown.

6. Brown Derby (1926) Building-as-symbol. One of L.A.'s best remaining (but rapidly deteriorating) examples of the whimsical and fantastic architecture with which the city was so long identified. 3377 Wilshire Blvd., Wilshire District.

7. Los Angeles City Hall (Austin, Parkinson, Martin and Whittlesey, 1928) Surely the city's most instantly recognized landmark, thanks in large part to its frequent depiction in films and TV (*War of the Worlds, Dragnet*, etc.). For its first 30 years, this eclectically styled building was the tallest, by law, in L.A. 200 N. Spring St., downtown.

8. Bullock's Wilshire (John and Donald Parkinson, 1928) L.A.'s first "suburban" department store. An art deco landmark of superb massing and details. The major entrance was placed at the rear, adjacent to parking, and thus set the pattern for subsequent development along Wilshire, 3050 Wilshire Blvd., Wilshire District.

9. Samson Tire Factory (Morgan, Walls and Clements, 1929) The set for Griffith's *Intolerance* may be gone, but we still have this exuberant L.A. rendition of an Assyrian palace. A spin down the Santa Ana Freeway would not be the same without it. 5675 Telegraph Rd., City of Commerce.

10. Lovell Health House (Richard Neutra, 1929) A quintessentially modern house for the quintessential L.A. client — a prominent naturopath — that helped to put L.A. on the map, architecturally. Its much-publicized opening, L.A. style, brought 15,000 wide-eyed Angelenos on tour through this elegant steel-frame structure. A major monument of the International Style. 4614 Dundee Dr., downtown.

11. Pan Pacific Auditorium (Wurdeman and Becket, 1935) A design of great energy that successfully carries the great plain hulk of the attached exhibition hall. This Streamline Moderne landmark now awaits restoration and reuse. 7600 W. Beverly Blvd., West Hollywood.

12. Union Passenger Terminal (Donald and John Parkinson, 1939) L.A.'s most monumental expression of Spanish Colonial Revival design sources and a gesture, perhaps, to the historic plaza area adjacent. This was the last of the great passenger terminals built in the U.S. 800 N. Alameda, downtown.

13. The Towers of Simon Rodia in Watts (1921) On a small wedge of land in the heart of Watts, Rodia singlehandledly created one of the great works of folk art in the world. He fashioned the soaring towers from salvaged materials—pipes, rods, bottles, tiles, and pottery. "I had it in my mind to build something great," he said, "and I did." 1765 E. 107th St., Watts.

14. Four-Level Freeway Interchange (Chester H. Gish, 1954) L.A.'s most renowned freeway landmark, "the stack," where the Hollywood, Harbor Pasadena, and San Bernardino freeways interlace. An appropriate urban symbol for the auto-oriented city. Downtown.

15. Pacific Design Center (Cesar Pelli/Gruen Associates, 1976) The audacious architectural statement— true Los Angeles fashion— becomes at once a stunning focal point and a surprisingly neutral backdrop. The monumental 600-foot-long "Blue Whale," a refined horizontal extrusion, challenges its neighborhood's small scale, yet manages to coexist all the same. 8687 Melrose Ave., West Hollywood.

Art: An Info Gallery

by Hunter Drohojowska

AN AMATEUR'S GUIDE TO GALLERY BEHAVIOR

Ice-white walls, track lighting, museum-gray carpet, sparę, stark, sterile environment—it's all about as inviting as a sojourn to the arctic for New Year's Eve. Visiting an art gallery for the first time can be like a trip to a foreign country: it helps to know the language and the customs of the natives. One could write a book, I suppose, but three basic tips should suffice as an introduction.

1. Reject intimidation Just because the receptionist refuses to acknowledge your entrance and wears shoes that would cost you an entire paycheck, shun that creeping sensation of insecurity. Try to remember that gallery employees are paid less than your maid and this person is undoubtedly living with the folks in the Valley, waiting for Mr. or Ms. Right.

2. Attend openings The liquor is free and freely flows. Regardless of all those foolish invitations that are circulated, openings are rarely by invitation only. The news travels by word of mouth, for openings are primarily social gatherings. It is always too crowded to see the art, which is fine because no one is discussing art, anyway. Frequent conversation topics include real estate legal fees, casual sex, real estate again, the Dodgers, and

William Wilson. Openings are where the line between life and art is virtually invisible. Even the receptionist will suddenly become quite friendly.

3. Ask prices No better way to permeate the membrane of the art organism. Now that you're looking at art and drinking with artists, you'll want to demonstrate support in the best way you know how—with your checkbook. Without the correct perspective, however, this move can send you right back to the cold zone of intimidation. Art is expensive, but there is one little-known trick to survival: the layaway plan.

That's right. In this chic, status-seeking business of snobs and socialites, most everyone buys on time. Let's be realistic. Even before the Age of Reagan, how many people had a couple grand at their disposal? Most galleries require one-third down and payments made monthly. Isn't that knowledge a great equalizer? Remember, a gallery is really a small shop selling knickknacks that sometimes wind up on the covers of art magazines and then attain an astronomical value. If you actually do buy a piece of art, you'll find that your mailbox will overflow with invitations to openings, the art community will be most welcoming, and the receptionist will now want to go on a date. Everyone loves a collector.

BEST BLUE CHIP GALLERIES

Flow Ace Gallery This is L.A.'s answer to Leo Castelli in New York. In fact, director Douglas Chrismas represents many of the same big names, including Robert Rauschenberg, Jasper Johns, Andy Warhol, and Ed Ruscha, as well as high-powered Europeans such as Mario Merz, Joseph Beuys, and Klaus Rinke. 185 Windward Ave., Venice; 392-4931. 8373 Melrose Ave., West Hollywood; 658-6980.

Margo Leavin Gallery The woman who brought this year's N.Y. art star Julian Schnabel to L.A., Leavin represents an interesting range of artists from both coasts who are well known for work of intelligence and sophistication. Among these are Jennifer Bartlett, Lynda Benglis, Judd Fine, Joe Goode, and Gary Stephan. 812 N. Robertson Blvd., West Hollywood; 273-0603.

L.A. Louver Gallery This is primarily L.A. blue chip—William Brice, Fredrick Hammersley, Charles Garabedian, and Larry Bell, with more than a nod towards California's original assemblage movement in artists such as Edward Kienholz, George Herms, and the estate of Wallace Berman. Director Peter Goulds, who is British, also represents a smattering of English painters such as Leon Kossoff and David Hockney. 55 N. Venice Blvd., for contemporary graphic art, and 77 Market St., both in Venice; 392-8695.

Larry Gagosian Gallery Gagosian reps young, successful, and pricey art stars from N.Y., especially those with a debt to photographs, neoexpressionism, or graffiti. Included are Robert Longo, Cindy Sherman, David Salle, Keith Haring, and Jean Michael Basquiat, as well as such blue chippers of the past as Ellsworth Kelly, Frank Stella, and Richard Serra. 619 Almont Dr., West Hollywood; 276-6051.

BEST PREDICTABLE GALLERIES

James Corcoran Gallery More L.A. blue-chip-quality stuff, vigorously acquired by competitive Los Angeles collectors. Rarely a bad show, rarely a great show, never a surprise. Most of the work leans to inoffensive good composition: Chuck Arnoldi, Billy Al Bengston, Laddie John Dill, Tom Holland, Ken Price. 8223 Santa Monica Blvd., West Hollywood; 656-0662.

Molly Barnes Gallery Purportedly one of L.A.'s "dealers to the stars," Barnes predictably exhibits work that is borderline schlock. The gallery's surprising exceptions are artists with a sense of humor: Bruce Houston, Rick Oginz, and Lowell Darling. 750 N. La Cienega Blvd., West Hollywood; 854-1966.

OTHER VOICES, OTHER ROOMS

Los Angeles Contemporary Exhibitions (LACE) Fairly established in its own right, at least LACE operates in an artist-run democratic spirit. Executive director Joy Silverman and program coordinator Jim Isermann have somehow managed to retain enthusiasm and diversity, featuring every medium from performance to painting, and avoiding soporific predictability. 242 S. Broadway, downtown; 620-0104.

BEST FOR THE RISKY, UP–AND–COMING ART

Richard Kuhlenschmidt Gallery Although open only on weekends and by appointment, this select venue is one of the most farsighted, adventurous, and flat-out intelligent galleries in town. It sustains respect from artists and critics alike, and the collectors are catching on fast. Kuhlenschmidt is known for showing artists, from both New York and L.A., whose imagery is influenced by the conceptual movement and pop art. Artists shown in the past include Robin Winters, Sherrie Levine, Richard Prince, Kim Hubbard, Bill Leavitt, Jim Isermann, Mitchell Syrop, and Jim Morris. 4121 Wilshire Blvd., Los Angeles; 385-8649.

Ulrike Kantor Gallery Kantor was one of the first to grab the new raw young talent in L.A., promoting work that is predominantly neoexpressionist and symbolist. She also shows artists from her native Germany, such as Milan Kunc and Roger Herman. Others include George Rodart, George Condo, Victor Henderson, Marc Pally, and Manuel Luna. 800 N. La Cienega Blvd., West Hollywood; 273-5650.

Rosamund Felsen Gallery Felsen is an ambitious, idealistic dealer who has recently begun to represent some imaginative young artists difficult to pin down to any genre other than eclectic, eccentric, and smart. Artists Jeffrey Vallance, Mike Kelly, Lari Pittman, and Alexis Smith—all work in acknowledgment of popular culture. Felsen also represents Robert

Ackerman, Chris Burden, Richard Jackson, and Grant Mudford. 669 N. La Cienega Blvd., West Hollywood; 652-9172.

BEST ALL—PURPOSE ART STOP

The Art:170 Building includes three contemporary art galleries, Jan Baum, Roy Boyd, and Topo Swope, as well as Prints and Arts of Japan and Artworks, a delightful shop selling books made by artists, postcards, sundries, et al. Le Grand Buffet, the upstairs restaurant, serves snazzy, low-priced lunches. 170 S. La Brea Ave., Los Angeles; 934-2205.

BEST PLACE TO HOLD A BENEFIT

Kirk De Gooyer Gallery De Gooyer, one of L.A.'s most generous dealers, often opens his museum-size space for private fund-raising and social functions. His artists provide the decor, with large-scale splashy abstractions, at times figurative. He represents Michael Dvortscak, Cheryl Bowers, Gary Lang, Stanley Somers, Robert Walker, Robert Hernandez, and Jacquelyn Dreager. 1308 Factory Pl., downtown; 623-8333.

BEST GLASS WITH CLASS

Oktabec Gallery Remember the awe with which people refer to the glasswork from the early years of this century—the work of Lalique and Galle? Well, it's for sale at this store, along with the fragile art of contemporary glassworkers. 8627½ Melrose Ave., West Hollywood; 659-8621.

Ivor Kurland/Summers Gallery Contemporary sculptural glass is a specialization, all right, and you can find it here. Some pieces look like ashtrays or vases; others, some humorous, some decorative, are wall-bound, like paintings. 8742A Melrose Ave., West Hollywood; 659-7098.

Garth Clark Gallery Not glass but ceramic art, the sort that transcends the onerous label of pot or dish. Clark is something of an art historian in his knowledge of the subject. 5820 Wilshire Blvd., Los Angeles; 939-2189.

Janus Gallery Primarily a contemporary art gallery representing ceramists who've broken the craft barrier in their designs and attitudes. The artists include Peter Shire, Elsa Rady, Juan Hamilton, and Mary Corse, the latter two sculptors who work in elegant fired clay. 8000 Melrose Ave., West Hollywood; 658-6084.

BEST MELDS OF FUNCTION AND ART

Functional Art Store The owners concentrate on the unique area of furniture and domestic stuff made and sometimes interpreted by fine artists. They have changing exhibitions, and represent Astrid Preston, Phil Garner, Marlo Bartels, Jim Ganzer, and others. 207 Ashland Ave., Santa Monica; 392-8796.

Whiteley Gallery A relatively new space representing folk-art of environments created by Sanford Darling. The appealing works are exhibited in arrangements with architecturally inspired furniture such as original Eames chairs and replicas of Isamu Noguchi tables. 111 N. La Brea Ave., Los Angeles; 933-1113.

Artful Crafts: Where to Find Them

by Sharon Bell and Kathi Norklun

BEST CERAMICS

The Clayhouse has a studio in the back and a high-fire kiln that produces stoneware and porcelain. Some of the artists represented in the front gallery use the studio; others come from various points on the West Coast, from San Diego to Washington, with one addition from Michigan. The Clayhouse sells glass and ceramics, but specializes in pottery, both functional and decorative: they even have a bowl of porcelain earrings. The studio and kiln are open to use by anybody; there are workshops and lessons in pottery making, and the Clayhouse also sells supplies. 2909 Santa Monica Blvd., Santa Monica; 828-7071.

BEST AMERICAN FOLK ART

Peace and Plenty is hidden behind a grillwork door. Push the buzzer and be welcomed into a two-level loft hung with antique quilts, all in excellent condition and tagged with their generic and particular histories. There are many familiar, traditional patterns as well as more eccentric ones. Contemporary and historic folk art is also offered for sale. The little gift items—tiny piecework patches or cut-out tin ornaments—are irresistible. An excellent book collection on folk art and quilting stands upstairs beside a collection of woven coverlets. A shop for the collector. 1130 Wilshire Blvd., Venice; 396-8210.

BEST CONTEMPORARY AMERICAN CRAFTS

Del Mano Gallery, a spacious fine-crafts showcase, features work by contemporary American artisans. There are cases of jewelry, including cast and worked pieces; ceramics, glass, and woodworks; and, in the back, a boutique of "wearable art"—fine-artist-designed fabrics done up in simple styles—and silk wall hangings. It's the kind of place to go to pick up a Richardson porcelain plate, decorated with children, white rabbits, and goldfish, or pieces of Correia glass. Various artists are featured in monthly exhibitions; additionally, "theme" group exhibits, such as the recent "Containers," include a fascinating variety of interpretations in materials that may range from felt to metal. 11981 San Vincente Blvd., Brentwood; 476-8508.

OTHER GALLERIES THAT CARRY THE BEST IN CONTEMPORARY CRAFTS

A Singular Place, 2718 Main St., Santa Monica; 399-1018.

Freehand, 8413 W. Third St., Los Angeles; 655-2607.

Wild Blue, 7220 Melrose Ave., Los Angeles; 939-8434.

BEST CRAFTS OF ALL WORLDS: OLD AND NEW, ETHNOGRAPHIC AND AMERICAN

The Craft and Folk Art Museum Shop features the finest in contemporary American ceramics, jewelry, "wearables," and woodworks, as well as such ethnic arts as Mexican folk art, Papuan (New Guinea) ceremonial objects, and Japanese folk toys. Stephanie De Lange (ceramics), Kerry Feldman (functional glass), and Max Karst (jewelry) are among the 100 or so artists the shop represents; displays are always changing. (Are you ready for Olympic Souvenirs by Artists?) The excellent book department at the rear of the store includes hard-to-find material on ethnographic arts. 5814 Wilshire Blvd., Los Angeles; 937-5544.

BEST ETHNOGRAPHIC ARTS

Gallery K represents authentic, primarily western and central African work, also Indonesian and Philippine traditional sculpture. Proprietor Barry Kitnick, senior member of the American Society of Appraisers, does a lot of work for places like UCLA. There are occasional special exhibitions, and a rotating collection of artifacts displayed to the public. The gallery will go to great lengths to research a piece for a client, including the ritual context, and will present the findings. Prices range from the $100s to the $1,000s. 8406 Melrose Ave., West Hollywood; 651-5282.

The Fowler Museum is an eccentric collection in the 19th-century sense of collecting curios: everything from rare Chinese snuff bottles to antique Chinese ivory, from toy banks that respond when a coin is dropped into them to Balinese *kris*, wavy-shaped daggers. There is a collection of porcelain plates made for the coronation of Tsar Nicholas I and two pottery camels from tombs of the T'ang dynasty. A collection in the spirit of times before ethnographic arts were aesthetically respected, relics of past times and cultures. 9215 Wilshire Blvd., Beverly Hills; 278-8010.

David Stuart Gallery Down a walkway off La Cienega is a sheltered, green courtyard. Up the brick stairway is a gallery with a wide-ranging collection of pre-Columbian artifacts: Chimu metalwork ceremonial cups, several sizes of Colima pottery dogs, Inca silver, and Mixtec mosaics. David Stuart has been in the business for decades, buying and selling to museums and private collectors. 748½ N. La Cienega Blvd., Los Angeles; 652-7422.

Harry A. Franklin Gallery was begun by a self-taught collector of African art who hung around Paul Wingert and other anthropologists back in the '30s and '40s. Twenty-five years after the gallery opened, his daughter Valerie Franklin continues the tradition of selling museum-quality sculpture to museums and private collectors. Ms. Franklin describes the gallery as service-oriented: she will do appraisals, or search out a particular kind of work for a client. The gallery, an elegant suite of rooms in a bank building, is open by appointment only. It has a large inventory; no contemporary crafts are represented, but rather "traditional tribal sculpture" from South Africa that has not been influenced by European contact. Also some Oceanic and pre-Columbian work. 9601 Wilshire Blvd., Beverly Hills; 271-9171.

Sonrisa imports the finest in Mexican folk art at the most reasonable prices. The most unusual items in the shop are those made for Día de los Muertos (Day of the Dead), the Mexican equivalent of Halloween. Little cardboard coffins that expose a rising skeleton when you pull a string, skull-shaped papier-mâché maracas, wildly painted devil masks, and even miniature funeral processions carrying decorated black coffins are available. The best buys are the incredibly intricate, multicolored tissue-paper cuttings with morbid themes: skeleton families playing with skeleton babies, or mama and daddy devil swinging baby Satan at a playground are only two dollars each, with over a dozen cheerful versions from which to choose. 1256 W. Temple, downtown; 250-7934.

A Guide to the Best Museums

by Ann Edelman

Museum hours are correct as we go to press. They are, however, subject to change. If in doubt, call first. Because entrance fees are also subject to variation, especially with current budget cuts, these are not listed. Some museums are free, some ask for a small donation, and several have a fixed admission charge.

Cabrillo Marine Museum Inventively designed by architect Frank Gehry, the museum houses exhibitions of Southern California marine life, and is informal, entertaining, and just plain fun. You can learn about food chains and who eats what, and visit the Touch Tank where you can get acquainted with various denizens of the deep. Outside is a whale skeleton with a sign that says Please Touch. Nearby are some tidepools that can be explored in the season, and the museum sponsors whale-watch trips and grunion runs. On the way back from San Pedro, at Banning House in Wilmington, an elegant Greek Revival mansion that railroad and shipping magnate Phineas Banning built in 1864. 3720 Stephen White Dr., San Pedro; 548-7562. Tues.–Fri., noon–5 P.M.; Sat.–Sun., 10 A.M.–5 P.M..

California State Museum of Science and Industry is a hands-on, push-button museum. Permanent exhibitions deal with mathematics, energy, communications, transportation, water resources, and the like. A giant incubator hatches 150 chicks a day, math is made accessible with soap bubbles and moving demonstrations, and an old car and a working engine teach people how motors work. The Hall of Health graphically illustrates the functioning of the human body, you can learn all about teeth in the Dental Exhibition Hall, and the Hall of Economics and Finance offers information on all aspects of banking and economics. The Space Museum, a new aerospace complex now in the process of development, promises visitors a chance to explore the wonders and mysteries of outer space. Some of the museum's changing exhibitions, showcasing a wide range of topics, are outstanding, as are those of the Afro-American Museum of History and Culture, temporarily housed here. Daily, 10 A.M.–5 P.M.. 700 State Dr., Exposition Park, downtown; 744-7400.

Craft and Folk Art Museum features changing exhibitions of ethnic and contemporary folk art. Some of the intriguing shows of recent months were Art and Architecture of Nepal, Black Folk Art in America, Korean Art and Artifacts, and an installation of works by Chicano muralists from East Los Angeles, where museum visitors watched the artists at work. The museum shop sells the creations of America's finest craftspeople, and upstairs, at the Egg and the Eye Restaurant, you can choose from over 50 different omelets. The museum sponsors films, lectures, workshops, and all kinds of special events, including the memorable, magical Festival of Masks, which will be held in July of 1984 to coincide with the Olympics. Tues.–Sun., 11 A.M.–5 P.M.. 5814 Wilshire Blvd., Los Angeles; 937-5544.

George C. Page Museum in Hancock Park houses the bones of the creatures who thousands of years ago were trapped in the nearby bubbling tar pits. The building looks something like an Egyptian pyramid, and is adorned with a bas relief depicting life in the Ice Age. Inside are skeletons of dire wolves, mastodons, giant sloths, and various extinct birds. On exhibition are two astounding holographic displays: one gives flesh to the bones of a sabre-toothed cat; the other reconstructs a 9,000-year-old woman whose skull and leg bones were found in the tar pits. Tues.–Sun., 10 A.M.–5 P.M. 5801 Wilshire Blvd., Los Angeles; 936-2230.

Hebrew Union College Skirball Museum draws from its extensive collection to present four permanent exhibitions that illuminate Jewish history. A Walk Through the Past utilizes art objects from ancient civilizations to traverse the course of Jewish life from the age of the patriarchs to the Exodus. The Realm of Torah is a multilayered exhibition that uses ceremonial objects, prints, photographs, and explanatory texts to elucidate the many facets of Torah. A collection of Hannukah lamps includes the Rothschild menorah. And kids love the Five Senses Show, which presents, in a sensory environment, objects relating to the Jewish festival year. Tues.–Fri., 11 A.M.–4 P.M.; Sun., 10 A.M.–5 P.M. 32nd and Hoover sts. (near USC), Los Angeles; 749-8611.

J. Paul Getty Museum It's worth the trip just to admire this detailed replica of a Roman seaside villa, with its colonnaded walkway, frescoes, mosaics, and authentic landscaping. It's a perfect setting for the free chamber-music concerts the museum sponsors, and the ocean view is spectacular. The collection of Greek and Roman antiquities on the ground floor is outstanding, and on display upstairs are European paintings from the Renaissance to impressionism. There are some magnificent Oriental rugs, and the Getty is famous for its period rooms filled with ornately embellished European furniture. Special exhibitions are held periodically. Mid-June–mid-Sept., Mon.–Fri., 10 A.M.–5 P.M.; mid-Sept.–mid-June, Tues.–Sat., 10 A.M.–5 P.M.; it is necessary to make parking reservations by writing or calling a week in advance. 17985 Pacific Coast Hwy., Malibu; 459-8402.

Long Beach Museum of Art is housed in a brick-and-cedar-shingle craftsman-style mansion built in 1912. The museum specializes in the work of Southern California artists from 1890 on; the major portion on exhibit dates from the '50s to the present. Also on display is a large collection of modern German paintings. Most notable, however, is the videotape collection, with over 600 works in the archives. The museum functions in conjunction with a media-arts center, where videotapes are produced and edited, and exhibitions of the works of video artists are mounted year-round. A beautifully landscaped lawn provides a setting for contemporary sculpture. Wed.–Sun., noon–5 P.M. 2300 E. Ocean Blvd., Long Beach; 439-2119.

Los Angeles Children's Museum Kids love this touch, feel, experience museum, where the word *don't* is taboo. They can climb aboard a city bus, throw pillows, paint their faces, immerse themselves in arts and crafts, and generally have a ball. The workshop for the day could be anything from "Make Something Out of Q-Tips That You've Never Seen Before," to a group project creating a giant dragon out of various colorful discards. A 99-seat theater features plays, mime, and puppetry for children, and, between performances, creative kids can invent their own productions. Sat.–Sun., 10 A.M.–5 P.M.; Wed.–Thurs., 2:30–5 P.M.; extended hours during the summer, and group tours can be arranged. 310 N. Main St., downtown; 687-8800.

Los Angeles County Museum of Art, situated in beautiful Hancock Park, is now the largest general art museum in the western United States, with over 100,000 square feet of exhibition space. Particularly outstanding are the collections of Indian and Tibetan art, costumes and textiles, 19-century European sculpture, and 17th-, 18th-, and 19th-century European paintings. There's also a choice selection of Oriental and American art. Check out the many changing exhibits, some of which are truly terrific. Tues.–Fri., 10 A.M.–5 P.M.; Sat.–Sun., 10 A.M.–6 P.M. 5905 Wilshire Blvd., Los Angeles; 937-2590 or 857-6111.

Los Angeles County Museum of Natural History Housed in a handsome Spanish Renaissance–style structure, the museum offers a varied and fascinating bill of fare: dioramas of marine life and land animals; gem and mineral displays; reptiles, insects and birds; fossils, including dinosaur skeletons; and for archeology and anthropology buffs, displays of pre-Columbian and South Pacific art and artifacts. The Hall of American History shows memorabilia from the American past, and one room contains a collection of old automobiles. There are always changing exhibitions, and the museum sponsors special events, such as travel films, concerts, a crafts fair, and an annual Native American festival that features demonstrations by American Indian artists. The gift shop is excellent, and the deceptively small bookstore has an outstanding selection of scientific books. Tues.–Sun., 10 A.M.–5 P.M. 900 Exposition Blvd., Exposition Park, downtown; 936-2230.

Museum of Contemporary Art, L.A.'s newest museum, provides exhibition space for a full complement of contemporary art, from paintings and sculpture, to installations, commissioned works, photography, architecture and design, and performance art. In addition to showing the work of established contemporary artists from all over, the museum encourages and involves emerging California artists. A new and innovative building designed by Arata Isozaki is scheduled to open in 1986. Meanwhile, the museum is housed in a spacious, renovated warehouse building. Sat.–Mon., 11 A.M.–6 P.M.; Wed.–Fri., 11 A.M.–8 P.M.. 152 N. Central Ave., downtown; 382-MOCA.

Museum of Neon Art Neon, invented in 1910, was used primarily for signs until the '60s, when artists began to use it in a fine-arts context. And MONA is probably the only space in the country that exhibits, documents, and preserves works of neon, electric, and kinetic art. Old neon signs, saved from oblivion, glow with glorious colors, alongside inventive and original works by contemporary neon artists. Kinetic sculptures whirl and jump, accompanied by striking sound effects. Typical of kinetic art is Dave Quick's *Little Nuke:* push a detonation button, and a giant chicken lays a plastic egg which sets off a nuclear accident. Special exhibits are mounted year-round, and the museum offers classes. Wed. and Sat., noon–5 P.M. 704 Traction Ave., downtown; 617-1580.

Museum of Rock Art is a space in Hollywood (where else?) that features continuing exhibitions of photography, posters, graphics, and other artwork relating to the world of rock and roll. A video room shows classic film clips and original rock performances from the museum's collection, the largest in L.A. Special exhibits are held periodically; museum hours vary. 6427 Sunset Blvd., Hollywood; 463-8979.

The Norton Simon Museum of Art The spacious galleries of this striking modern building exhibit an extraordinary collection of art: Indian and Southeast Asian sculpture; old master paintings and drawings; Goya etchings; impressionist works by Cézanne, Toulouse-Lautrec, van Gogh, and Renoir; and paintings by Degas, Picasso, and the German expressionists. Sculptures adorn the lawn, and there's a fine view of the mountains on a clear day. The bookstore has one of the best selections of prints and art books in the city. Thurs.–Sun., noon–6 P.M. Orange Grove and Colorado blvds., Pasadena; 449-3730.

Pacific Asia Museum This beautifully wrought reproduction of a Chinese house, many of its materials actually imported from China, is incongruously situated in the midst of downtown Pasadena. The museum, once a private home, then the Pasadena Art Museum, now features changing exhibitions of Asian and Pacific art. The inner courtyard, with its fountain, Japanese garden, and pool filled with koi, is peaceful, and the museum has several small, informal shops that carry unusual Oriental merchandise, both new and antique. Wed.–Sun., noon–5 P.M. 46 N. Los Robles Ave., Pasadena; 449-2742.

Southwest Museum has one of the finest collections of North American Indian art and artifacts in the world. Housed in a 1914 mission-style building with a spectacular view of the city, the museum is one of L.A.'s earliest. The tunnel entrance has a series of dioramas depicting Indian life in the Southwest. On display are historic pottery, Navajo blankets, and a full-size Cheyenne tepee. Exhibitions change periodically. Tues.–Sat., 11 A.M.–5 P.M.; Sun., 1–5 P.M. 234 Museum Dr., Highland Park, between downtown and Pasadena; 221-2163.

Browsing the Best Libraries

MOST COMFORTABLE

Brand Library A pure-white, mosque-like building standing out sharply against the foothills of Glendale, the Brand is one of the most pleasant public libraries to visit in the area. This elegant structure houses the art and music collections of the Glendale Public Library, and the holdings in records, tapes, and art books eclipse any other accessible collection around. Because the building was formerly a residence, the Brand has a personable air to it, and the collection has the aura of a private library. Also, in an attached wing is a gallery where year-round displays by local artists can be found. If this isn't enough, the park that surrounds the Brand, with its scenic hiking trails and playground for children, is reason enough to spend a day there. 1601 W. Mountain St., Glendale; 956-2051.

BEST ONE–AND–ONLY LIBRARY

The Central Library You're not likely to find another public library with the enchanting interior design of this famed place. The frescoed walls, the lovely rococo hanging globe in the catalog room's dome, the tiles, the parquet, the marble all combine to make this building an especially refreshing antidote to its carpeted, metal-and-plastic successors. In addition, the collection here is sizable, and so thorough in some areas that it's a viable substitute for a university library. 630 W. Fifth St., downtown; 626-7461.

BEST THEATER ARTS LIBRARY

The Margaret Herrick Located at the Academy of Motion Picture Arts and Sciences, the Herrick Library has one of the nation's best motion-picture history, biography, and production collections. There are more than 16,000 books and bound periodical volumes, and the library subscribes to more than 200 film and television journals. Unique and only-in-L.A. special collections include Louella Parsons, Hedda Hopper, and the Lux Radio scripts. Reference use by appointment only. 8949 Wilshire Blvd., Beverly Hills; 278-4313.

BEST SPECIALTIES COLLECTION

Special Collections, UCLA If you've ever wanted to read a Gertrude Stein first edition, or have a peek at Henry Miller's personal archives, Special Collections at UCLA is at your service. Or rather, you're at their service, which is slow (some things can't be gotten on the spot). You must also abide by their research rules, which have been politely termed repressive, what with proctors monitoring you behind glass windows, etc. But all of this can be excused in the face of the many rare items that can be viewed. Among the more outstanding are the Japanese American Research Projects Collection and the Early Children's Books, which include gems for tots of the 18th and early 19th centuries. Inquire at the University Research Library's main desk about obtaining a reader's card. University Research Library, UCLA campus, Westwood; 825-4731.

BEST ART LIBRARY

Beverly Hills Public Library—Fine Arts Division This is an excellent small collection, with holdings on art, film, theater, and photography. Special collections include the Dorathi Bock Pierre Dance Collection and American and European auction catalogs. Also notable are over 4,500 slides on 20th-century artists and 2,000 art exhibition catalogs. Open to the public for reference use only. 444 N. Rexford Dr., Beverly Hills; 550-4720.

BEST PLANT SCIENCES LIBRARY

Los Angeles State and County Arboretum Plant Science Library Whew! If you think the name is long, you should see the list of holdings on everything you always wanted to know about green life. There are more than 23,000 books and items on every subject from botany and horticulture to plant pathology and landscape architecture. 301 N. Baldwin Ave., Arcadia; 446-8251.

BEST NATURAL HISTORY LIBRARY

Los Angeles County Museum of Natural History Research Library This place has more "ologies" than you even knew existed. How about herpetology? Or malacology? And, of course, paleontology, mineralogy, ornithology, and anthropology. There are also interesting special collections dealing with L.A. and California history, such as the L.A. Theatre Programs (pre-1900) and the Southern California Newspaper Collection (pre-1900). The Western History Collection includes a permanent exhibit of early photographs of Los Angeles and vicinity. Open to the public with certain restrictions. 900 Exposition Blvd., Exposition Park, downtown; 744-3387.

BEST GENEALOGICAL LIBRARY

Church of Jesus Christ of Latter–Day Saints Want to trace your roots? You can do it right in West Los Angeles. The Genealogical Library of the Mormon Temple will make it easy for you to research the branches of your family tree. Library holdings include census, land, historical, and family records, some dating back to the 15th or 16th century. There are 10,000 books and thousands of microfilm records covering the whole world, except for Russia. Additional materials can be ordered from Mormon headquarters in Salt Lake City. This is a community service, so you do not need to be a church member to use it. 10777 Santa Monica Blvd., Westwood; 474-5569.

BEST PLACE TO PUT A LIBRARY

The Huntington Library, Art Gallery, and Botanical Gardens were established in the early 1900s, when railroad magnate Henry E. Huntington decided to build a grand mansion in the grandest Southern California suburb of them all: San Marino. Hank's thirst for botanical knowledge led him to import plants from every continent; his 200-acre estate now contains a dozen different gardens. (See, er, Best Lovers' Spots.) The art gallery, housed in the mansion, focuses on 18th- and 19th-century British fine and decorative arts; among the paintings are Gainsborough's *Blue Boy* and works by Turner and Constable. The original collection also includes 18th-century French decorative arts; recent bequests of 17th- and 18th-century European and 18th-, 19th-, and 20th-century American paintings round out the holdings. The library is, for the most part, restricted to researchers, but 200 rare books, including early editions of Shakespeare and a beautifully illuminated *Canterbury Tales* (circa 1410), are on permanent display. Tues.–Sun., 1–4:30 P.M.; closed the month of October; advance reservations required for Sunday visits. 1151 Oxford Rd., San Marino; 792-6141.

Arcades and Amusements

by Les Paul Robley

BEST VIDEO ARCADES

Westworld Electronic Amusement Center is an arcade with a difference — no pinballs, foosballs, or air hockey tables clutter its ultramodern interior. In fact, two-player games of any kind are banned from the premises so as to avoid overcompetitive behavior among the customers. The arcade is known for the latest coin-op video games, and usually they have them in multiples.

It's also one of the cleanest arcades in the city, in keeping with its policy of removing forever the stigma of the reprehensible pool parlors of old. Uniformed employees frequently patrol the area to help any overenthusiastic gamer who needs to make change or has lost his quarter in a hungry machine. Food and drink of any kind (flammable or non) are outlawed, and UCLA students under 16 are banned during school hours. Children must be accompanied by an adult after 9:30 P.M.. 10965 Weyburn Ave., Westwood; 208-8827.

Castle Park Arcades Normally situated right next to a freeway, one would have to be blind to miss a Castle Park arcade. In the center of the grounds is a large picture-postcard fairy-tale castle, complete with moat and drawbridge. Inside are a plethora of arcade coin-op favorites, not to mention pinball, billiards, rifle-shoot-ing coin-ops, and skeeball alleys. The more elaborate Riverside arcade center has three (that's right, three) Austrian crystal chandeliers to light the various split-level playing areas. A stairway that looks as if it were built of Leggos leads down into a foosball pit. Under construction is a real dungeon, equipped with chains and torture devices, to house such popular Dungeons and Dragons–type games as Exidy's Venture and Midway's Wizard of Wor. For the more physically oriented, there are a few assorted miniature golf courses, complete with their own smaller versions of castles, giant water slides, and bumper boats. In Riverside, there's also a museum that's kind of a coin-op heaven. Here, old-time games can live out the remainder of their existence in relative peace and harmony, free from the arcaders who continually bend their joysticks or spill coke on their display screens. 4989 N. Sepulveda, Sherman Oaks (990-8102); 12400 Vanowen St., North Hollywood (765-4000); 2410 Compton Blvd., Redondo Beach (644-1166); and 3500 Polk Ave., Riverside (714-785-4140).

THE MAGIC MOUNTAIN AMUSEMENT OASES

What can a person do at Magic Mountain if he's acrophobic, and recoils in horror from anything that treats him like a basketful of clothing going through tumble dry? Along with other line-weary ride-aholics, he can while away his afternoon in the cool complacency of one of five separate video oases in the park. Decor-wise, the most interesting arcade resides in the mining camp area across from the Roaring Rapids river-rafting attraction. Set inside an unusual location for a video arcade—a large barn with the words Livery Stable on the front—are all sorts of electronic game paraphernalia. New coin-ops like Stern's Frenzy, Sega's Zaxxon, and Bally/Midway's TRON head the popularity polls.

The park's largest arcade is located near the rollicking Buccaneer ride, boasting over 100 coin-ops out of a total of 250 on the entire mountain. Situated right at the doorway are a plethora of Ms. Pac-Man and Donkey Kong machines. Also on hand are about 25 skeeball alleys with prizes ranging from gigantic stuffed Pac-Man to cuddly centipede-like dolls.

The smallest arcade (considered small only when compared to the three other biggies) makes up for its size by housing one of everything in the way of coin-ops: from Kicks to Bosconian to Mousetrap, as well as old standbys like Asteroids and Defender.

Those who brave the two water-flume rides, the Log-jammer and the Jet Stream, can dry their clothing in the warm atmosphere of the only outdoor arcade on the premises. Here one encounters vigorous tests of dexterity, like electronic shooting galleries, ring tosses of all kinds, and a device that digitally measures the speed of your pitching arm. There are more than a dozen other amusements that take you back to the days of local county fairs.

The final arcade lies next to the Mountain Express roller coaster ride, and is predominantly filled with coin-ops, skeeball, and, of course, money-changers. The most popular game seems again to be TRON; there's a line to play in the arcade's sole machine. A number of park employees frequently patrol the area to help any overactive gamer who's lost a quarter, needs to make change, or has simply passed out from heat exhaustion in the hot noonday sun.

DISNEYLAND'S BEST ARCADES

Main Street Penny Arcade Dominating the entrance is a glass-enclosed "lady" who turns her head, speaks, and tells your fortune for a dime. Behind her stretch two rows of 20 authentic Cail 'O Scope flip viewers that show you a silent comedy, Tom Mix Western, or maybe an old Felix the Cat cartoon for a penny. Surrounding these are steam shovels that hoist out trinkets, hands of lead that you must squeeze, a Love Tester to measure your virility, and player pianos that show you everything inside except the little person moving the keys. It all comes magically together, endowing the Main Street Penny Arcade with just the right touch of nostalgia.

Teddi Barra's Swingin' Arcade in Bear Country, Frontierland Here lie some quaintly unique three-dimensional machines that are available exclusively in this park and Walt Disney World in Florida. One extremely addicting game is named I'm Gomer—Fly Me Through Bear Country, and is a blending of elements from Bear Country and the Haunted Mansion ride. The player must control a departed denizen of the earth (or "ghost" if you're a believer) and, with the aid of a joystick, fly him over tombstones and under bridges, collecting all kinds of points for good piloting. The interesting thing about the game is that Gomer is truly a spirit—you can see through him and he comes complete with auto-reverse and a vanishing act when the game is over.

The arcade is nestled amidst a forest of fragrant pine trees. The Old West atmosphere is quite authentic, and if you get tired of flying ghouls, shooting skunks, or playing Totem-Up, you can rest your fingers and settle down for a nonalcoholic beverage at the Mile-Long Bar next door.

The Tomorrowland Starcade is Disneyland's homage to the land of video-arcade paraphernalia. Even though the theme here is space and future technologies, the two-level arcade has over 200 coin-ops of almost every electronic game conceivable—from 3-D sit-ins, cabaret-style Pac-Mans, and Deluxe Asteroids, to large wall screens of Missile Command whereby the entire arcade can see how skillful or terrible you really are. New games like Frogger, Tempest, Avalanche, and QIX seem to appear first on the top level, and then work their way to the bottom to compete with the Starcade's three favorites: Starcade 500, Space Chase, and Gorf. There are also six air hockey tables up above for the more athletically gifted.

On the lower level there's even a big screen horseracing game called Space Chase. Here, six players control a horse named after a planet, and they compete against one another and the computer-controlled pacer horse in leaping over hurdles to get to the finish line.

BEST AMUSEMENT PARK AMUSEMENTS

Roller Coasters
Most Visceral: Colossus (Magic Mountain).
Best Theme: Big Mountain Thunder Railway (Disneyland).
Smoothest: The Revolution (Magic Mountain).
Roller Coaster with the Most Historic Value: The Corkscrew (Knott's Berry Farm). This was the first loop roller coaster built in this half of the century. Loops were made earlier, but the materials to make them safe were not available.

Landscaping
Best Use of Topography: Magic Mountain.
Best Landscaped: Disneyland.

Water Rides
Fastest: Jet Stream (Magic Mountain).
Smoothest: Roaring Rapids (Magic Mountain).
Best Theme: Pirates of the Caribbean (Disneyland).
Runner-up: Timber Mountain Joy Ride (Knott's Berry Farm).

Highest View Tower
Sky Tower (Magic Mountain). Two hundred feet tall from base to head, taking base elevation above sea level into account.

Best Eating
At Knott's Berry Farm: Hollywood Beanery, Roaring Twenties area.
At Disneyland: Blue Bayou Restaurant, New Orleans Square.
At Magic Mountain: Anywhere outside of the park.

Best Steam–Train Ride
The 1890s-style steam train at Disneyland.

Best Dark Ride
Haunted Mansion (Disneyland).

Least–Known Amusement Park
Santa Claus Land.

BEST PARKS

Barnsdall Park, home of the late, lamented Garden Festival, is a peaceful, hilly oasis between Hollywood and downtown. It's a real people's park, used by folks of all ages who want to get away from the hullabaloo of Hollywood. It's a park with much activity: an arts and crafts center for adults, outstanding children's programs at the Junior Arts Center, concerts, plays, art exhibitions featuring local artists, and tours of the Frank Lloyd Wright Hollyhock House. 4800 Hollywood Blvd., Hollywood.

Chatsworth Park in the West Valley is big and offers much recreational activity. Most notable, however, are the spectacular rocks, great for climbing, hiking, or merely viewing in all their splendor. Take the Ventura Freeway west to the Topanga exit, go north to Devonshire, then west to the end.

Crestwood Hills is a wooded, rustic, secluded, intimate park tucked away high in the hills above Brentwood. There's a baseball diamond, a picnic area, and a playground. But above all, this park is a great place to get away from it all, to roam around the hilly terrain, or just to relax. To reach the park from Sunset Boulevard, turn north on Kenter Avenue to Hanley, then right on Hanley, and wind around until you hit the park. 1000 Hanley Ave., Brentwood.

Hollenbeck Park is one of the oldest and prettiest of the city's parks, famous for its blooming coral trees in the spring. There's a lake with a picturesque wooden bridge on the park's rolling, tree-shaded terrain, a scene used in the '20s for silent movies. In September, crowds turn out for the annual two-day festival, La Feria de los Niños. Boyle Ave., between Fourth and Sixth sts., East Los Angeles.

Moco–Cahuenga Canyon is a verdant, cool, secluded spot just minutes from Hollywood. A stream, with moss-covered rocks, waterfalls, and wooden bridges, meanders through the canyon. Banks of luxuriant ferns carpet the ground, and overhead a forest of venerable trees, including a beautiful stand of sycamores, shades the visitor. A great place for friends and lovers. Near the intersection of Western Ave. and Los Feliz (go north on Fern Dell Dr. to Red Oak Dr.); the entry gate is on the east side.

Orcutt Ranch Park is a gem, and a favorite for weddings. It's a horticultural center, with nature trails, an abundance of gorgeous and fascinating plants and flowers, a rose garden, and 16 acres of citrus trees. The old Spanish-style ranch house is still standing. Take the Ventura Freeway west to the Topanga exit, north on Topanga to Roscoe, then west on Roscoe to 23600 in Canoga Park.

Palisades Park, a lovely tree-shaded oasis that snakes along a bluff above the ocean, is populated by just about everyone—bikers, joggers, schmoozers, card players, winos, and lovers. The sunsets can be spectacular, and it's fun to watch the boats on a good sailing day. Ocean Ave. in Santa

Monica, north of the Santa Monica Pier.

Vasquez Rocks County Park is perhaps the best of all, and a rock climber's delight. Huge, angular, jagged rocks rise from the desert floor; one can spend all day playing hide-and-seek and climbing around on them. Long ago, legendary bandit Tiburcio Vasquez used it as a hideout. Hot in the summer, it's perfect for an evening picnic when the air is cool and clear and the sunset turns the rocks into a kaleidoscope of glorious colors. Drive north on Interstate 5 to a clearly marked turn-off.

BEST SMALL PARK

Wattles Park Once the backyard of a wealthy socialite, this tiny garden of Eden is wonderfully uncrowded. There's a co-op garden, tended by country-hungry city dwellers, and a rose garden, in a very romantic state of disrepair, with a picturesque long trellis and half-buried benches. A circular fish pond, choking with overgrown weeds, is on the verge of disappearing under the growth. At the northern end of the park, a stone-lined path snakes up the canyon walls, and if you climb carefully through the brush and dust, you'll be rewarded with a wonderful view of the city. Curson Ave. at Franklin, West Hollywood; open 7 A.M.–dusk.

The Great Outdoors

BEST HIKES AND WILD PLACES

The Santa Monica Mountains cut through Los Angeles west to east, stretching for almost 50 miles from Point Mugu on the ocean to Griffith Park in the heart of the city. It's a land of steep canyons, jagged rocks, chaparral-covered hills, sycamore and walnut groves, and grasslands dotted with gnarled California oaks. Hawks swoop around the skies, and there are deer, coyote, small rodents, and even an occasional bobcat or mountain lion. One finds spectacular views of ocean, city, and valley in this mountain range, and in the spring a profusion of wild flowers explodes on the hilly terrain.

Here are some prize hiking areas, guaranteed to keep you busy for the next 15 years. If you are a serious hiker, pick up a copy of Milt McAuley's *Hiking Trails of the Santa Monica Mountains,* and one of Sierra Club's *Day Walks in the Santa Monica Mountains.* And you can also call the Park Information Center at 888-3770.

Point Mugu State Park The largest and perhaps most beautiful of the parks, Point Mugu is a hiker's paradise, with 70 miles of trails, both rugged and gentle. There are superb views from the rocky bluffs above the ocean, and La Jolla Valley has one of the best remaining stands of California native grasses. Big Sycamore Canyon has very different terrain, with cottonwood, sycamore, and big-leaf maple trees, and dogwood and lush ferns growing near the springs. And masochists, don't despair. There's a really tough 26-mile all-day "Walkabout"! Pacific Coast Hwy., 15 miles south of Oxnard; 706-1310.

Topanga State Park Closer to town is Topanga State Park, a lovely area of rolling hills covered with grassland and chaparral, dotted with oak groves, and graced with its very own stream. There are 35 miles of trails, among them the 6-mile hike from Trippet Ranch, which climbs to a spot with fine views of Topanga and Santa Ynez canyons, drops through a chaparral forest to the stream, then veers up the hill again for a superb view of the ocean at an overlook. Another favorite hike is the scenic 9-mile route ending at Will Rogers State Park in Pacific Palisades. Turn east off Topanga Canyon Blvd. onto Entrada Rd., just north of the town of Topanga, then keep bearing left till you reach the parking lot; 454-8212.

Malibu Creek State Park This rugged, rocky area was formerly the Century Movie Ranch. Along the creek that runs through the land are waterfalls and a rock pool, and a manmade lake, with fresh fish and water birds such as herons and coots, gives it special character. Two entrances, one at the corner of Mulholland Dr. and Cornell Rd., and one on Las Virgenes–Malibu Canyon Rd.; 991-1827.

Paramount Ranch This is a versatile bit of land. Movies were made here for over 20 years; a Western-town movie set is still used by television studios. And, of course, the lovely, rolling terrain, dotted with massive, twisted oak trees, becomes Merrie England in the spring when the Re-

naissance Faire is in residence. But for the average biped, it's simply a beautiful area, great for walking, horseback riding, picnics, and just lazing around. Near Mulholland Dr. on Cornell Rd., two miles south of the Ventura Freeway; 888-3770.

Charmlee County Park Easy, gentle trails run through meadows and oak woodlands. The bluffs that overlook the Malibu coastline are a fine place for whale watching and picnicking. Entrance is four miles inland from Pacific Coast Hwy., on Encinal Rd.

BEST PLACE TO JOG

Lake Hollywood is really quite incredible. Less than three minutes from Hollywood Boulevard, you can run for almost 3.5 miles around a crystal-clear lake surrounded by towering pine trees. Lizards scurry with your approach, a hawk or two soar above, and squirrels, skunks, and coyotes sniff your trail. You'd think a lot of people would know the virtues of Lake Hollywood, but apparently not, since even on a weekend you'll encounter five or six people — at the most. You run on some sort of closed access road, so wear the proper shoes and bring along a beverage because the actual lake is fenced in and there are no drinking fountains. The road is open weekdays, 7 A.M.–noon and 2–7:30 P.M., and weekends, 7 A.M.–7:30 P.M. To get there, take Cahuenga north, make a right on Dix (that's a block north of Franklin), and a left on Holly Drive up the hill to Deep Dell Place. Make a sharp right, continuing to Weidlake Drive, where you turn left (don't be put off by the Not a

Through Street sign). Continue until you reach the lake entrance. It is with much reluctance we expose this inner-city jogging paradise, so keep it to yourself.

BEST JOGGING PATH

Ocean Avenue/San Vicente This path is the height of aestheticism for the track-weary runner. Beginning in Ocean Park along the beach-front bike path, continuing along Ocean Avenue through Santa Monica, and on up the scenic tree-lined median of San Vicente Boulevard, one can sweat and puff while admiring the view that encompasses the ocean, the beaches, and the Santa Monica Mountains. Truly one of L.A.'s unique gifts to its inhabitants, this beautiful route can almost make shin splints and heat prostration worthwhile.

BEST POLO MATCH WATCHING

Will Rogers State Park Don't know a chukker from a checker? Doesn't matter. Just remember that the rules for this sport resemble those used for hockey, and you're all set. On weekend afternoons you can bring a picnic, lie around on the grass, and watch lightning-fast horses gallop for goals. If you grow bored with this very British sport, take a look at the Will Rogers ranch, which is just a few feet away. The late comedian picked a beautiful spot for his home some 50 years ago, and a staff of excellent guides make the half-hour tours into more than just another dull museum ride. Other than that, walk the scenic hillside trails, toss a frisbee, or just relax. The city seems far away up here. 14523 Sunset Blvd., Pacific Palisades.

BEST PLACES TO PLAY TENNIS

Free The city of Los Angeles, with tax monies provided by the residents, has some magnificent parks, many with outstanding tennis facilities. Rustic Canyon in remote Santa Monica Canyon was once a private club and it still looks like it, with gargantuan sycamores and eucalyptus overhanging the courts. Palisades Park in Pacific Palisades features eight courts in a shaded basin. And the Vermont Canyon courts in central Griffith Park are also in a rustic setting. There are many others, so check the phone book under "City of Los Angeles—Parks and Recreation" for addresses and telephone numbers. Also, though the tennis boom is said to have died, there's still a plethora of tennis addicts about, causing the city to implement a reservation system on a fee basis at some facilities.

Rustic Canyon, 601 Latimer Rd., Santa Monica; 454-5734.
Palisades Recreation Center, 851 Alma Real Dr., Pacific Palisades; 454-5445.
Vermont Canyon, N. Vermont Ave. (above Los Feliz Dr.), Los Angeles; 664-3521.
Balboa Park, 17015 Burbank Blvd., Encino; 995-6570.

Fee For those tennis fans who don't want to go looking for a court at a public park and who don't have their own club, there are a few establishments that rent courts by the hour, saving players time and trouble. The best of these is The Racquet Center, where one can obtain a court for about eight dollars an hour from 8 A.M. until 10 P.M. For night play, these lights are as good as you'll find. There are several good pros teaching here if you want a lesson and there are various programs for instruction, competition, and recreation. Similar rental facilities are Tennis Place in midtown and Tennis Village in Santa Monica. We must mention Al's Tennis Shop and Hackers Haven, where you'll find the only public clay courts in the Southland. Two Har-Tru courts suddenly appear as you drive down a side street in Lawndale, and Al only charges six dollars an hour, lights or no. That's a deal, folks.

Racquet Center, 10933 Ventura Blvd., North Hollywood; 760-2303.
Tennis Place, 5880 W. Third St., Los Angeles; 931-1715.
Tennis Village, 2701 Ocean Park Blvd., Santa Monica; 450-8430.
Al's Tennis Shop, 4416 W. 154th St., Lawndale; 679-5504.

BEST PADDLE TENNIS

Venice Beach, right near Muscle Beach Sometimes the obvious is the best after all. Paddle tennis has been hot for a couple of years, with private courts opening up. Most aficionados agree that the very best facilities are at Venice Beach, where there are eight city courts. For one thing, it's cool,

for another, many of the city's tournament champs train here. Regulars say it's democratic and informal, though you may have to wait a long time for a court, especially on weekends.

BEST MINIATURE GOLF

Golf 'n Stuff Golf 'n Stuff is where the 605 and Santa Ana freeways meet in Norwalk. For miniature golf, it boasts a total of four far-from-miniature courses. There are realistically designed French chateaux, missions, and steeple-topped churches with attention to detail that equals the villages in Disneyland's Storybookland Canal ride. For the stuff part, it has an arcade and a Little Indy racetrack with twists and banks that resemble the real thing. What's more, there are no rails or guide walls to keep you from weaving in and around other racers. 10555 E. Firestone, Norwalk; 863-8338.

BEST PERFORMANCE BEACH

Muscle Beach Shakespeare said all the world's a stage, and L.A. took him literally. If William were to visit Los Angeles today, he wouldn't want to miss Muscle Beach, a fenced-in outdoor weight-lifting pen on Venice Beach where men the size of bulls sweat and snort under the hot sun. Seemingly unaware of the thousands of passersby, these bare-chested brutes flex their muscles and pump amazing poundages of iron to the applause of the delighted crowd. Bikini-clad girls squeal and gawk at their favorite hunks. (Arnold Schwarzenegger, naturally, stops in now and then.) Japanese tourists take pictures. Big bellies graze on pizza and beer in the bleachers, belching occasional cheers. But the big boys rarely blink an eye in response, for they're in full control of their audience, and they love it. Near Ocean Front Walk and Windward Ave., Venice Beach.

BEST SURF SPOTS

Harrison's Reef at the County Line County Line, just north of Bass rock between Pete's Reef Restaurant and Leo Carrillo Park, is a favorite among surfers, for the waves can get well up to six or eight feet, even in the summer. On weekends, one will usually find cars with surfboards attached all along this stretch of Pacific Coast Highway. The beach has a generally sandy bottom with a few small rocks. Kelp beds begin about 100 yards out in 40 feet of water with the reef at 300 yards. This makes the waves less choppy, with a nicely formed curl, but also smaller than they normally could be. Closest bathroom facilities are at Leo Carrillo or Pete's Reef.

Zuma and Westward Beach Zuma is off the 29800s of Pacific Coast Highway south of Trancas Canyon Road. Westward Beach is farther south, concealed from Pacific Coast Highway by Point Dume. To get there take Westward Beach Road seaward from Pacific Coast Highway. However, be forewarned that a parking fee is charged, and it gets pretty crowded in the summer. Zuma is by far the more popular surfing area, with

breakers larger on the southeast end. A strong current moves toward this point parallel to the beach in the summer. Riptides are prevalent in winter, seen as muddy dark streaks moving out to sea, with an occasional surfer in the middle of it. About 100 yards out from the lifeguard headquarters is a man-made reef, which is said to be composed of items such as a jeep and toilet fixtures.

Malibu's Surfrider Beach Once home of the famous Malibu outriggers and the '60s traditional style of long-board surfing a la the Beach Boys and Frankie Avalon, Malibu is somewhat different from the way the old-timers remember her. But despite the changing attitudes of the '80s toward surfing, namely, competition amongst the waves and the predominance of a young, short-board surfing crowd, the near perfect form of Malibu's waves and her record of being one of the world's most populated beaches remains virtually intact. During the summer months, a southeasterly swell brings the sandy beach nice two-foot waves, perfect for beginning surfers and boogie boarders, that is, if they can find room amidst the regulars that haunt the area. The strong westerly current is blocked somewhat by the protuberance of Point Dume. A reef constructed by the California Fish and Game Department in the '60s lies about a half mile south of Malibu. It's composed of various automobiles, a Culver City streetcar, concrete shelters, and more than 325 tons of quarry rock.

The Newport Wedge The famous wedge—dubbed the "dirty ol' wedge" by local body surfers—is a daredevil spot for, you guessed it, the sport of body surfing. A breakwater constructed near the area creates some truly mammoth waves in the wintertime (some ten feet high) that come crashing down on helpless swimmers in often only one foot of water. So you have to land just right if you don't want your back to come out looking like a pretzel. According to the surf movie *The Endless Summer,* some $3,000 worth of swim fins were lost there in just one year.

BEST SCUBA DIVE SPOTS IN L.A.

Malaga Cove Just south of Torrance Beach, at the beginning of the Palos Verdes Peninsula on the west side, is a well-protected cove that is usually calm while other areas are being buffeted by big swells. Beach access is next to the church at 300 Paseo Del Mar, and is provided by means of a paved fire road that winds down to the water's edge. There are two easy entrance points for all levels of divers (beginning to advanced): a rock entry near the road, or a sandy beach a little farther north. The area is frequently used by instructors for their basic scuba classes.

Fair visibility and a generally sandy bottom (disrupted occasionally by large rocks) make this a splendid area for exploring and hunting. The cove is known for its large lobster population and big spider crabs. There's also a nice variety of subjects for photography, including octopus, starfish, geribaldi, calico bass, perch, and a few angel sharks in the sand near the rocky edges. The bottom slopes gradually to about 30 feet deep a quarter of a mile out, becoming rockier the farther west you travel. Some giant bladder kelp is expected on this west end.

Christmas Tree Cove (Patterson's Cove) and Point Vincente These adjacent coves provide one of the clearest dive spots in all of L.A., with game and surrounding surface area most resembling Catalina. In fact, all of Palos Verdes Peninsula would offer great diving if it weren't for the usually treacherous descent down the cliffs. It may look easy, but with tanks and other assorted gear on your back, it's no joke. Both coves offer paths off the ocean side of Paseo Del Mar, with Point Vincente's safer to navigate. Entries are made via rocky beach and must be timed to coordinate with the low-to-moderate swells. The bottoms angle sharply, leveling off to a maximum depth of 30 to 40 feet. Visibility averages about 15 feet, with a maximum of 30 feet during the winter months.

Reefs, prevalent in both parts, make the photography and game generally interesting. Abs and scallops are abundant—the reefs attract numerous fish, including geribaldi (migrating from Catalina in the summer), opaleye, and sheephead. A CalTech dive club, the Kelpers, is currently involved in a kelp restoration program with California Fish and Game to reduce the huge sea urchin population at Point Vincente. Their hope is to bring back the kelp that was destroyed by the sewage pollution of the past.

2.

ENTERTAINMENT AND NIGHTLIFE

The Silver Screen

BEST MOVIE THEATERS

Mann's Chinese; UA Egyptian Theater In Westwood? Forget it. Lots of plastic people, synthetic atmosphere, and institutional chic, but no good theaters are to be found in that sterile corporate pleasure center. Hollywood is still the place to see movies properly; while tunnel-visioned entrepreneurs have twinned or quadrupled most of the grand old movie palaces on the boulevard, you can still immerse yourself in old-style grandeur at the Chinese and Egyptian theaters. The Chinese has a large, evenly lit screen, a six-track stereo system that fills every square foot of the spacious auditorium with crystal-clear reproduction, and sumptuous art deco decor that breathes history into every nook and cranny. The Egyptian runs a close second in decor, and the screen is wider and more curved than that of the Chinese, but they haven't shown a good 70mm movie there since *The Wind and the Lion* in 1975. As a third choice, the Cinerama Dome's okay if you like being herded into line by loud-mouthed ushers and being monitored by armed guards under the exit signs.

BEST MOVIE AUDIENCE

The World A good theater is more than just a place to consume images projected on a screen. A good theater is a combination of form and content in which each complements the other. The best place to observe the movie theater as theater is the World, on Hollywood Boulevard at Gower. For content, it always has the best schlock triple bills in town (such as the immortal *Blood Eaters, New Year's Evil,* and *Fists of Fury*), and its raucous audience is always in top form. When they're watching the screen, they cheer and jeer like no one else; when they're not watching the screen, which is most of the time, they're performing their own real-life versions of dramatic situations—from sex, violence, and verbal abuse, to eating, snoring, and having a good time in general. You'll spend most of the evening looking around you instead of at the screen, partly because the audience is so entertaining, but mostly because you'll feel very unsafe. But keep a low profile, and you'll be glad you came. *Editor's note:* Turn to The Best of the Worst section, where you will get another view of the World.

BEST REVIVAL–HOUSE SCREEN

Four Star Theater For the ultimate comfort in viewing those OBGs, the Four Star Theater has installed a brand-new Dolby sound system a la the Pacific Dome, with the big screen to accompany the aural improvement. Remakes of such classics as *Bus Stop* and *The Grapes of Wrath* in 70mm— can you imagine? This isn't revival; it's complete regeneration! 5112 Wilshire Blvd., Los Angeles.

MOST ELEGANT PORNO THEATER

The Mayan From the same architects (Morgan, Walls & Clements) who gifted our landscape with such monuments as the Wiltern Theater, The Chapman Market, and the U.S. Royal Tire complex (off the Santa Ana Freeway), which resembles a walled Babylonian Shangri-la, comes this wildly ornate theater. Built to resemble a pre-Columbian palace, it features seven Mayan warriors glaring down at you as you enter the brightly painted facade. The theme is continued inside, where only hardcore porno films are shown, with an occasional Spanish mad-slasher double bill. 1040 S. Hill St., downtown.

BEST AVANT–GARDE VIEWING

If Wertmuller, Truffaut, and Bergman seem artistically tame to you now, perhaps it is time to explore the world of the experimental filmmaker. Brakhage, Rainer, Frampton, and Strand are a few of the established "names," but there are literally dozens of stimulating individuals working in this medium. Following are the major sources for viewing 8mm and 16mm artwork in the L.A. area.

In addition, occasional programs and/or series are held at the Academy of Motion Picture Arts and Sciences, 8949 Wilshire Boulevard, Beverly Hills 90211. For information, call 278-8990.

Encounter Cinema Regular screenings on Tuesday evenings at Melnitz Auditorium on the UCLA campus. Check for times, admission fees, and other schedule information. P.O. Box 69673, Los Angeles 90060; 463-1809 or 825-2345.

Pasadena Filmforum Regular Monday-night screenings at the Bank Street Theater in Pasadena. Light refreshments available. Call for specific times, fees, and other programming information. P.O. Box 5631, Pasadena 91107; 358-6255.

sive. Filmex invites the community to become members of its financial support group, the Filmex Society. Your best bet is starting at $100 for the year, which includes a monthly screening of a major yet-to-be-released motion picture for you and a guest, discounts on tickets for the festival and on selected UCLA Fine Arts productions and certain magazines, plus you get an insider's view of Hollywood and the industry. A bargain in the long run, and a membership doubles as an aid to a major force in L.A.'s cultural happenings. 6525 Sunset Blvd., Hollywood; 469-9400.

BEST OLD–FASHIONED MOVIE THEATER

Aero This mid-size cinema sits on quiet Montana Avenue and has a definite ma-and-pa quality. From the young ticket cashier to the overstuffed sofas and ancient coke machine in the lobby, entering the theater is like walking backward into a 20-year time warp. It's a class act even down to the bathrooms, which feature real bars of soap and nonfluorescent lighting. Ticket prices for second-run double features are three dollars. 14th St. and Montara Ave., Santa Monica; 395-4990.

BEST REVIVAL HOUSE OVER A FIVE–YEAR PERIOD

New Beverly Cinema There are a lot of revival theaters in L.A., but this is the one that has consistently shown a respectable amount of less-mainstream material that can't be seen on late-night TV. The programmers manage to include at least three nights of obscure, hard-to-see films on every weekly calendar. 7165 Beverly Blvd., just west of La Brea; 939-4038.

BEST MOVIE ATTRACTION

The Filmex Society L.A. is the home of The Los Angeles International Film Exposition (Filmex), the largest film festival in the U.S., and it is not exclu-

BEST MOVIE THEATER BALCONY

Hollywood Paramount and The Picwood Before multicinemitis infected L.A., there were more balconies in local theaters than you could shake a ticket stub at. The only two worth mentioning now are these. The Paramount's balcony is deep, dark, and full of ghosts from the theater's long history. And its outer reaches are remote enough for you and your companion to indulge in what balconies were made for indulging in. On the other hand, the Picwood's balcony was made strictly for watching movies; it's light enough to see your way around at all times, but it's also roomy and the sightlines are excellent. To relive the ultimate primal moviegoing experience, slouch down in the front row and dangle your feet off the railing—it's the next best thing to being a kid again. The Paramount, 6838 Hollywood Blvd., Hollywood. The Picwood, Pico and Westwood blvds., West Los Angeles.

MOST COMFORTABLE MOVIE THEATER

Plitt Theaters The Plitt I and Plitt II in Century City are maintained as showcase theaters for the Plitt Corporation. They feature the finest in projection technology and plush seats that sway back and forth without disturbing the people in front or behind you. The sound system is magnificent and the screens in both theaters are among the largest in the city. These days the theaters tend to be covered with detritus and almost impossible to walk on due to the sticky floors, but Plitt generally cleans up their act just before Filmex, which is held annually here. ABC Entertainment Center, Century City.

The Cinerama Dome is the ultimate in technical and comfortable movie-going. Here you can thrill to 70mm prints with Dolby stereo, as you relax into the ultraplush high-back seats. The Dome's most famous feature is the wraparound screen, and speakers are strategically placed around the circular theater, resulting in amazing stereo separation. Parking, which is always a major drawback at the Plitt theaters, is readily available adjacent to the theater. Drop in sometime for a late-afternoon showing, when you'll have this fabulous theater almost all to yourself. 6360 Sunset Blvd., Hollywood.

BEST CONCESSION STAND

The Beverly Theater This small revival house outdoes itself here. First kudos go to the fact that they serve real butter, not that repulsive yellow "butter flavor" oil. Also on the menu: hot apple cider, apple juice, Hebrew National hot dogs, frozen Milky Ways, Unknown Jerome chocolate-chip cookies, and—last but not least—cherry cokes! 7165 Beverly Blvd., Hollywood.

The Beverly Center Cineplex This 14-screen complex is impressively weird, with a long hallway of rooms, each the size of, say, a large bathroom, showing the latest in movie musts. Their concession stand, however, is very nearly regal, featuring such haute cuisine delights as fresh cappuccino, Perrier, nachos, Toblerone chocolate, and, of course, trail mix. Beverly Center, La Cienega and Beverly blvds., Beverly Hills.

BEST ANCIENT MOVIE PALACES

by Les Paul Robley

The Los Angeles This 2,020-seat movie house was built back in 1931, when moviegoing was truly an event. Like an imitation of one of Mad King Ludwig's Bavarian fairy-tale castles, it is said to be the most opulent motion-picture theater in the country. The lobby seems as spacious as the auditorium, almost a self-enclosed little city.

Architect S. Charles Lee fashioned its style after French Renaissance, garnishing it with crystal chandeliers and a crystal fountain surrounded with marble fish at the head of a grand staircase. Traces of its glorious past are still evident, such as a restaurant, ballroom, and two glass-enclosed crying rooms for parents with noisy offspring (these are no longer in use). Downstairs is a huge ladies' room with stalls the size of an average bathroom. Opposite this was once a periscope screen, a kind of camera obscura, built for those with weak bladders who didn't want to miss any of the show.

Still present is a downstairs nursery, a balcony and mezzanine inside the auditorium, and an orchestra pit near the screen. Now used as a bilingual house by Metropolitan Theatres (American movies shown with Spanish subtitles), it's worth the price of admission just to take in the timeless atmosphere. 615 S. Broadway, downtown.

The Million Dollar Theatre The outside really looks like it cost a million dollars to build. Constructed in 1917 by building architect Albert C. Martin and theatre architect William L. Woolett, this is probably one of the oldest movie palaces in the United States. The 2,200-seat auditorium has remained virtually the same throughout the years, containing churrigueresque organ screens and pits, and sunken panels in the ceiling. The exterior is also churrigueresque revival, an elaborately florid architectural style originated by the 18th-century Spanish architect José Churriguera, and brought to Los Angeles from Mexico nearly 200 years ago. Numerous gargoyles ornament the building, peering down at local passersby (these were used originally for drain spouts). A decorative, cornicelike sculpture crowns the theater's top. The Million Dollar's facade features Texas steers sculpted in the form of a coat of arms.

Suitably, the theater is currently in use by the Metropolitan Theatre Circuit as a Spanish movie house. Old theaters never seem to die—they just become Spanish houses, porno palaces, or turn into Korean churches in their old age senility. 307 S. Broadway, downtown.

The Orpheum Theatre Speaking of the Orpheum Theatre, the one on 630 South Broadway is now known as The Palace and is the oldest surviving Orpheum in the U.S. The Orpheum vaudeville circuit later joined forces with Radio Pictures to become the O in RKO Pictures.

Two blocks south on Broadway, a bookend for this historic lane of movie palaces with the Million Dollar holding up the other side, is the new Orpheum Theatre (well, not really new; it was built in 1925). Architect G. Albert Lansburgh designed the interior (as he did the former Orpheum), and the team of Schultze & Weaver (designers of the original Biltmore Hotel chain) were responsible for the exterior. The mammoth auditorium offers a beautiful gold-leaf ceiling, hanging chandeliers, and bronzed light fixtures for overwhelmed visitors to gawk at. Like The Los Angeles Theatre, this cinema is currently used by Metropolitan as a bilingual house. 642 S. Broadway, downtown.

The Tower Theatre The year 1927 was an important one for theaters, since it marked the date that movies made the transition to sound. Many a stable film career was ended by this sudden change of events, and the great movie palaces were not invulnerable to it either. Projection booths had to be newly equipped for sound, high-frequency horns installed in the auditoriums, and acoustical improvements had to be made in some of the larger auditoriums.

When it came time to build new cinemas in Los Angeles, designers were presented with specific proportional changes in their interiors. The long, narrower auditoriums grew in popularity, since more customers could be seated in them without the gripes and arched necks experienced by patrons on the periphery. Amplified sound made this architectural change possible, since the older auditoriums had to be constructed under the restraints of the stage and vocal limitations of its live performers. For theaters built after 1927, these restricting factors never had to figure prominently in their design.

One such house was The Tower Theatre, the first in L.A. to be built exclusively with the talking picture in mind. Now owned and operated by the Pacific Theatres chain, it contrasts sharply with the older palaces on the block, especially its sister theatre, the

Cameo on 588 South Broadway Avenue (the only surviving nickelodeon in California). Anyone who's ever had the opportunity to look down from the projection booth at the 810 seats below will see that it's like looking over the edge of the Grand Canyon. The booth has two Century projectors that have been converted to accept large 6,000-foot feed and take-up reels, and one Simplex E-7 projector.

The building's front displays a large stained-glass window featuring a filmic theme, and a high clock tower (from which it gets its name). The earthquake of 1971 caused the tower to lower slightly in its seat. Legend has it that should the tower ever fall, it will mark the end of talking pictures in Los Angeles. Broadway at Eighth St., downtown.

Radio and Television

BEST STATIONS FOR LOCAL MUSIC

KXLU (88.9 FM), Loyola Marymount; KSPC (88.7 FM), Claremont College; and KNAC (105.5 FM), Long Beach Both noncommercial college stations, KXLU and KSPC have blended the best independently released records, both local and imported, with particular attention to the local talent via such shows as "Stray Pop," one of the more innovative and popular shows on local radio. KNAC has to compete with the heavy commercial market in L.A. and therefore modified its programming accordingly, but even so it is the best commercial radio station for giving local music air play and programming the more enterprising of the new music.

BEST REGULARLY SCHEDULED CLASSICAL MUSIC RADIO PROGRAM

"The Opera Box" The great thing about this show is host Jim Svejda's enthusiasm for his subject, and his superior research. The format regularly features either a single great opera singer, a compendium of representative recordings by singers at a single opera house, or greatest recordings of selections from a single work. Whatever the format of a particular show, Svejda is always fair in dealing with his subject's limitations and always gives his obvious passion, opera, a religious fervor that's contagious. KUSC (91.5 FM); Tues., 8 P.M.

BEST R & B RADIO SHOW

"Blue Mondays Edition" Johnny Otis can be credited with being one of the founding fathers of Los Angeles rhythm and blues. His first hit dates back to the mid-'40s, and his later talent discoveries are legend: Big Mama Thornton, Etta James, Esther Phillips, and the Robins. When Otis jumped into the rock-and-roll ring, he landed with a splash — the chart topper "Willie and the Hand Jive." This year, the Los Angeles bandleader has returned to the airwaves with his two-hour radio show. Otis's rap is the real thing, as he recalls the ups and downs of three decades of music. A natural preacher, he spins out lines as if he's in your living room. "Blue Monday" always features one or two special guests, ranging from hit makers to session musicians, making it like old-home week around the microphone. Callers get a healthy dose of platter chatter and vinyl matter, courtesy of Otis's extensive record collection and a headful of memories. KPFK (90.7 FM); Mon., 9–11 P.M.

BEST REGGAE RADIO SHOW

"**The Reggae Beat**" Roger Steffens is probably the single person most responsible for the increased popularity of reggae in L.A. This is due in no small part to his four-hour reggae program that is possibly the best in the nation, complete with interviews and in-studio performances from the biggest international reggae stars, plus the vast, almost legendary vaults of reggae recordings collected by cohost Hank Holmes. "The Reggae Beat" has spawned many other reggae shows on radio, including ones on KNAC, KXLU, and KJLH. KCRW (89.9 FM); Sun., 2–6 P.M.

BEST COUNTRY WESTERN STATION

KLAC (570 AM) With its flag-waving jocks, commercials, and old-timey fiddles, KLAC used to be the kind of station that you'd turn up extra loud when you wanted to get even with the neighbors. But it's finally toned down its old-shoe image. Musically there isn't *that* much difference these days between KLAC and its FM rival, beautiful music KZLA, whose slogan is "we play the music and get out of the way." At old 570, however, there's still that effort to get the listener involved in "family." DJs are still personable, if quieter, and guest artists and syndicated shows such as "Live From Gilley's" and "Silver Eagle" are regular features. And KLAC's first with new music, such as Bob Segar's "Shame On the Moon."

BEST NONCOMMERCIAL COUNTRY STATION

KCSN (88.5 FM) This station is a welcome change from the Kenny-Sylvia-Alabama axis, with the best alternative country programming on the dial. Last year they decided to devote every day of the week from 1 to 4 P.M., and seven hours on the weekends, to some of the "Americana Music." The result has become a virtual feast of tasty licks, with individual shows on old-timey and bluegrass, '50s to '80s C & W, western swing, rockabilly, and various mixes thereof. You can get KCSN, located at California State University, Northridge, by fiddling with your aerial or turning on KLAC and pushing the FM button.

BEST BLUEGRASS AND FOLK RADIO SHOWS

"**Folkscene**," hosted by Roz and Howard Larman, features traditional and contemporary folk music, live guests, and a calendar of live-folk-music events. KPFK (90.7 FM); Sun., 9:30 P.M.–midnight.

"**Alive and Picking**," hosted by Mary Katherine Aldin, features bluegrass, folk music, and old-time country. KCSN (88.5 FM); Sat., 7–10 A.M.

HIPPEST AM STATION

KGFJ (1230 AM) is a great station that plays rap records, regular soul, and black hits, and even trendy British scratch and techno-disco faves. On Saturday nights, from 11 P.M. to 2 A.M., they offer nonstop party dance music, commercial free.

BEST JAZZ PROGRAM

Chuck Niles Here's a dude who mixes excellent cuts with tidbits of real inside info garnered from 30 years of having been out there on the scene, hanging with the best. Two songs have even been written to him, "Be Bop Charlie" by Bob Florence, and "Niles Blues" by Lewis Belson. Niles favors straight-ahead jazz with an accent on the blues and on hard-driving be bop, and his selection is always intelligent and . . . right there, man! KKGO (105.1 FM); Tues.–Sat., 7 P.M.–midnight.

BEST RADIO SELF–HELP TALK SHOW

"The Bill Ballance Show" One of the more insipid offshoots of the "me decade" has been the proliferation of self-help radio talk shows, where there is usually a holier-than-thou host ready to take on any caller with some whimpering romantic problem or life-style conflict. A pleasant contrast to the garden variety of transparently pretentious airwave shrink can be found in the frisky Bill Ballance, a daytime talk vet who has settled on Thousand Oaks's KGOE. Ballance walks the humorous line between put-on and understanding, and his razor-sharp wit is worth whatever mundane topic he's chosen for the day's discourse. He gives no quarter in his conversations with women— mostly of the married Valley mentality—and he is as quick to spot a phony as he is willing to applaud the zanies. Ballance seems to have a direct line to the feminine mind, and somehow he makes the rest of the radio "pop" psychologists appear irrelevant. So if Toni Grant makes you want to tie your antenna in a knot, an easy spin of the dial will renew your faith in the power of positive humor. KGOE (850 AM); weekdays, 9 A.M.– noon.

MOST "SPONTANEOUS" CLASSICAL MUSIC HOST

Tom Dixon "Tomorrow evening at the Music Center, cellist Lynn Harrell will perform, uh, ah, heh heh, let's see . . . Have you ever tried to read your own scribble? I can't make mine out at all. . . ." Such gushing faux pas are commonplace every weekday afternoon, when host Tom Dixon bravely fumbles and bumbles his way through KFAC's "Good Afternoon Listening." It's a kick, a little like the days of live TV when Betty Furness couldn't open the Westinghouse refrigerator's automatic door. Dixon is always messing up words and phrases, dates and times, composers' names, advertisers' names — you name it, he's botched it. On top of it all, he seems to take a perverse, sophomoric pleasure in courting public humiliation. One day he confessed, in high spirits, to "the big boo boo" he had made earlier: "I played the Ravel minuet at the wrong speed — 45 instead of 33⅓! Well, I'll tell you all about it later — it was a real doozer! ..." So's Tom, but that's okay; he grows on you, in a reverse chic sort of way. "Good Afternoon Listening," KFAC (92.3 FM); Mon.–Fri., 1 P.M.

BEST RADIO STATION IN FREEWAY TRAFFIC

KPRZ (1150 AM) A great mixture of '30s, '40s, and '50s music that is really relaxing and an inspiring counterpoint to contemporary music. Mainly swing, ballads, and big-band sounds, the programming is dubbed "the music of your life," but the rhythmic makeup of the styles reflects, whether it's true or not, a far less stressful time.

BEST SIGNOFF IN LOCAL TV HISTORY

Channel 7 does do something right. They air an inspirational signoff worth staying up for. It's right before the national anthem and it's called *High Flight,* a poem about the glory of flying, a metaphor for living, a gentle assurance of an afterlife, or a subtle religious sermon, take your pick. Part of it goes, " ... sunward I've climbed and joined the tumbling mirth of sun-split clouds and done a hundred things you have not dreamed of." It concludes with, "I trod the high untrespassed sanctity of space, put out my hand, and touched the face of God."

STRANGEST NOSTALGIA RADIO STATION

KPRZ (1150 AM) It's hard not to like this new station. As their jingle goes, they play, "The Music of Your Life — The Great Sounds of the Last 40 Years." This isn't the quality nostalgia of, say, KGIL ("Ballads, Blues, and Big Bands, Too"), but it is the lounge-act schlock of the last 40 years. For an occasional touch of class, they'll throw in some Ella Fitzgerald, Henry Mancini, or Duke Ellington, but the main course dished out here is the likes of Patti Page, Perry Como, Rosemary Clooney, Jerry Vale, Tony Bennett, and Frank Sinatra.

KPRZ will surprise you, though; sometimes they play great stuff hardly ever heard on any other L.A. station, like songs from the iconographic Yma Sumac, or Keely Smith and Louis Prima duets. Another highlight is the swinging weather report. There's this big band tune and every 10 or 15 seconds it's interrupted with a report of environmental conditions around the country — "St. Louis, cloudy, 75 degrees" — then back to the music until they've covered the whole damn U.S.A. KPRZ is easy to find; assuming that you have a button on the car radio set for KRLA, just slowly turn the dial, and it's the very next station to the right.

A GUIDE TO JAZZ RADIO

KPFK (90.7 FM) Limited coverage here at Pacifica radio, but it's first class. John Breckow, an avowed jazz lover and record collector, hits the airwaves twice a week with shows that are both musically pleasing and informative. Breckow's style is to choose an artist or type of music and work around that, and while his annotations are often lengthy, he's not just reading off the back of the albums: he knows his jazz. He's on Fridays from 8 to 10 P.M., and midnight Sunday to 6 A.M. Monday. Jay Green, another collector with a varied taste in acoustic styles, presents a bonanza of interesting, swinging material starting at midnight, Friday.

KLON (88.1 FM) Hard to hear in much of central Los Angeles, this outlet from California State University, Long Beach (though it's not a student station—almost all of the staff are full-time pros) serves southern L.A. with a mainstream format from 9 A.M. to 4:30 P.M. and 6:30 P.M. to 1 A.M., weekdays; noon to 5 P.M. and 6 P.M. to 1 A.M., weekends. Another delightful commercial-free offering. Program director Ken Borgers is on weekdays, from 9 P.M. to 1 A.M., followed by music director Dan Jacobsen, 1:30 to 4:30 P.M. At night you can hear Bob Epstein from 6:30 to 10 P.M., and Dave Burchette, 10 P.M. to 1 A.M.

KKGO (105.1 FM) The town's only round-the-clock jazz station presents a format that ranges from the newest contemporary fusion pieces to big bands to classics, the idea being that you'll hang in through a cut you don't like if you know that one you will is upcoming. Morning man Jim Gosa (5:30–9 A.M., weekdays) mixes it up well, choosing the best cuts from old and new albums and adding pleasant chatter to keep you company. Laura Lee (9 A.M.–2 P.M.) and Joe Huser (2–7 P.M.) roll you through midmorning into the evening with melodic selections, then Chuck Niles, a mainstream addict, pulls out delicious straight-ahead cuts and tasteful contemporary items from 7 P.M. to midnight. Sam Fields handles the graveyard shift.

KCRW (89.9 FM) Jazz coverage is good—Tom Schnabel's "Morning Becomes Eclectic" offers a basic jazz format with sidetracks into classical and ethnic areas, plus the almost nightly "Strictly Jazz." From 10 P.M. on Monday and Wednesday through Friday and from midnight on Sunday, Tuesday, and Saturday, jazz from all spectrums is played, sans commercials. Of particular interest are the shows of Will Thornberry, a longtime pro who often schedules excellent interviews and in-depth musical profiles (Thursday, 10 P.M.); Bo Liebowitz, a collector of vintage straight-ahead works (Wednesday, 10 P.M.); Junebug (Sunday, midnight), who leans toward the avant-garde edge; and Nina Lenart's "Latin Dimensions" (Friday, 10 P.M.). "Jazz Alive" airs Mondays at 10 P.M.

MOST INFORMATIVE RADIO STATION

KPFK (90.7 FM) is the radio station that gives a glimpse of what the media could accomplish if it really cared. Featuring what is probably the most varied and informative programming in politics and the arts, KPFK has a certain inevitable amount of mass appeal. Every type of music, from classical to reggae, or bluegrass dulcimer to Yemenite wedding songs, is explored, along with well-researched commentary that makes the shows more than just another foray into easy listening. The news is probably the finest and most revealing in the country, putting the networks deeply to shame. There are also sci-fi shows, poetry shows, theater shows, history shows; there are shows on Asian, Latin American, feminist, gay, and senior citizens' issues . . . and on and on. Particularly noteworthy is the insightful, hard-hitting political coverage of such programs as "Morning Magazine," "Middle East in Focus," and "Family Tree." A subscriber-dependent operation, KPFK is well worth your financial support, as you're bound to click with at least one of their regular programs.

BEST BLACK MUSIC AND AFFAIRS RADIO STATION

KJLH (102.3 FM) The black radio station that translates into Kindness, Joy, Love, and Happiness. Owned by Stevie Wonder, the programming reflects his musical attitude of good rhythm and blues, jazz, and funk, leaving out the school of screaming. Newscasts center on the black community, both local and national, reflecting their views on public issues. On Sundays, we can all go to church and listen to some fine gospel. KJLH concentrates on supporting the black community by accentuating the positive and eliminating the negative. Musical programming is as smooth as black silk.

BEST RADIO BROADCASTER

Rick Dees Before Rick Dees came along, nobody in L.A. got out of bed before noon. Today, most everyone gets up at 6 A.M. and takes a shower with the Lord of Lampoonery, who brings theater back to the airwaves where it belongs. Dees is a master satirist who pokes fun at our metropolis in such a way that we laugh at ourselves, not each other. Even the time, temperature, and traffic reports play into his fantasies: an effeminate time fairy tells you the hour, the temperature is read in "Dees Degrees," and the traffic update is followed by an hysterical woman screaming,

"Don't take the car! You'll kill yourself!" No minority group is spared Dees's acerbic jibes, and he's thus appreciated—or condemned—by just about everyone. Why, the queen of England, on her visit to L.A., remarked, "Rick Dees? I don't always understand him, but I like his taste in clothes." "Rick Dees In the Morning Show," KIIS (102.7 FM).

BEST METHOD FOR INTERRUPTING MOVIES FOR COMMERCIALS

Channel 5 gets kudos for actually taking the time to lift a snippet of the soundtrack from whatever movie they're showing, and using it to somewhat unobtrusively fade in and out of commercials.

BEST TELEVISION ANCHORMAN

Hank Plante For straightforward midday news, nothing beats Channel 9's 1:30 P.M. report. This is strictly of the no-frills, tear-it-off-the-wire-service-and-read-it variety. And they've got the right guy for it in Hank Plante. He just sits and reads, unpretentiously, seldom making mistakes. There are no minicam reports or consumer advocates or staff psychologists or movie critics. A welcome relief.

BEST ACTRESS IN A TV COMEDY

Tawny Little Schneider The anchorwoman of KABC's "Eyewitness News" has a great deal of competition but no true peers. Tawny is a former Miss America turned newscaster who says, "I just wasn't the beauty queen type ... I was so bright and outspoken." Tawny does the news as though she has just been dry cleaned. Her starched visage never wrinkles, and through the bombing of Beirut the viewer knows she has one thing on her mind: her lipstick. Viewers have come to appreciate her deep sense of humanity through coverage of such historical moments as movie stars filing into the Dorothy Chandler Pavilion for the Academy Awards. During the 1982 segment, she squealed and giggled like a high school girl. If you've ever wondered what happened to Valley girls when they grow up, or you've never seen Ted Baxter in drag, tune in "Eyewitness News" on KABC, Monday through Friday at 11 P.M.

BEST LOCAL RELIGIOUS TV PROGRAMS

There's certainly no shortage of crackpot religious TV shows jamming the airwaves, but three stand out as distinctive entertainment.

Church in the Home, a live service direct from Skid Row, is performed by Reverend Fred Jordan and broadcast on Channel 11 (usually at 11:30 A.M.). Before the transients can get a promised meal, they must listen to the stuttering Rev. Fred relate God's word. The best part is when he takes a minicam through the alleys to gather tragic life stories. Once a very intoxicated Indian used the forum to express, in a graphic, expletive-undeleted diatribe, his feelings on the white man's insensitivity. In the middle of his attack, he passed out.

The Trinity Broadcast Network out of Huntington Beach (UHF Channel 40) is also always good for a laugh. Jan and Paul Crouch host this 24-hour plea for funds. Jan is prone to whimpering, crying, and "jumping for Jesus." During a fund-raising festival, she kicked off her shoes and ran around the studio like a wigged-out witch doctor, waving her hands and shouting "hallelujah" whenever anyone pledged $100. But the highlight is when the Crouches' greasy son arrives to report on the evils of punk rock music. He shows album covers, reads lyrics, and once took a video camera to a Circle Jerks concert. "Hold onto your seats," he cautioned before they ran the tape of Keith Morris mooning the audience. Afterward, Jan and Paul got on their hands and knees and prayed for "punkers."

Dr. Gene Scott is a Pentecostal preacher who is constantly threatened with having his broadcasting license revoked by the FCC because of questionable finances. Basically, Gene just sits there night after night, screaming about government injustice and asking for money. One night, when he was in the middle of a particularly vicious verbal assault, he leaned back to make another point and fell completely backwards out of his famous sheepskin-covered chair. His newest gimmick is on-the-air baptism. For a minimum contribution, we assume. UHF Channel 56.

The Club Scene

BEST DANCE CLUBS

Did you know that the lifespan of a white rat is 2½ to 3 years? Well, that happens to be longer than the lifespan of many of L.A.'s dance clubs, which hatch and expire with sometimes dizzying speed. Nonetheless, a few stalwart places have been around long enough to make us feel that they'll still be rockin' by the time this book comes out.

Club Lingerie Affectionately known as Club Underwear by certain regulars, this dance club has been continuously open, under different names, since 1942, and street info has it in business since the mid-1930s. Eclectic is the word for Lingerie's booking policy, which has had Big Joe Turner backed by the Blasters on one night and Johanna Went on another. It's known for good reggae, new wave, and R & B artists of national stature. Friday nights there's The Veil, an innovative new music disco, and Wednesdays are devoted to rockabilly. But all the action isn't onstage; the waitresses are known for their sartorial splendor and the patrons often exercise equal imagination. 6507 Sunset Blvd., Los Angeles; 466-8557.

The Palace This has got to be the "best fancy pants" club around. It's a gorgeous, multileveled venue that features a kind of electronic dance

Muzak, but they book quite a variety of acts, ranging from the upright trendy to the downright terrific of rock 'n roll, new wave, and other pop styles. The Palace is also an after-hours spot, serving soft drinks after 2 A.M. Sunday night: Gay Disco. 1735 Vine St., Hollywood; 462-3000.

O.N. Klub Also known as the House of Sweat, this club delivers the best in reggae and ska, with a sprinkling of new wave and rockabilly thrown in. Beer and wine are served, and Tonto's Kitchen offers popcorn, hotdogs, and sissy drinks. There are usually from one to three bands a night, but O.N. is famed primarily for its reggae offerings, being one of the first clubs in the city to promote this musical style. Wednesday night: Folk Night. 3037 W. Sunset Blvd., Silverlake; 665-1286.

Candilejas Club This is one of the best Latin clubs in L.A. For over-21s of the salsa persuasion, there's a large salsa orchestra playing live Thursday through Sunday, and shaking the rafters till 4 A.M. on Friday and Saturday. In 1965, there were over 200 salsa clubs in L.A.; the numbers may have diminished since then, but not the spirit. Dress code: T-shirts, shorts, sneakers—no! Designer jeans—si! 5060 Sunset Blvd., Hollywood; 665-8822.

Cathay De Grande This club used to feature punk bands until the boys in blue cracked down. Now they've compromised with lots of new wave, rockabilly, and R & B, with an average of three bands a night. The downstairs club opens at around 10:30 P.M. with live music, and upstairs there are rock videos and dancing from 5 P.M. on. How to dress? Well, there are still many patrons who show up in vintage prom dresses and gray-felt "poo-dle" circle skirts. 1600 N. Argyle Ave. (at Selma), Hollywood; 461-4077.

BEST FOLK MUSIC

McCabe's Guitar Shop McCabe's is one of the oldest folk clubs in L.A., having been established back in the '60s. They book live music every Friday and Saturday night (the rest of the week it's a folklore center and guitar shop), with performers ranging from folk to bluegrass to blues to zydeco to old-timey. Alumni include Emmylou Harris, Jackson Browne, Linda Ronstadt, Jennifer Warren, and many more. The atmosphere is intimate and sometimes collegiate, with coffee and brownies served at the intermissions and guitars and banjos adorning the walls. 3101 W. Pico Blvd., Santa Monica; 828-4497.

The Banjo Cafe L.A.'s only bluegrass club, they proudly state, and that's what you get six nights a week (closed Sunday), along with delicacies like chili, pizza, and burgers on the menu. Admission varies; the performers run the gamut from local favorites to Ralph Stanley, Don Reno, and the like. 2906 Lincoln Blvd., Santa Monica; 392-5716.

BEST COUNTRY CLUB

The Palomino They no longer scrape the cowboys up with the broken glass here, as they did in 1952, when the Thomas Brothers bought the place. Nowadays, this is a high-class honky-tonk that books rock acts too (no dancing). But at 31—(possibly the longest continuously run club in the U.S.), "The Pal" is *the* place for anyone remotely interested in the country scene. History whispers from the old wood walls, which display hundreds of pictures of then-unknowns such as Patsy Cline, Jim Reeves, George Jones, Johnny Cash—you *name* 'em, they've played here (and when nobody else wanted them). But *you* want to be here because there's still history being made. You never know who's going to jump onstage to perform—folks'll tell you about the time Freddy Fender or Marty Robbins got up at Talent Night, or Jerry Lee Lewis invited Kris Kristofferson onstage. (And Clint Eastwood shoots his films here.) Ambience is '50s "joint," with dim lights and hand-painted fluorescent signs. Drinks aren't cheap, but the new Sunday Western barbecue with three bands—all for $2.95—*is* a bargain. 6907 Lankershim, North Hollywood; 764-4010.

BEST R & B CLUB

Five Torches You might have a hard time convincing anyone but the most persistent of aficionados, but, yes, Los Angeles does have a rhythm and blues nightlife. Once home to the grandest of R & B traditions, the city saw disco pummel live black music into submission, with only the hardiest of clubs surviving. And no other spot has thrived with more class than the Five Torches, a medium-size room with a stage situated next to the front door. Here, live music still reigns king; it's finding out who plays when that keeps the club a secret. But when Bobby "Blue" Bland or Z.Z. Hill is scheduled, the faithful flock out in force to see and hear living proof that R & B is burning bright. The club features no pretentious ambience, which is one of its charms. It's the music that people have paid to hear, and with all eyes on the bandstand, it's the music that makes the nightclub so special. For coming attractions, consult *Scoop* newspaper or watch the posters on telephone poles south of Pico Boulevard and Crenshaw Boulevard at Imperial Highway. 11344 Crenshaw Blvd., Inglewood; 777-8295.

BEST REGGAE CLUB DJ

Ron Miller Ron started booking reggae shows at the Twenty Grand Club before anybody had heard of any reggae singer other than Bob Marley. Since then, he has played in just about every club and with every band connected with reggae. He helped many starting "toasters" hone their vocal skills, like Jah T. from the band Idren. He is an unmistakable figure in his Detroit Red Wings hockey shirt, full beard, and shades, fiddling and turning the knobs to his sound system.

BEST FREE FUN

Maple Leaf Club This claims to be the only organization in America devoted to preserving ragtime music, and they do it in style. Every meeting provides musical surprises; besides ragtime there is boogie woogie and stride piano, small groups, larger groups and occasionally a singing group. The late Eubie Blake was even known to make an unexpected appearance, playing his latest ivory ticklers. Now in its 15th year, the club has members from all over the world and showcases the best local ragtime talent. (Meets bimonthly on last Sunday of every odd-numbered month.) Variety Arts Center, 940 S. Figueroa, downtown; 623-9100.

BEST JAZZ CLUBS

Hop Singh's Hop Singh's took quite a while to finally open. Announcements preceded the fact by at least three years and, in this case, the wait was worth it. Hop Singh's is the town's largest casual nightclub. The chairs don't match, neither do the tables, but in exchange for uniformity, there's plenty of room for your feet and you can see the bandstand from every corner. Owner Rudy Onderwyzer, formerly of Shelly's Manne-Hole and the Lighthouse, also arranged for some interesting murals to grace three of the walls, giving us something visually stimulating should the musical offering need a respite. The room seats 350 easily, and top names such as Phil Woods, the Great Guitars, and Buddy Rich can be heard here with frequency. Minors are welcome. 4110 Lincoln Blvd., Marina del Rey; 822-4008.

Baked Potato This club is about the size of your living room and when the music's loud, which it is usually, it's *very* loud. Still, this is the same Baked Potato where Tom Scott, Lee Ritenour, and Larry Carlton played week after week before they reached grander climes, and top contemporary, or fusion if you will, groups can still be found here nightly. The house band is Quest, led by co-owner and pianist Don Randi. Incidentally, the name of the club refers to the junior-football-size spuds that make up the menu. Amazingly, the prices for these royal Idaho products haven't gone up in five years. 3787 Cahuenga Blvd., North Hollywood; 980-1615.

Donte's Donte's is the senior jazz room in L.A. For over 15 years, the best local bands have paraded through this spot, where the decor seems to change as fast as the acts. It now sports a flat black paint on all the walls and ceilings, save for some walls which are of wood paneling. It's a pleasing contrast, as is the variety of musicians that owner Carey Leverette presents. Freddie Hubbard, Joe Pass, the Capp-Pierce Juggernaut big band, and Carmen MacRae (she recorded here) are just a few of the regular passersby. During the week, new and upcoming bands are spotlighted, while name draws appear on the weekends. Leverette keeps a first-class chef aboard and the food tastes like it. (The wine list, however, could use some help.) 4269 N. Lankershim Blvd., North Hollywood; 769-1566.

Bars and Hangouts

BEST CHIC NEIGHBORHOOD BAR

Chrystie's The kind of friendly neighborhood bar you wouldn't be afraid to live upstairs from. Located next to the Wilshire Theater in Beverly Hills, Chrystie's offers a warm and comfortable cocktail lounge and restaurant. Leather booths line the small room. The bar itself is done in deco leather, with beveled-glass accents. You can sit on high stools and the facing wall, thank God, has no mirror. Instead of watching a narcissistic indulgite go gaga over his or her reflection, there's a chance for some decent conversation. Chrystie's, by the way, is one of the few places in L.A. open for a late supper, serving hot food until 1 A.M. 8442 Wilshire Blvd. (near La Cienega), Beverly Hills; 655-8113.

BEST PUB

Ye Old King's Head One needn't be English to enjoy Ye Olde King's Head, but one will hear sundry British accents among the throng. "Home of the British fish and chip," the King's Head is close to the Santa Monica beach and is a noisy, lively joint replete with British emigres. Two dart boards are always busy, and a crowded bar serves Watney's, John Courage, Newcastle brown, and Guinness. Besides fish and chips, there's such English staples for the palate as Cornish pasties, Scotch eggs, shepherd's pie, and sherried Midlands trifle. The sandwiches are sufficiently fat that you can barely get your jaws around them. The decor is pleasant brown wood and no-nonsense, and the walls are covered with a miscellaneous array of portraits, shields, mirrors advertising English ales and beers, and other odds and ends. A separate section adjoining the bar and dart room is somewhat quieter, for dining and conversation. The pub is fun, the food and drink quite good. If you've been to London, it will bring back memories. Mon.–Sat., 11 A.M.–1:30 A.M.; Sun., noon–1:30 A.M. 116 Santa Monica Blvd., Santa Monica; 394-9458.

BEST HOLLYWOOD NEIGHBORHOOD BAR

Boardner's is a bar that lies literally in the heart of Hollywood, right between Sunset and the Boulevard, between ritzy and low rent. There are plenty of places that cater to a clientele either so high up or so low down that the average drinker is intimidated by the surroundings. Drinking at the Brown Derby, on one side of the social spectrum, or, say, Jackie's at the other, is best left to the regulars. Boardner's is a neighborhood bar to those who don't live around it, an oasis in a declining part of Hollywood. The drinks are hearty, the talk is seasoned Hollywood and street stuff, and the booths comfortable. There's enough history wafting around the room that it takes several visits just to get straight what happened to whom when. By day, workers from the nearby *Hollywood Reporter* fill up Boardner's; at night, an adventurous mix of drinkers trickles down from Hollywood Boulevard. The bar is a vanishing breed and should be seen to be believed. 1652 N. Cherokee, Hollywood; 462-9621.

BEST HOLLYWOOD NOSTALGIA BAR

The Frolic Room There's a real '40s feel to this place, from the neon on the outside to the recessed circular light fixtures suspended from the ceiling inside. But what most people cherish most about this joint is the wallpaper. Not just any ordinary wallpaper, but carefully restored wallpaper by Hirschfield, the famed caricaturist. It looks pretty old, but is actually in excellent shape and features the likes of Marilyn Monroe, Einstein, Picasso, and even Eleanor Roosevelt. As to clientele, the Frolic Room has one of the most eclectic; overdressed theatergoers, punkers, straights, gays, and long-forgotten starlets all coexist peacefully on the Walk of Fame's favorite alcoholic oasis. 6245 Hollywood Blvd. (right next door to the Pantages Theatre); 462-5890.

BEST HIDEAWAY BAR

The Coronet This tiny, hidden-away joint has long been a refuge for working actors, screenwriters, English rock stars, and serious drinkers who like its low-key, dimly lit, no-assholes-allowed atmosphere. Actor-owner Nick Faltas keeps the jazz station playing until 2 A.M. closing. The best place for a nightcap after an obscure French flick at the nearby Cineplex. 370 N. La Cienega, Beverly Hills; 659-4583.

BEST WESTSIDE BARS

Chez Jay is a Westside tradition for good food at decent prices. The bar here is actually very small, and usually crammed with people waiting for a table in this popular eatery. Nevertheless, it's a great place to meet an incredibly eclectic kind of crowd; and if you're the kind of person who likes to drink sociably—in the literal sense —rather than out of depression, Chez Jay is the place for you. 1657 Ocean Ave., Santa Monica; 395-1741.

West Beach Cafe really starts jumping around 11 P.M. every night, after the dinner crowd has split. A crowd heavily flavored with Venice art-scene types and movie-industry types begins to settle in until closing time, drinking champagne by the glass, mixing business and pleasure quite nicely. The room, with its ever-changing displays of modern art is, for a change, *not* underlit, fostering gregariousness rather than tête-à-têtes. The West Beach features a dazzling selection of cognacs and armagnacs, but don't expect to get off cheap, especially if you're thirsty. A champagne cocktail (albeit a *very* good one) costs five dollars. 60 N. Venice Blvd., Venice; 399-9246.

BEST NEIGHBORHOOD BAR SERVING TWO ETHNIC GROUPS AT DIFFERENT HOURS

The Escape Bar is two neighborhood places in one. The English-speaking crowd comes directly from work and is overseen by Pat, a super lady and barkeep. Around 8 P.M. the Korean lettering over the door (meaning "Love Room") takes on significance. In come the Asian customers and seductive ladies, live music replaces the mellow jukebox, and the prices go up. There's even the back room with half-hidden booths sheltered by white ruffled curtains. Third Street near Kingsley, Los Angeles; 386-1594.

MOST DECADENT PRIVATE CLUB

The Meat Rack Located in trendy East Hollywood is the West Coast's kinkiest and most fashionable pay toilet. The Meat Rack is the ultimate experience for the anonymous male sex junkie. For a nominal charge one can fulfill those darkest of fantasies. Spanking, spitting, and water sports are not unusual in this members-only club, so don't wear white Levi's or go in bare feet. Guests wander through the maze in sometimes total darkness while the sweet aroma of poppers fill the air. The walls are (dis)tastefully decorated with the raunchiest sexual graffiti. First-time visitors don't know whether to barf or go blind. For the exact address, ask around. Oh, yes, for gay males only.

BEST MECCA FOR GROUPIES

Le Parc Hotel Elvis Costello, the Police, the Clash, Santana, Kool & The Gang, and a constant parade of rock heavies make classy Le Parc Hotel their home away from home. The discreet third-floor bar is the best place for you smart, sharp-looking girls seeking to comfort cute, rich, lonesome, tour-weary rock stars. 733 N. West Knoll, West Hollywood; 855-8888.

BEST PUNK HANGOUT

Danny's Dogs This is the home of the famous Oki Dog, teriyaki burrito, and some of the best fries in town if the grease is clean. It's also the home of a host of colorful characters who provide free entertainment, both on the street and behind the counter. Danny's is known as the Ma Maison of the east of Fairfax crowd and the police visit frequently, but eating an Oki Dog veggie burrito is still on this side of the law, even for punks. Santa Monica Blvd. and Vista, West Hollywood.

BEST PLACE TO HEAR PUNK MUSIC

London

BEST BEER SELECTION

Barney's Beanery Have you ever heard of Old Peculiar Ale? How about Brassin de Garde? Or Paulaner Hell Urtyp? Well, for the answer to all your beer trivia questions, plus the actual beers themselves, pay a visit to Barney's, where these three and more than 197 other brands can be found. There's no reason to be bored with the commoners when you can excite your adrenals with the pride of Norway or Hong Kong or Thailand or Jamaica. Why, this beer-tasting excursion could almost substitute for an around-the-world drunk. 8447 Santa Monica Blvd., Hollywood; 654-2287.

BEST AFTER–HOURS HANGOUT

Lhasa Club Truly a fascinating place featuring a little bit of everything

and everyone, Lhasa was created by Frenchman Jean-Pierre Boccara as a "unique performance art space," the like of which has yet to be seen either here or in Europe, according to the young owner. Boccara books comedians, bands, and all manner of performance artists, and hosts film and video screenings of both silent classics and brand-new avant-garde works. Lhasa has also recently opened an art gallery, with limited hours, to bring the creations of new artists both here and abroad to the attention of L.A. At present, Lhasa has no liquor license, but its combination cappuccino and juice bar feaures an array of tasty snacks and concoctions. And, as befits any such bastion of eccentricity, the patrons are every bit as intriguing as the acts; on any given night you're apt to see partygoers dressed in everything from leather to '50s prom attire and sneaks. L.A. at its hard-core artyest. 1110 N. Hudson Ave., West Hollywood; 461-7284.

BEST PIANO BARS

Hong Kong Low Piano bars haven't really made the leap into the modern world, but for a pleasing glimpse of the past, they can't be beat. It takes a special sort to re-create the ambience of a living room, but that's what the good piano players do when a few customers gather around the keyboard and the songs start rolling. Hong Kong Low (downstream from the former Hong Kong Club punk rock room) features one of the most ingratiating musicians in town. Besides the set of standards that are part and parcel of every piano bar's repertoire, the woman who tinkles the ivories here has a built-in rhythm section in the odd assortment of windup monkeys who bang and clang away while she sings. It's quite a sight when she slips into "Margaritaville," turns on the juice, and sets the monkey loose. Add the tambourines and maracas that are handed out to her sing-along partners around the piano, and you've got a beat-happy symphony. 425 Gin Ling Way, Chinatown; 628-6717.

Club 22 If what you want is "Melancholy Baby," any place with an old, beat-up spinet will do. At Club 22, what they offer is a cross between Mardi Gras and a tribal wedding ceremony. Santos, an Argentine tinkler who also plays synthesizer, passes out bongos, tambourines, and various other percussion instruments to the customers and from there on in anything can happen. Remember playing the rattles in kindergarten? This is twice as much fun. 9424 Brighton Way, Beverly Hills; 274-7766.

BEST ARTIST HANGOUTS

West Beach Cafe Reeks of art. The menu features a monthly guide to the work on the walls. Caters to collectors, dealers, and artists who can afford it. Very upscale, but a real oasis for Sunday morning brunch. 60 N. Venice Blvd., Venice; 399-9246.

Al's Bar is without question the primo hangout for serious hard-core downtown artists. They've recently relinquished live music in favor of offering loft-dwelling neighborhood art types a comfortable, friendly bohemian wateringhole, complete with a well-stocked jukebox, small patio, cozy booths, pool table, TV, and mural-covered walls. 305 S. Hewitt St., downtown; 687-3558.

BEST VIDEO BAR

Revolver Chicly dressed people stand about in a sterile room, all staring at television monitors on the walls. Are they waiting for their flights to arrive? Well, in a manner of speaking. But this is not LAX: it's L.A.'s hottest video bar, Revolver. Gone are the days of sipping your beer to the jukebox at the corner bar; this '80s pub runs video shows continuously, featuring name performers and newcomers in a variety of comedic and musical reviews. But of more interest than the stars on the screen are the "stars" in the bar. They include high-tech, high-fashion groupies who would like to work in the entertainment industry. Most of the crowd is gay, male, and very good looking, although some, we must admit, are a bit snooty. For these, the video screen provides the perfect direction in which to stick their noses in the air. 8851 Santa Monica Blvd., West Hollywood; 550-8851.

SOME WELL–KNOWN PICKUP BARS

Merlin McFly's You needn't be a young, flawless physical specimen to score here, but it helps. But why do such pretty people look so vacuous? Maybe it's the noise level, which precludes any but nonverbal interaction. Or maybe it's the automatic swivel of heads as a new body walks in the etched-glass front doors of this ferny, woody saloon. Lots of brass around the bar—and we don't mean just the rail. With a little eye contact you ought to be able to get something going, especially if you can read lips. 2702 Main St., Venice; 392-8468.

The Ginger Man Lots of brass here, too, combined with red brick and beamed ceilings. But this clientele is much too bourgeois, cool, and hip to do the puppet-swivel checkout routine. These chic Important and Assistant Important people will cast a casual glance that classifies you instantly according to financial and professional status, as well as looks. Definitely not the place for your Wrangler jeans, no matter how great you look in them. 369 N. Bedford, Beverly Hills; 273-7585.

Hamburger Hamlet This particular Hamlet is often described as "CPA City," and the bar area is teeming with an odd mixture of the suit-and-tie bunch and the pressed-designer-jeans crew. If you're not fussy about the quality or sparkle of introductory repartee ("You come here a lot?"), you should do okay here, on sheer numbers alone. Circle the bar a few times, or set yourself up at a backgammon table. And smile—a lot of these grownups tend to stand around self-consciously and stare, like junior high kids at a school dance. 11648 San Vincente, Brentwood; 826-3558.

Joe Allen's This West Coast branch of the New York original is refreshing in the sense that the customers don't seem to flaunt their wonderfulness. Lots of writers and actors congregate here for dinner and in the late evening hours, and while things can get wild and raucous, there isn't much of the phony posturing often found at other establishments. When your own initials are enough, this is the place to come and relax, drink, and enjoy the talk. An interesting place for pickups, but by no means a meat market. 8706 W. Third, West Hollywood; 274-7144.

The China Club as a conception rates somewhere between *The Lady from Shanghai* and Studio 54. The decor is so deco-chic that in the event that nothing else looks good, you can always feast your eyes on the interior design. The '30s to '50s splendor in the form of fresh flowers and pink lighting contrasts splendidly with the shiny black furniture, paintings, mirrors, and atomic-age accoutrements. It wouldn't be too surprising to see Gary Cooper and Marlene Dietrich glance up from a tête-à-tête in one of the dim corners near the bar. If your mood veers toward those who are wealthy, witty, kinky, or all three, you've come to the right place; the regular clientele includes new-wave musicians, artists, writers, designers, owner of coke empires, etc. 8333 W. Third St., West Hollywood; 658-6406.

L.A.'s Live Theaters

by Joie Davidow

Theater in L.A. falls into three categories. The first is the big houses, where splashy, big-name productions on their way to or from New York are the only fare with enough pull to fill so many seats. The mid-sized houses, which are the mainstay of theater in New York, exist only in small, but increasing numbers here. These 400- to 500-seat spaces accommodate fully professional productions of a less extravagant nature—thought-provoking small-cast plays, clever little musicals. The third category is by far the largest. Thanks to an agreement with Actors' Equity, professional actors can waive their rights to Equity minimum wages, so long as they work in a theater seating 99 or less. Originally designed as a means of allowing actors to showcase their talents for casting directors and agents, the Equity-waiver theaters in L.A. have flourished in recent years, becoming a venue for high-caliber productions and interesting experimentation. In a typical season, there are more than 400 Equity-waiver productions in L.A., some of them featuring such big-name actors as Jon Voight, Gena Rowlands, Paul Michael Glaser, Gregory Harrison, Tyne Daley, and Salome Jens.

THE MAJORS

The Pantages A beautiful art deco palace, worth a visit just to goggle the awesome architecture. Since the theater has a pit, it's used almost exclusively for big musicals. Beware, though, the acoustics are not the greatest, and there are seats under the balcony to avoid if you like to hear your shows. The Pantages is in the domain of the Nederlander Organization, which brings its big hits in from Broadway. For your intermission pleasure, the refreshment counter in the middle of the lobby sells soft drinks, nuts, and candy; there's also a very busy bar to your left, downstairs, and a second bar, upstairs, is open occasionally. 6233 Hollywood Blvd., Hollywood; 462-3104.

The Ahmanson This monolithic black space is not famous for its acoustics either, but it books a season of pre-Broadway tryouts and post-Broadway sure-fire ticket sellers. You can get a drink at intermission here too—if you're fast enough to beat the crowds. The Ahmanson offers a subscription season, and there's usually a splashy post-Broadway musical booked in for the whole summer. Music Center, 135 N. Grand Ave., downtown; 972-7343.

The Wilshire Another art deco marvel, with a magnificent bar in the middle of the lobby. The occasional big musical or star-filled hit plays here, but the place is more often lamentably dark. 8440 Wilshire Blvd., Beverly Hills; 467-1199.

The Music Center Pavilion In the summer, the Civic Light Opera plays here. The acoustics are fine, and the sound system is excellent, as it's also the home of the Los Angeles Philharmonic. Music Center, 135 N. Grand Ave., downtown; 972-7211.

The Shubert Theater A huge, splashy place, where huge, splashy musicals like *Evita* and *Dreamgirls* run forever. The theater gets an audience of out-of-towners from the classy Century Plaza Hotel across the way. Bars in both upstairs and downstairs lobbies. ABC Entertainment Center, Century City; 553-9000.

THE MID–SIZED HOUSES

The L.A. Stage Company This nicely appointed, air-conditioned facility has been given new life by artistic director Susan Dietz, who rescued it from a fate worse than death as a cinema. Past productions have included *Uncommon Women and Others, The Fox,* and the long-running *Nuts.* The off-Broadway hit, *Sister Mary Ignatius Explains It All for You,* also had a long run here. In keeping with Dietz's policy of promoting local talent, a full season of locally produced plays is offered. 1642 N. Las Palmas, Hollywood; 461-2755.

L.A. Stage Company West The success of her Hollywood theater prompted Susan Dietz to open this Beverly Hills facility. Air-conditioned with 348 seats and a wine bar in the plush lobby, the theater is a home for plays new to L.A. A locally produced version of Caryl Churchill's hit, *Cloud 9,* was the critically acclaimed inaugural offering. 205 N. Canon Dr., Beverly Hills; 859-2643.

Coronet Theater This smallish theater, situated in a pretty little courtyard set back from the street, is the home of the L.A. Public Theater, produced by Peg Yorkin. The quality of productions is usually good, and past efforts have featured name actors such as Mariette Hartley, Adam Arkin, and Shelley Hack. The delightfully funky bar, adjacent to the theater, is always full of colorful characters. 366 N. La Cienega Blvd., West Hollywood; 659-6415.

The Huntington Hartford Theater This is a book-in house, which doesn't generate its own season but serves as an L.A. address, mostly for shows that played successfully off-Broadway. There's a very comfortable upstairs bar with plenty of seating. You can order drinks before the show, and they'll be waiting for you at intermission. 1615 N. Vine St., Hollywood; 462-6666.

The Mark Taper Forum The Music Center's plush and modern smaller theater space offers an interesting season in the three-quarter round, under the artistic direction of Gordon Davidson, usually including a decent sampling of new plays. There is a narrow bar on the ground floor. The Music Center, 135 N. Grand Ave., downtown; 972-7654.

The Westwood Playhouse This attractive space in the Contempo Westwood Center is reached by walking through a Scandinavian furniture store. Drinks are served from a bar in the pretty little patio in front. The theater is primarily used for one-person shows and book-ins like *Little Shop of Horrors.* 10866 Le Conte Ave., Westwood; 208-5454.

Long Beach Light Opera Although this company is housed in the Terrace Theater, a sleek, modern 3,000-seat-plus facility, it has not been a fully professional theater until recently. In seasons past, an amateur cast backed one or two big stars, but a recent agreement with Actors' Equity qualifies the company for a League of Resident Theaters contract, which means that they can pay regional theater wages to all their actors, the same fees paid in most mid-sized houses. The company specializes in musicals, from *Bittersweet* to *Grease*. Convention Center, Long Beach; 432-7926.

New and Planned Theaters At press time, a number of mid-sized houses were in the works, many of them planned for completion in time for the 1984 Olympics. The Nederlanders plan to build a pair of mid-sized theaters on Hollywood Boulevard across the street from the Pantages, with a shared lobby. The historic Pasadena Playhouse is in the process of being refurbished, with the smaller Balcony Theater already open, and a mid-sized auditorium scheduled to be in use soon. The Aquarius Theater on Sunset, home of the long-running *Zoot Suit*, is being rebuilt and renamed the Earl Carroll Theater, as it was called in its glory days. And a number of Equity-waiver companies have serious expansion plans. Most notable of these is the Los Angeles Actors Theater, which is in the process of building a facility downtown that will house three theaters, an art gallery, a bookstore, and a cafe.

SMALLER THEATERS

Since there are so many of these Equity-waiver-sized houses (more than 100 at last count, and multiplying rapidly), we can only take space to mention a few here, with no particular advocacy or insult to those not included. While many theaters offer season subscriptions, tickets are almost always available for single performances as well.

Actors for Themselves Producer Joseph Stern puts on expensively mounted shows in the Matrix Theater, one of the most modern and handsomely appointed facilities in town. Since Actors for Themselves is an organization of well-known, established actors, you'll often see outstanding casts here. 7657 Melrose Ave., West Hollywood; 852-1445.

American Theater Arts In a nicely remodeled building, formerly a mortuary, director Don Eitner runs both a theater season and an acting school. The season's offerings generally include revivals such as Kaufman and Hart's *Once in a Lifetime,* as well as the occasional new or lesser-known play. 6240 Hollywood Blvd., Hollywood; 466-2462.

Back Alley Theater This small facility in the Valley initiated an adaptation of D.H. Lawrence's *The Fox,* which moved up to a mid-size house in L.A. and then on to New York. In addition to their schedule of productions, the company runs a writers' workshop to which such playwrights as Beth Henley and Paul Zindel, both

Pulitzer Prize winners, contribute. The theater has only 60 seats, but it's air-conditioned. 15231 Burbank Blvd., Van Nuys; 780-2240.

Gene Dynarski Theater Character actor Gene Dynarski handcrafted this attractive little theater space, used mostly for book-ins by small production companies. 5600 Sunset Blvd., Hollywood; 465-5600.

Globe Playhouse Inside this barnlike structure is a replica of Shakespeare's original theater of the same name. Only Shakespeare is produced here, naturally, and this company does it all, although the quality of productions varies widely. 1107 N. Kings Rd., West Hollywood; 654-5623.

Los Angeles Actors Theater Under the direction of Bill Bushnell, Diane White, and, more recently, consulting director Alan Mandell, this company continues to do interesting work, including many premieres. Scheduled to move into a new facility downtown sometime in 1984, they currently offer quality seasons in their two small Hollywood spaces. Many outstanding actors, playwrights, and directors have been associated with the theater, including Israel Horovitz, Joseph Scott Kierland, Esther Rolle, Viveca Lindfors, and Salome Jens.

Stages Under the artistic direction of Paul Verdier, this theater has maintained a close association with playwright Eugene Ionesco, producing many of his plays, often with Ionesco himself in residence. A tiny but attractive space, the quality of the work here is usually high. 1540 N. McCadden Pl., Hollywood; 465-1010.

Odyssey Theater Ensemble With three Equity-waiver spaces under the artistic direction of Ron Sossi, the Odyssey continues to present works that take chances, and often succeed, sometimes spectacularly. The fascinating variety of offerings includes everything from Brecht to Sondheim to Sam Shepard. A series of one-man shows plays in one of the theater's smaller spaces. 12111 Ohio Ave., Los Angeles; 826-1626.

OTHER THEATERS WORTHY OF SPECIAL MENTION

The Bank Playhouse in Pasadena is located in a refurbished bank. The Delacey Street Theater, home of the L.A. Repertory Theater (but located in Pasadena), is a tiny space, offering work of high quality. The Pan Andreas Theater on Santa Monica Boulevard in West Hollywood is a rental space, but an attractive one. The pretty little Callboard Theater is on Melrose Place. The Studio Theater at the Colony presents a full roster of plays in the Los Feliz–Atwater area. Company of Angels is a respected resident company in the heart of Hollywood. The Melrose Theater is a comfortable, air-conditioned facility with a resident company. The Pilot Theaters are twin facilities in West Hollywood that are always busy with plays and poetry readings, as is Richmond Shepard's multi-theater complex, also in West Hollywood. Theater West is an organization of writers, actors, and directors that, in addition to producing plays, presents workshops and seminars, some of which are open to the public. The many spaces run by Ted Schmidt now include the Cast, the Cast-at-the-Circle, and the old Company Playhouse on South La Cienega. Theater Exchange, on an unlikely residential street in North Hollywood, offers a very respectable season of old and new plays. The Powerhouse Theater in Santa Monica is worth exploring, as their offerings are often either adventurous or experimental, and are usually refreshing, at the very least. And the Victory Theater, in Burbank, has a good track record for producing interesting shows.

Dance in L.A.
by Anne Haskins

Dance performances are going on everywhere in L.A.; it's just a matter of knowing where to look for them. And while this may not be New York or Paris, who cares? There's still a substantial amount happening in the L.A. dance world, with a correspondingly substantial amount of room for new and experimental companies and spaces. What L.A. doesn't have in terms of tradition, it makes up for in energy; as a center for "performance art," for instance, you're apt to encounter some of the worst as well as some of the most innovative dance pieces imaginable. At any rate, it's tough to be bored here, dance-wise or otherwise. And the following will give you a brief idea of where to go in L.A. to see dance, both local and international.

UCLA consistently puts forth a tremendous effort with its Art of Dance series. While tap, ballet, and ethnic groups are not slighted, the emphasis is definitely on modern dance, and the artists range from such living legends as Martha Graham and Merce Cunningham to exciting contemporary companies like the Alvin Ailey Dance Theater. In addition, UCLA often provides L.A. with its first look at young innovators (New York's Laura Dean, for instance), as well as showcasing local companies. And many of the artists and troupes combine their performances with more intimate lecture-demonstrations and master classes. Call 825-9261 for information on upcoming dance programs.

The Music Center Pavilion and Shrine Auditorium Large dance companies on tour show up most frequently at the Music Center's Dorothy Chandler Pavilion and the cavernous Shrine Auditorium. American Ballet Theater visits annually, usually at the Shrine and usually in February or March. (A word of caution: avoid the Shrine's orchestra seats from about the 9th to the 20th rows—a trough makes it impossible to see the dancers' feet, and sometimes much below their heads.) As the resident Music Center dance company, the Joffrey Ballet is scheduled to perform at least one season a year at the Chandler, which is a good theater for dance. In addition to the Joffrey, other companies such as Bella Lewitsky's occasionally perform there. Lewitsky, by the way, is awaiting the completion of her own dance theater space in a combination performance and studio complex going up near the Music Center. When completed, the Lewitsky Theater may well provide a space designed specifically for dance companies, something L.A. has long needed. The Music Center, 135 N. Grand Ave., downtown; 972-7211. Shrine Auditorium, 3228 Royal St., downtown; 749-5123.

Los Angeles Ballet and other locals The Los Angeles Ballet remains something of a gypsy in its hometown; besides a series of free performances each summer at the John Anson Ford Theater, the company has wandered from the Huntington Hartford to the Beverly Theater to the Pantages, in search of a permanent home. Meanwhile, other local dance companies perform throughout the year and throughout the L.A. area at The House (1329 B Fifth St., Santa Monica) and the Embassy Auditorium (847 S. Grand Ave., downtown), two intimate performance spaces that attract performance artists as well as dancers. And, look for more dance in art galleries. As dance and performance art increasingly explore common ground, the forms are also sharing performance stages.

Los Angeles Area Dance Alliance (LAADA) The best way to plug into the local scene is through LAADA, an association of local dance companies. The relatively inexpensive LAADA membership fee is a wise investment for serious dance watchers, since it provides discounts on dance-concert tickets, opportunities to participate in various special events, access to classes, and a subscription to *Dance Flash,* a bimonthly newsletter with a complete listing of dance events around L.A. For checking the pulse of local dance, the LAADA-sponsored Dance Kaleidoscope, held each summer, is a sure bet. This four-day dance festival at the John Anson Ford Theater offers a smorgasbord of the best of local dance companies, about 20 of which are selected to perform from the more than 70 that audition. And during the year, LAADA-sponsored choreographers' showcases, Monday night works-in-progress series, and other events provide a range of opportunities for dance lovers. LAADA headquarters are at the Pilot Theaters, 6600 Santa Monica Blvd., Hollywood; 465-1100.

A Miscellany

BEST MALE EXOTIC DANCE SHOW

Chippendales in West L.A. is not the best male exotic dance show in Los Angeles. It's the best in the world. For ladies who savor beefcake, Chippendales serves chateaubriand. The man who started the show four years ago, Steve Banerjee, is an Indian whose Ghandiesque eyes belie the fact that he has turned a local strip show into an international marketing concept. Over the years, Banerjee has researched the answer to the Sphinx's riddle: what turns women on? Like most gurus, he does not share his secrets but alludes to "a certain look" and "the power to command the attention of women." Mere observation of the Chippendales Men reveals smiles that could turn the tides of oceans and chests that extend past stomachs and not vice versa, à la the usual male fare. Steve insists male stripping is not a fad: "Women have been looking at men's buns for many years." And he has found a timeless key to what pulls at women's heart strings and purse strings. Chippendales now markets calendars, lingerie, and jeans, and the guys appear on national television spots. Wed.–Sun. nights. 3762 Overland, Culver City; 202-8850.

BEST FEMALE IMPERSONATORS

The Queen Mary Nightclub It's risky business picking the best female impersonators in town. You could get your eyes scratched out. It is with fear and trepidation, then, that we crown the Queen Mary (the nightclub, not the ship). The Queen's troupe is led by mistress of ceremonies Butch Ellis, who is a cross between Phyllis Diller and Madame and twice as nasty. Butch's court is lovely, and for some of these ladies modern science has added a few new twists or, better said, curves, to the art of female "impersonation." While audiences are impressed by the remarkable feminine presence of the performers and their portrayal of stars such as Judy Garland and Bette Midler, the most delightful surprise of the show is the superb dancing. The cast of impersonators and supporting male dancers dazzle-step their way through numbers from *West Side Story, Best Little Whorehouse in Texas,* and *Victor/ Victoria*—and do it with gymnastic pizzazz. Wed.–Sun. nights. 12449 Ventura Blvd., Studio City; 506-5619.

BEST BURLESQUE SHOW

Kitten Natividad at the Body Shop No real fan of Russ Meyer would dare miss an opportunity to see one of his chestiest starlets perform. Kitten Natividad, best known for her starring roles in *Up* and *Beneath the Valley of the Ultra Vixens,* is the main attraction of the Body Shop's floor show. She comes onstage in a large formal gown and begins stripping to "Tie a Yellow Ribbon 'Round the Old Oak Tree." The act climaxes when Miss Natividad strips down to a G-string and takes a bubble bath in a giant glass tub, while offstage bubble machines add to the experience. The song playing, of course, is "Tiny Bubbles." There's a five-dollar cover and a two-drink minimum. 8250 Sunset Blvd., West Hollywood; 656-1401.

BEST JUKEBOX

Yee Mee Loo's For anyone who's ever found themselves trying to shout over a live band, jukeboxes are a much-valued substitute. They take requests, can be turned up and down or ignored altogether, and sit like a friendly fixture in the corners of America's wateringholes. Finding one with a sympathetic selection of songs is not unlike meeting an old friend, and feeding them quarters is the audio equivalent of any video game. A good jukebox is head and shoulders above a bad band, and for those with the proper predilection, searching out a great one can take on aspects of looking for the Holy Grail.

Several local spots have real contenders — the Firefly on Vine; Hinano's on Washington Street in Venice; Barney's and Ports, both on Santa Monica, and Brennan's on Lincoln Boulevard in Venice. But for sheer bravado, The Countdown Lounge on Ventura Boulevard rang in with the sharpest roster. It was actually worth the ride to the Valley. But like all good things, the bar got in the way of progress and when last spotted the place was an auto-rental agency. Running a close second, though, and still going,

is the music machine at Yee Mee Loo's, a congenial room with a box that includes sides from the big band era, vocal classics from the romantic '50s, and a smattering of singles from the '60s to keep away cries of complete nostalgia. The bar itself is a treasure, hidden away from the main drag of Chinatown, and attached to the standard formica restaurant. It's always nighttime at Yee Mee Loo's, and it seems like Frank Sinatra is usually in the air. 690 N. Spring, Chinatown; 624-4539, 972-9044.

MOST COMPREHENSIVE THEATRICAL EVENING

The Variety Arts Center As one of L.A.'s landmark structures, what better location could the Variety Arts Center have than across the street from L.A.'s landmark restaurant, The Pantry? With its five floors of constantly buzzing activity, the center is probably the most unique place to spend a free or nearly free evening. There's a main theater on the ground floor that seats 1,160 (Clark Gable spoke his first line on that very stage), and the Screenery on the mezzanine, which shows movies from the '20s, '30s, and '40s. The renowned library on the second floor has a joke file of more than 50,000 items from W. C. Fields, Eddie Cantor et al. On the third floor is Tin Pan Alley, where singers, dancer, and comedians perform nightly, and where, on Wednesday nights, old radio shows are enacted, complete with sound effects. The fourth floor consists of the lavish

Variety Arts Theatre Roof Garden and Restaurant, which contains, among other things, the original "Tonight Show" set. 940 Figueroa, Los Angeles; 623-9100.

BEST SEATS AT THE DOROTHY CHANDLER

The Loge and Balcony Surprisingly, the sound is fuller, of a more comprehensive clarity in these uppermost levels, especially where a symphony orchestra is concerned. Which is nice to know, considering how much less tha tickets cost up there, compared to the middle of the orchesra, where admittedly vocalists in opera or with the Philharmonic make a more dazzling effect. As far as the worst sound goes, avoid the rear of the orchestra, under the Founders' Circle overhang, where the sound is flat, devoid of brilliance, the bass indistinct.

BEST DIVES

One of the strange psychological necessities among the more erudite among us is the strange compulsion to occasionally drop the high-booty pose, put on the rags, and go slummin'. Now the folks that inhabit those parlors of inequity with cheap drinks and nasty glares don't want condescending rich folk telling them their hangout is "quaint," but if you've got either a bit of the social scientist or the bum in you, these are some night spots where the beer is cheap and pretensions are left at the door.

The Blacklite Cocktail Room Not only is there a great neon sign announcing this bar's presence, but the interior is decorated with photos of famous local boxers and a couple of guys with cauliflower ears will sit at the bar and tell you of their glory days in the ring. The atmosphere is low key, casual, and as Ms. Davis once said, "Wot a Dump!" But hell, it's a *nice* dump. 1159 N. Western Ave., Los Angeles; 469-0211.

Harold's Cafe Possibly the oldest gay bar in L.A. The red counter is sagging, and the more expensive liquor bottles are gathering dust, since who's gonna spend money on booze when beer is only 35 cents a glass! Real low-down, brightly lit, with signs warning you not to carry weapons, and a blackboard with the names of 86'd patrons like "Miss Destiny." Farther up the street is the even more intimidating Waldorf, primarily a black bar now, and not a good place to hang around if you have an aversion toward six-foot black transvestites carrying bricks in their purses. 555 S. Main, Los Angeles; 972-9941.

HOST WITH THE MOST(EST)

Zachary Just what this city needs: a real live, snappy-jive professional emcee. The "Fabulous" Zachary has been plying his perky patter on stages around Los Angeles, always quick with a string of superlatives and a dazzling grin. Whether he's describing rock-and-roll bands, charming chanteuses, or questionable newcomers, the energetic Zachary can bring to life even the most reserved audience. In his ever-present tuxedo—be sure and check the shirt studs if you get close enough—Mr. M.C. gives the evening a touch of show-biz class by recalling the bygone days of formality when diamonds really were a girl's best friend. Besides his onstage introductory chores, Zachary is also an accomplished cabaret pianist, and has worked any number of nightclubs tinkling the ivories. Which is what led him to emceeing. "I've always loved being onstage," he recalled recently between introducing Adore O'Hara upstairs at the Cathay de Grande, and Randy Chance & the Atomic Bomb downstairs. "But of course I couldn't play piano all the time, so I just figured why not keep my tux on and offer to introduce the acts. I love it; it's simply *fabulous. Fabulous!!*" It is, too.

3.

FOOD AND RESTAURANTS

BEST TUNA SANDWICH

The Breadwinner It seems impossible to become inordinately enthused about those dear, dry little flakes swimming aimlessly in a sea of mayo, with an occasional particle of celery, pickle, or pimiento to brighten the blob. But the tuna salad at The Breadwinner is full of surprises—not your run-of-the-mill scoop on a bed of wilted lettuce, that's for sure. A mound of white albacore meat, lemon juice, and caraway seeds glued together with a *minimum* of Hellman's holds court atop a throne of lettuce, red cabbage, zucchini, carrots, celery, cauliflower, and sprouts. Sunflower seeds, raisins, cherry tomatoes, and radishes garnish the display like so many crown jewels. This ingenious dish comes in two sizes: small ($2.95) and large ($3.70), and there's an abundant selection of dressings to round out the creative experience. 225 Santa Monica Pl., Santa Monica; 394-7029. 200 S. Beverly Dr., Beverly Hills; 550-0590.

BEST BARBECUE

Carl's Barbecue, or Bar-B-Que as the signs say, is the ultimate in onomatopeia among foods. Who knows from where the name came, but its mere mention can moisten the mouth into a delerious fever. What usually passes as barbecue in these parts is more like roast beef in tomato sauce. For the real deal, the quest leads to Pico Boulevard, just west of La Brea, and a small hole-in-the-wall shop called Carl's. The men who man the fires at Carl's know exactly what they're doing when they set a rack of ribs on the pit, or smoke their briskets and birds to tender perfection. It's all in the wood, and only the best cooking logs are used here. Then, when the meat has been smoked just enough, the ritual of applying the sauce takes place. And this is where Carl's leaves the rest of the competition at the starting gate. Their sauce, from mild to *hot*, is a natural wonder. The blending of spices and liquids that goes into this elixir is a recipe for the ages, something that defies description. The mix has been known to cause a sweaty euphoria and has gotten devotees to travel miles for a taste. There are other barbecue stands better known than Carl's, but there are absolutely none that do it better. 4988 W. Pico Blvd., Los Angeles, 934-0637.

Harry's Open Pit Still popular after all these years, this small establishment can become frantically crowded at dinner hours and on weekends, as it offers very reasonably priced barbecued beef, chicken, and fish. Decoration consists of British signs and souvenirs and a large-screen TV. A main objective of the owners seems to be to make it as easy as possible for the customer to become totally sloshed for the least amount of money. Shots of tequila with lime are always 25¢, and 20-ounce schooners of Henry Weinhard's are only $1.05. The atmosphere brings to mind a singles bar without the anxiety: lots of people, lots of food, lots of booze. 1434 Crescent Heights Blvd. (near Sunset), Hollywood; 654-4773.

BEST MEXICAN DELI

El Rodeo What do you need to start your day, to really get you going? Naturally, you need eggs, some chorizo to scramble with 'em, some corn tortillas to wrap it all in, and some Mexican sweet breads dripping with butter to finish the meal off. All these things, and more, are at El Rodeo, where they also carry several kinds of Central American cheese products, avocados, Mexican beer, and Caramba and other soft drinks. And the adjoining restaurant specializes in barbecued chicken, which is always being sold as some kind of special two-for-

the-price-of-one deal. Wait, there's more: cheap breakfasts, menudo, tacos, carne asada, etc. The place is clean and recently remodeled, and the employees are friendly. 1721 Sunset Blvd., Echo Park; 413-6272.

THE ULTIMATE GROCERY STORE

Irvine Ranch Farmers Market A case a mile long is crammed with meats, and you can watch the butchers at work behind the counter. An adjacent case displays every kind of seafood—clams and crabs, shrimp and fresh trout. But the produce is the thing here, mountains of it, all artfully arranged in swatches of glorious color. The greens section is a thing of beauty. The Ranch Market doesn't just carry your ordinary, run-of-the-garden produce. There's fresh marjoram and sage and rosemary; fava beans and okra; mangoes, kiwi fruit, and red papayas from Hawaii; ollalie berries and radicchio. The selection of cheeses is too much, and there's fresh pasta of all kinds made daily, with accompanying Italian sauces. In addition to the usual fare, the deli counter has a selection of some 40 mouth-watering salads. There are canned and packaged goods, a bakery, bins of natural foods, and even a flower shop. And a conveyor belt, sort of a modern-day dumb waiter, whisks the groceries to your car. Beverly Center (ground floor), 142 S. San Vincente Blvd., Beverly Hills; 657-1931.

BEST
FRENCH FRIES

Joe Allen's At this show-biz hangout, there isn't a hell of a lot that's exceptional to eat, and the best entree isn't even on the posted blackboard menu—hamburgers and french fries. For $1.75, you get a large order of steak-fry-style potatoes. Broad and thick cut, they are always delicious, crispy golden on the outside and perfectly cooked on the inside. 8706 Third St., West Hollywood; 274-0101.

BEST SUSHI

Up until a few years ago, many Angelenos equated visiting a sushi bar with the experience of visiting a cannibal's stew pot. It simply was not considered decent to (A) partake of raw flesh in any form and (B) enjoy doing so. But things have changed drastically. Far fewer people comment "Raw fish! Blecchh!" when you mention the delectable mixture of uncooked tuna, or salmon or eel, rolled in sweetened rice and nori, and enlivened with the peppy accouterments of pickled ginger and sinus-flushing Japanese horseradish. In fact, it's a pleasure to see sushi bars springing up all over town, every hour on the hour. So, if you want to try an alternative to those Golden Arches, we recommend:

Teru Sushi Remember when your mother said, "Finish your spinach or no ice cream!"? You shut your eyes, held your nose, and swallowed. Well, what if she had said, "Finish your sea urchin!"? If it had been made at Teru Sushi you would have requested seconds and to hell with the ice cream. Teru Sushi excels in the art of sushi,

perhaps because unlike many "ethnic" restaurants in America, the staff's ethnicity matches that of the restaurant. That's right, the sushi chef is not Cuban but Japanese, and he shouts out a warm *irasshaimasai!* ("welcome") as you enter the restaurant. 11940 Ventura Blvd., Studio City; 763-6201.

Aki This is a traditional Japanese restaurant noted for an exquisitely light and flavorful tempura, and they added sushi to their menu seven years ago. Dean and Tom, the sushi chefs here since the bar opened, are first-rate, handling the preparations with deftness and artistry, while at the same time remaining convivial and personable. Specialties include the salmon, which is pickled rather than the usual smoked, and the Spanish mackerel sashimi, which is arranged inside a lemon shell with cucumber leaves, resembling a delicate flower. Hint: the chefs will gladly offer suggestions on what to order. 11513 Santa Monica Blvd., West Los Angeles; 479-8406.

Also recommended:

Sushi King, where the bar is open quite late. 1330 Wilshire Blvd., Santa Monica; 395-0120.

Hide, a small bar in the Japanese community with an authentic ambience. 2050 Sawtelle Blvd., West Los Angeles; 477-7242.

Shibucho, a fine midtown bar open until the wee hours. 3114 Beverly Blvd., Los Angeles; 387-8498.

Isshin Sushi, an intimate little place with wonderful and plentiful selections at incredibly low prices. 10861 Lindbrook Ave., Westwood; 208-5224.

BEST SHISH KEBOB

Shemrun If Lancelot were to meet Guinevere for a romantic feast in the forest, they would rendezvous at Shemrun. And what would they partake of? Omelets and quiche? Not on your life. They'd drown their torrid taste buds in Shemrun's tender moist shish kebob. Named for a mountainous resort in the Middle East, Shemrun, tucked away in the beautiful hills of Topanga Canyon (L.A.'s countryside within the city), offers a variety of dining experiences. You can dine outside on the terraced garden patio under a tree that shoots through the floorboards and listen to the frogs croak as night falls. You can sup in the lounge with the locals and hear how Pearl's vehicle was rescued from a mud slide last week. Or, you can join Lancelot and Guinevere in the formal dining room for shish kebob, chicken kebob, or a variety of culinary delights, both Continental and Middle Eastern, made to regal perfection. And if you really do want quiche or omelets, Shemrun whips them up superbly—weekend brunches are not to be missed. 1105 N. Topanga Canyon Blvd., Topanga; 455-2222.

BEST CURRIES

Canard de Bombay This place is expensive ($15 to $20 per), but for the best in rich, flavorsome Indian food, this is L.A.'s answer to the top-quality Indian cuisines of New York and London. Well worth the price for the right occasion. 476 S. San Vincente Blvd., Los Angeles; 852-0095.

MOST FANCY-SCHMANCY INDIAN RESTAURANT

Paul Bhalla's The minute you enter this place, you'll forget you're in L.A., or for that matter in North America. From the carved teak and etched brass to the Indian art, mood lighting, and waitresses bespangled and bejangled in colorful belly-dancing attire, Paul Bhalla's is definitely an eating *experience*. But more important than the decor is the food; for at least six consecutive years, Paul Bhalla's has been awarded a four-star rating and it would be difficult to leave here either disappointed or unsated. Your meal comes complete with soup, dal, yogurt salad, rice, bread, and entree, and if you're tempted beyond that, do try one of the excellent appetizers or the special breads (the pizza-style onion-cinnamon, for instance), carried piping hot straight from the oven. Oh, while we're at it, have you ever tried a muddy elephant? The bartender will tell you all about it. 10853 Lindbrook Dr., Westwood; 208-8535.

BEST CALAMARAKIA

Fran O'Brien's Former Washington Redskin O'Brien and his friend Jimmy Demetri, an expert and experienced chef, joined forces to open this restaurant, which has an atmosphere rather like a cross between an Irish pub and a New York saloon. The cuisine is

Greek, and, says the jovial O'Brien, "We teamed up to give people a Super Bowl menu." Here's a sampling of the succulent appetizers: calamarakia, young squids that are fried and served hot with fresh lemon; tzatziki, a dip made from yogurt, cucumber, fresh garlic, and fresh herbs; and saganaki, Greek kefalotiri cheese flamed in a skillet. Entrees, served with lots of accompaniments, include souvlaki (lamb shish kebob), marinated and skewered with green peppers, onions and mushrooms; shrimp Aegean Isles, baked with shallots, scallions, tomatoes, white wine, and seasonings, then topped with feta cheese; and such favorite Greek staples as moussaka and stuffed grape leaves. For the indecisive, there's a selection of specialties one can sample—roast lamb, moussaka, dolmathakia, pastitsio, and spanakopita. Portions are ample, prices moderate, and wine, beer, mixed drinks, and coffee are served. 3321 W. Pico Blvd., Santa Monica; 829-3459.

BEST BAGEL

Feeling runs high among bagel fanciers. Some like the texture smooth, others prefer it chewy. However, everyone agrees that what you must have in a bagel is freshness, so consider the following sources.

Brooklyn Bagel Bakery churns out fresh bagels all day and into the night. They sell a variety of flavors—pumpernickel, whole wheat, raisin, etc.—and, of course, both water and egg. The onion bagels are the greatest, simply crammed with onions, and they come in two sizes, regular and miniature. Another taste treat is the onion stick, 2½ times the size of a bagel,

and stuffed with onions, poppy seeds, and garlic. And if you yearn for a fresh bagel at 2:30 A.M. on a weekend, Brooklyn Bagel is open till 3 A.M. on Fridays and Saturdays. 2217 Beverly Blvd., downtown; 413-4114.

I & Joy Bagels If you can forgive the pun, I & Joy's fresh bagels are so good that some varieties may be sold out at the end of the day. Among the savory flavors are garlic, onion, rye, whole wheat, pumpernickel, and raisin. A specialty is the bialy, a bagel that's doughier than a regular bagel because it's not boiled before it's baked. 11974 Ventura Blvd., Studio City; 760-9068 (also, five other locations in the Valley and West Los Angeles).

BEST JEWISH DELI

Nate 'n' Al's Okay, you got yours, but we *kvell* over knowing about this one. First of all, the rye bread here is the freshest and tastiest Jewish rye in L.A. The rest of the menu lives up to the bread. Nate 'n' Al's is like home —every waitress reminds you of Mom, and they wouldn't serve you anything they knew you wouldn't like. Our favorite meal is the roast chicken, done to perfection and served with potato pancake and a healthy portion of dressing and vegetables. The soups, sandwiches, egg dishes, smoked fish, side dishes, desserts, you name it—always fresh, top quality, and just plain good. 414 N. Beverly Dr., Beverly Hills; 274-0101.

Junior's We can't *kvell* over the regular eat-in menu at Junior's, which seems pretty average and slightly high priced. But the take-out deli's a different story. It's a veritable Fressing Emporium, with four separate sections: cold cuts, fish, cheeses, and salads; cold entrees (from kugel to lasagna); hot entrees; and a bakery that does itself proud with, among other gems, a chocolate whipped-cream seven-layer cake at just 99 cents per whopping slice. 2379 Westwood Blvd., Westwood; 475-5771.

BEST CROISSANT

Having tasted the best croissant in southern Spain, created by the unbeatable mixture of *pieds noirs* (French kicked out of North Africa) and low food prices (especially butter), our croissant expert was appalled three years ago by the American equivalent of this rather complex bread form. The few good croissant places that graced L.A. at the start of the fad usually gave way to new management, disdain for the American palate ("they'll never know the difference"), and impatience (it takes nearly three days for the risings and butterings of the dough if you want to do it right). But now, *dieu merci,* there are some real winners about which L.A. can brag, such as:

The Croissant Place The huge, all-butter plain croissant here is tops for taste and flakiness. Many fillings are available (the spinach in Mornay sauce is particularly divine), including the unlikely peanut butter and jelly, a delicacy in its own right when placed on this particular throne. There are also mini-croissants with fillings made to order. 8333 Santa Monica Blvd., West Hollywood; 654-7066.

Viktor Benes The name of this place invariably crops up in any discussion of the best croissants in L.A., and with good reason: their product is properly flaky, suitably light textured, golden in color, never overbaked (and consequently never dry), and remarkably cheap at 50¢ (the competition around town ranges from 75¢ to $1.25 for the plain variety). A very good almond croissant (almond-paste filling, almond slices on top) is available at the same bargain price. 8717 W. Third St. (between Robertson and San Vicente blvds.), West Hollywood; 276-0488.

Elysee This small combination bakery and espresso bar offers an excellent—and large—croissant, very buttery and sweet. A number of fillings, from chocolate and almond to chicken, spinach, cheese, and fruit, are available, too. And if you like chocolate mousse, they've got a great version here. 1099 Gayley Ave., Westwood; 208-6505.

Upper Crust has terrific croissants and 28—we said 28—kinds of quiche. 640 N. Robertson Blvd., West Hollywood; 652-5445.

BEST BAKERY FOR VALLEY GIRLS

Weby's Bakery is an institution in the Valley. Everything is fresh, fresh, fresh. You can, in fact, watch the goodies being made while waiting for your number to come up, and walk out with a loaf of corn rye that's still warm. In addition to bread, they have cookies, cheesecakes, bagels, and pies, and the apple, pecan, blueberry, chocolate chip, and raspberry coffeecakes are famous. In the super-dessert department, there's the Linzer torte, an ambrosial concoction of chocolate and raspberries, and the fruit-basket cake, four layers of white cake fused with layers of custard flavored with fresh peaches, strawberries, and bananas, then topped with whipped cream and a strawberry flower. For the chocoholic, there's a glorious moist chocolate cake with layers of chocolate mousse, iced with more mousse and covered with chocolate curls. And for special occasions, Weby's will bake and decorate cakes to order. 12131 Ventura Blvd., Studio City; 769-6062.

BEST GRAND MARNIER CAKE

Paris Pastry Everybody owes themselves a Grand Marnier cake at least once before they die. This genuine masterpiece elevates plain old chocklit cake to undreamed-of heights by soaking it in Grand Marnier orange liqueur, wedging a chocolate-flavored whipped-cream filling in between the layers, and covering the whole shebang with a triumphant European chocolate icing. It can be found in all its glory at Paris Pastry, where it currently resides as one of the most sought-after high-class party desserts in town. (Also not to be missed, while you're in the place, are the raspberry napoleons.) Oddly enough, the breads at Paris Pastry are not as outstanding as their desserts, so if you're in search of a good croissant, you may be disappointed. But one crumb of Grand Marnier cake cancels out any other complaints. 1448 Westwood Blvd., Westwood; 474-8888. 11650 San Vincente Blvd., Brentwood; 826-2131.

BEST GERMAN CHOCOLATE PIE

Polly's From the outside it looks like just another one of those orange-vinyled, dreadfully wallpapered excuses for a coffee shop. But once inside, a surprise awaits you. Polly's serves excellent Guatemalan and Colombian coffees, excellent sandwiches and specialty salads, and, above all, excellent pies. There are many flavors of the latter item to choose from, but the German chocolate, with its creamy chocolate-coconut base and mound of genuine whipped cream on top, is a topnotch dessert anytime. Fifth St. and Wilshire Blvd., Santa Monica; 394-9721.

BEST COOKIE

Bear's Brown Bag of Cookies in Santa Monica is populated with teddy bears, both large and small, and the motto is Eat More Cookies. That's easy to do. Bear's original cookie is a toothsome chocolate chip that comes with or without nuts. Other flavors are cinnamon oatmeal raisin, peanut butter chocolate chip, and milk chocolate with nuts. For a richer treat, try the Mississippi mud pie, the popular Bear's basic brownie, the crunchie fudgy sandwich, or, perhaps best of all, the Bear paw—ice cream sandwiched between two cookies, then rolled in chocolate chips. Batches of cookies are baked throughout the day, so everything is absolutely fresh, dripping with chocolate, and sometimes still warm from the oven. 2726 Main St., Santa Monica; 396-1375.

BEST ETHNIC MARKETS AND SANDWICHES

Are you stressed out on McGrease-burgers? Are you sick of talking food to an adenoidal microphone with zits? Then wait a minute. There are alternatives: one of these neighborhood-market sandwich counters. Talk to real people and enjoy a real sandwich, custom made.

Dario's Sandwiches A downtown tradition since 1925, Dario's Italian sandwiches warm both heart and stomach. The General Lee, for example, is hot roast beef, sausage, meatballs, and melted cheese on a French roll. Liquor and some Italian groceries are available. 410 Ord St., downtown; 628-4736.

Deli & Delites This international grocery specializes in "personalized pita pocket sandwiches," but also serves about 40 sandwich combinations on nine kinds of bread. With new inventions added frequently, it can take a week to make a selection. Plus a week to find Gemco Center. 6415 Vineland (Gemco Center), North Hollywood; 877-7919.

Venezia Deli This tiny market just south of the Fox Venice theater is classic mom and pop. Pop grinds and stuffs his sausages in the back room, while Mom cooks them and plops them into French rolls with a shower of great sauce. Meatballs, too, plus about 20 other sandwiches. The place is redolent of secret family recipes. 1515 Lincoln Ave., Venice; 823-0012.

Fernwood Market Tucked away in Topanga Canyon, this market seems pleasingly remote from big-city frenzy. But inside is a big-city delicatessen counter, piled high with huge sandwiches and sandwich makings. Hey, all you Vals, get a custom job on your way to the beach. 446 S. Topanga Canyon Blvd., Topanga Canyon; 455-2412.

BEST MEAL IN A SALAD

The Good Earth Some people can devour salads—any size salad—as quickly as an army of guinea pigs, snapping and munching and boring their way through forests of celery and fields of lettuce without so much as a pause for reflection. If you are one of these rodent people, you're sure to orgy at The Good Earth, where they serve not plain old salads but gourmet feasts. Here a dinner salad is not an accompaniment to the meal; it's the dinner. From the Mediterranean sunshine, a monster combo of greens, cheeses, fresh mushrooms, olives, chopped eggs, and artichokes, to the cashew chicken and Charlie Chan curried tuna, The Good Earth has the salad terrain covered. Arriving in a heap the size of Rhode Island, these items will provide you with at least 20 minutes of nonstop crunching, and a good half hour if you take breathers between bites. A guinea pig could not only devour one—he could live inside it. 10880 Weyburn Ave. (208-1441) and 1002 Westwood Blvd. (208-8215), Westwood.

RESTAURANT WITH THE MOST PERSONALITY

Patrick's Roadhouse If you're looking for a road-side cafe with an ocean view, Victorian–Salvation Army decor, and a host who scolds his patrons, hollers at his help, and sings along with Barbra Strident—have we found a place for you. Patrick's is definitely a restaurant phenomenon; check out, for instance, the genuine conch-shell hanging lamps, or the 19th-century marble washstand from which guests snitch coffee, cream, and syrup. At the center of the activity is owner-host Patrick Fischler, commonly known as Bill, a sort feisty fellow who cracks jokes at the drop of a fork, but who is also not above screaming at his clientele to "eat up, everybody, eat up—there are people waiting!" Yes, Patrick's just may be the only restaurant where they're happier to see you going than coming. But they're not packed for nothing; food's good, atmosphere's truly original, and the entertainment (??) is free. Pacific Coast Hwy. at Santa Monica Canyon; 459-4544.

BEST OMELETS

The Omelette Parlor This is one of Venice's weekend-morning traditions and we almost don't have to give out the exact address, as the line of people waiting patiently on Main Street will let you know you're there. For this reason, we don't recommend popping in here if you're in a hurry on a Saturday or Sunday; weekday mornings, however, are usually much saner.

Anyway, the omelets are varied, generous, and on the expensive side, although with home fries and a whole-wheat muffin spread with apple butter, you won't go away hungry. And the decor, with its wooden trolley-car booths (some of which have individual wall phones), mural-size photos of Venice Beach circa 1926, and Mexican-movie-poster wallpaper in the restrooms, is wonderful. 2732 Main St., Venice; 399-7892.

Zucky's won't win any prizes for its interior design; it's pure '50s vinyl and formica raucous. But the omelets, which feature everything from pastrami and cheese to zucchini, mushroom, and sour cream fillings, are first-class, as are the warm bagels, cream cheese, and preserves that accompany them. Best of all, they're served 24 hours a day. If you're not in the mood for eggs, visit Zucky's anyway; it's *the* Jewish deli hangout in Santa Monica, and you might even find a star or two tackling a matzo ball. 431 Wilshire Blvd., Santa Monica; 393-0551.

BEST COFFEE/ CAPPUCCINO

Slowly, slowly America is beginning to realize the difference between Maxwell House and a sublime Italian roast. Ever since croissants and quiche became staples in the L.A. diet, a comparably Continental liquid to wash them down with was also required, and so espresso, cappuccino, and café au lait made their belated appearance. One can now run into these beverages almost anywhere, but a truly fine cup of black gold is still rare enough to warrant special mention. Honors thus go to:

The Coffee Emporium Here coffee is brought in green and roasted fresh daily in one of the very few coffee roasters in Southern California. In addition to the regular Viennese and French roasts, one can sample such exotica as Yrgcheff Ethiopian or Zimbabwean. The small cafe also features Melior-style coffee, where with your very own French plunger pot, you can brew up a storm right at the table. 4325 Glencoe Ave., Marina del Rey; 823-4446.

The Rose One of the most genuinely "trendy pretentious" restaurants in L.A., the clientele at the Rose is infinitely more interesting than the food. Literally everyone has a screenplay here, and visitors range from the unemployed writer or actor to the likes of Coppola or Cher. Be forewarned that the eats are unexceptional and the prices phenomenal. But the coffee, cappuccino, and café au lait are excellent, as are many of the pastries, which explains why it's one of the favorite breakfast hangouts at the beach. 220 Rose Ave., Venice; 399-0711.

Farmer's Market We wouldn't ordinarily venture into the realm of this, the most outstanding tourist trap in the city besides Universal Studios. But the two redeeming features of Farmer's Market are the fresh produce and the 100 or so food booths, among which is the coffee stand that serves the best cappuccino in town, at a bargain price of only 95 cents. The espresso is rich, the steamed milk just right, and if you pick up one of the fabulous rolls or pastries at any of the neighboring stands, you've made your visit to this otherwise cornball place worthwhile. Corner of Fairfax Ave. and Third St., Miracle Mile District.

BEST CITY IN A RESTAURANT

Pioneer Boulangerie This unusual eating place takes up one square city block, features three separate restaurants, a bakery, wine cellar, deli, gift shop, and flower stall, and has true atmosphere *français,* from the quaint, latticed outdoor cafe to the rustic, provincial-style indoor cafeteria and the upstairs Basque dining room. Special features of the Boulangerie are the large brick-oven bakery, open for public viewing, from whence cometh renowned sourdough and french breads, not to mention croissants and pastries; the wide variety of wines and cheeses; and the dozens and dozens of soups (unfortunately overpriced) for which the restaurant originally became famous. We remember the Boulangerie when it opened across from the beach in Santa Monica seven years ago, a sweet, cozy little soup and salad bar where you could get a croissant for a quarter. The fact that it's now a seething metropolis, complete with waiters in red berets doubling as traffic cops, gives us pangs of nostalgic regret. Nonetheless, it's one of those unique spots that keeps both tourists and natives intrigued. Main St. between Bay St. and Bicknell Ave., Santa Monica; 399-7771.

BEST PALACE IN A RESTAURANT

Yamashiro The name means "castle on the hill," and that's precisely what it is: a replica of a Japanese mountain palace-retreat that dates from 1913.

Once you begin the ascent up the long, winding hill that leads to this isolated wonder, you begin to feel a little Twilight Zonish as the real world gradually disappears, giving way to imperial Japan in all its architectural and beautifully landscaped splendor. Yamashiro is enormous, with seemingly never-ending rooms (the most beautiful is an indoor-outdoor garden room with a huge pool, fountains, and foliage) that overlook one of the most spectacular views of L.A. For a romantic dinner or round of drinks, this place is primo, but if you happen on it on a rainy winter night, be prepared: with its tomblike quiet and chill, flickering candlelight, and the eerie sound of bare branches tapping against the dripping windows, Yamashiro can be spookier than hell. 1999 N. Sycamore Ave., Hollywood; 466-5125.

BEST THAI DELIGHTS

One of the redeeming features of L.A. is that you don't need to go to Bangkok if it's a mee grob or beef satay fix you're after. The city abounds with Thai restaurants, and if you're partial to, or simply want to explore, this delightful alternative to Chinese, here are a few safe bets.

Royal Thai Regal interior decor combines with excellent food and extra-reasonable prices to give the Royal Thai our nod of approval. For an exotic culinary escapade, try the pineapple paradise, an amazing blend of chicken, shrimp, Thai sausage, vegetables, and pineapple in curry-seasoned rice; the fried fantail shrimp, which entitles you to six plump prawns and a delicious hot-sweet-sour sauce; the barbecued sparerib appetizer (unlike any other you know); and, of course, the Thai tea and coffee, iced drinks that resemble milkshakes without the calories. Best of all, dishes are priced from $3.50 to $6.00. 10668 W. Pico Blvd., West Los Angeles; 558-9348.

Siam Hut The Siam Hut is — or used to be — a great little unpretentious, uncrowded spot. Well, fat chance of that remaining true now, but anyway, they have excellent soups, entrees, and rice dishes, all very affordable at $3.50 on up. A friendly word of caution: wear a sweater or two in the winter because this is one place that doesn't believe in turning on the heat. 11500 W. Pico Blvd., West Los Angeles; 477-5118.

Chao Praya One of the first Thai spots to be discovered by the Hollywood crowd, Chao Praya has managed to keep its prices down and its food quality up despite long waiting lines on weekends. The specialty here is their unique preparation of seafood dishes; try, for instance, the crab meat and ground pork with asparagus. 6307 Yucca Ave., Hollywood; 464-9652.

Chan Dara Although many of the dishes here are hot and spicy, they'll prepare any of them mild gringo style at your request. Good food at fair prices, with a nice selection of Thai beer. (Be advised: the restrooms have seat belts!) 1511 N. Cahuenga Blvd., Hollywood; 464-8585.

BEST BLINTZES

The Bagel Just south of Olympic in the Fairfax District, The Bagel Bakery and Deli holds court amidst thrift shops and Chinese restaurants, discount furniture and window dressings. The area is old and quaint, and so is The Bagel; part of its charm lies in its horrific '40s wallpaper and '50s vinyl booths. Yes, it's classic deli all the way, but unlike Canter's or Zucky's or Kenny's, The Bagel can brag about *their* blintzes—Yiddish crepes that are so big they seem puffed up with their own importance. An order of two is equal to four anywhere else, and definitely superior in quality; the pancake is thick, moist, and bright yellow, courtesy of much egg yolk, and the filling is an incredible blend of pot cheese and sweetened sour cream. To top it all off (literally) are side dishes of hot blueberry preserves and sour cream. *Oy vay!* 1052 Fairfax, Los Angeles; 939-2032.

BEST SOUP

The Tomato Soup at Chez Helène Called on to meet another deadline, we were sure that we already knew where to find the best soup—Chez Helène. Then we bumped into D. who insisted, "The best soup is a garlic soup at La Grange Au Crêpe." Unable to resist, we grabbed two soup enthusiasts as tasters and went off first to Chez Helène. Irony of ironies, it shared the same side of the street, one adjoining wall, and the garden patio with La Grange Au Crêpe. (Did they go so far as to share the same chef, we kidded?) After indulging in the aromatic delicacy of carefully combined foods, warm french bread, complementary champagne, and the excep-

tional tomato basil soup at Chez Helène, we asked Louise, the night manager, if she might divulge the recipe. She laughed, "Ah, but you don't want the recipe, because everybody is asking me the recipe, but no I am joking. You start with the mushroom, you see, and garlic, and you have the butter, and you have your tomato and your cream, but the secret is something the French call Genievre, a gin with herbs. It is the gin and then the basil that gives it this special flavor." We thanked her and went next door to La Grange Au Crêpe, where we encountered warm candlelight dining and an olfactory heaven. We nursed the last bits of their delightful garlic soup—but in conclusion, we all agreed the tomato soup at Chez Helène was the best. 1029 W. Washington Blvd., Venice; 392-6833.

BEST PHANTOM RESTAURANT

The Chinese–Islamic Restaurant We aren't sure of the exact name of this place, and the phone number and exact location are up for grabs. But one of our reporters does swear to having eaten there. This mysterious dive features cheap, exotic fare in low-rent surroundings (watermarks on the wallpaper, a roach or two on the watermarks), and the chef and owner, an affable Chinese Muslim who closely resembles the James Bond movie villain Oddjob, doesn't speak English but will laugh uproariously at *anything*. A fabulous layered sesame pocket bread is baked right on the premises, and the cold noodles (with beef and vegetables) are recommended, too. But wait: you won't find either of these on the menu! No kidding, the best strategy—should you actually *find* the Chinese-Islamic Restaurant — is to check out other people's orders and ask plenty of questions. On Ninth St., somewhere near Alvarado and MacArthur Park; downtown.

BEST FALAFEL

Noura Real men might not eat quiche anymore, but they do eat falafel. The best in town is that served at Noura in West Hollywood. For those of you who eat first and ask questions later, falafel is spiced mashed chickpeas formed into balls and deep fried. When well done, as they are at Noura, they're crispy on the outside and deliciously soft in the middle, the way Allah meant them to be. They're served in pita bread with plenty of vegetables, pickles, and delicately seasoned tahina (sesame-seed condiment) on top. If you've got a galvanized iron stomach, you can also add a red-pepper hot sauce. A large falafel will set you back $2.25. Noura also serves a great tabbouleh salad of cracked wheat, mint, and parsley. 8479 Melrose Ave., West Hollywood; 651-4581.

Me and Me Well, there are Noura devotees, and then there are the followers of Me and Me, particularly the Fairfax location, where all falafels are cooked to order and seem to possess the perfect combination of texture and spice. Another bonus is the actual geographic placement of this small, cozy stand: it's in the heart of Little Israel, the old Jewish section of L.A., where you get the unusual benefit of another time and place. 465 N. Fairfax Ave., Los Angeles; 655-4748.

Also recommended:

Falafel King, which features an excellent seven-salad plate. 10940 Weyburn Ave., Westwood; 208-5782.

Hungry Pocket, noted for its extra-spicy falafel. 1715 Pico Blvd., Santa Monica; 450-5335.

BEST FISH MARKET

Gordon's If you're tired of fish markets where they use "fresh" to mean that they just took it out of the freezer that morning, you might try Gordon's, which in its former incarnation was the well-known fish counter at the Day-Lite market on La Cienega. Father and son Jack and Mike Yosha do their own filleting, as well as offer imaginative advice and recipes for virtually any kind of fish. Gordon's supplies fish to many of the city's finer restaurants. Daily fresh fish specials are posted on the blackboard. 9116 W. Pico Blvd., Beverly Hills; 272-9977.

BEST ISRAELI SALAD

Shula & Esther's You laugh. But some day you are going to crave a real Israeli salad, the kind they serve on the Golan Heights. When that day comes, Shula and Esther's is the place you want to go. Don't get sidetracked by the other menu offerings; go for the combination hummus and tahina plate — eggplant, turkey salad, egg salad, coleslaw, red cabbage, chopped liver, and Israeli vegetable salad—all for only five dollars. 519 N. Fairfax, Los Angeles; 852-9154.

BEST MARGARITAS

El Cholo Don't fret if you have to wait for a table here. They make the best margaritas in town—$7.90 for a tall frosty pitcher. Or if you're on your way to take the law boards and have to go easy, you can get them by the glass for $1.85. 1121 S. Western Ave. (near Wilshire), Los Angeles; 734-2773.

BEST DESSERT DRINKS

Fellini's They cost four dollars and up, but that's a paltry price to pay for unforgettable after-dinner decadence. Mom's shortcake, for instance, is a lethal mixture of amaretto, Häagen-Dazs ice cream, fresh strawberries, and whipped cream, and the others are just as good, or bad, as the case may be. Owner Gary Gilson is proud of his dessert drinks, which he claims are "not done" anywhere else. "They take time," he explains, "and most bartenders don't want to be bothered." By the way, if you're in the mood for something you can chew, give the hot homemade pecan pie a whirl. 6810 Melrose Ave., West Hollywood; 936-3100.

BEST BURGERS

Freeway Cafe One of the best hamburgers in town can be devoured at the Freeway Cafe, an old wooden stand overlooking that beautiful expanse of concrete, the Hollywood Freeway. But don't let the simplicity of the exterior fool you. This is not a pit stop, but a veritable palace of delight for the connoisseur of ground beef. One can order a tasty burger topped with mushrooms, avocado, chili, or bacon, and prices are reasonable, though the hours are not (open Monday through Saturday, but never after 4 P.M.). This is the place for a taste of life in the fast lane. 3222 Cahuenga Blvd. West, Hollywood; 851-3307.

Fatburger refers to itself as "The Last Great Hamburger Stand." Here you'll find your basic, luscious, juicy, 100 percent American burger. The first Fatburger, on Western Avenue, opened over 30 years ago, and the one on La Cienega has been a longtime fixture. Specialties range from the plain Fatburger (with seven condiments added if you choose) to the super-filling double king burger with chili, cheese, egg, or bacon. And the hours are divine: open 24 hours a day, 365 days a year. 3021 S. Western Ave., Los Angeles; 734-7490. 450 S. La Cienega Blvd., Beverly Hills; 652-8489. (Other locations in Westwood, Manhattan Beach, Santa Monica, and West Hollywood may have a different decor, ambience and hours, but the basic product's bound to be the same.)

BEST HIGH—CLASS BURGER

Hamburger Henry Here's where the rich go to get the Mercedes-Benz of burgers. The basic number is a third of a pound of juicy meat, cooked to order and served with lettuce, tomato, onion, pickle, chips, and fresh fruit. All of which is sandwiched inside of homemade buns, made fresh daily. But who wants that when you can choose from nearly 40 combos, some of which have won gold medals at the California State Fair? For instance: the bacon-avocado, topped with avocado slices, cheese, and strips of bacon; the Queen Mary, with baked ham, sauerkraut, and melted cheese; hamburger Rockefeller, with fresh spinach, bacon, and hollandaise sauce; and owner Henry Meyer's favorite, the Bombay burger, smothered in chutney and shredded coconut. 3001 Wilshire Blvd., Santa Monica; 828-3000.

BEST CHILIBURGER

The Original Tommy's The place that takes the cake—or should we say, takes the bun—for *the* unwaveringly best, most scrumptious, calorie-laden, pungent, sloppiest burgers in town. Not only is this little hut a happening place at 2 A.M., but it is also reasonably priced and the food is cooked and wrapped in such a speedy blur, you hardly have your order off the tip of your tongue before it's thrust at you in a greasy yellow wrapper. And they make the best goddamn chili

in town. Liz Taylor has Chasen's chili flown to her all over the globe, but only because she hasn't tasted Tommy's! There is a standing joke about Tommy's: if you get so drunk you forgot where you ate the night before, if you ate at Tommy's you'll remember the next morning. Word to the wise: if you order a plain hamburger, the help will ridicule you. "Oh, you want a sissyburger, eh?" You can eat a hamburger anywhere, but at Tommy's, chiliburgers are what it's all about. Beverly Blvd. at Rampart, Silverlake; 389-9060.

BEST PANCAKES

Musso & Frank Grill Forget steaks and chops. You came here to eat flannel cakes. As much a tradition as the restaurant itself, they are made from whole-wheat flour and served crisp and light, without any soggy cooking fat. Unless you keep super-late hours though, don't go looking for breakfast at dawn's early light, as they don't open until 11 A.M. An order of pancakes costs $3.10. 6667 Hollywood Blvd., Hollywood; 467-5123.

BEST SEAFOOD

Seafood Bay If this were in Rome or Athens, it would be written up in the guidebooks as one of those great but diminuitive places where only the natives go. Or as the *New Yorker* might say, "it's only a naive domestic seafood restaurant, but you'll be amused at it's presumption." And pleased by the low prices, too. Seafood dinners range from $3.95 to $9.95. Steamed clams or mussels are $3.30; chowder is 95¢. There are usually lines waiting for the few tables, so you might try eating at an off-time. No reservations are taken. The atmosphere is strictly candy-store casual. 3916 Sunset Blvd., Silverlake; 664-3902.

The Lobster doesn't look like much on the outside, or the inside either, for that matter. A couple of phony paintings of clowns and two of the sea hang over the 15 tables (including a unique one-sider), but who needs atmosphere when the food's this good? The menu goes on and on, featuring over 30 types of fish and shellfish dinners, many of them fresh catch. The meals aren't fancy — your entree comes with cole slaw, potatoes, and bread unless you order a complete dinner — but the fish and seafood is handled to perfection, never over- or underdone. As an appetizer, the huge shrimp cocktail with a delightfully tangy sauce is just right. Each evening, there are a few specials, dropping the already low prices even lower. Expect to wait, as they don't take reservations. Nor do they take checks or credit cards. After-dinner suggestion: a constitutional along historic Santa Monica Pier or the adjoining Palisades Park overlooking the ocean. 1602 Ocean Ave., Santa Monica; 394-9751.

Also recommended:

Paco's, where the Mexican-style fish preparations, heavily laden with garlic, are exquisite. 4141 Centinela Ave., Mar Vista; 391-9616.

Castagnola's Lobster House, featuring fresh seafoods from around the globe. 4211 Admiralty Way, Marina del Rey; 823-5339.

Malibu Sea Lion, where the ocean sprays against the windows. 21150 Pacific Coast Hwy., Malibu; 456-2810.

BEST SALAD BARS

R.J.'s This rib joint offers a salad bar of about 50 items, including pickled herring, artichoke hearts, innumerable sprouts, peppers, pickles, and condiments, and, at the dinner hour, shrimp and hearts of palm. Even the backdrop is outstanding. Flanking the ingredients is a veritable still life of the freshest fruits and vegetables, arranged with an artist's eye for color, balance, and form. The whole thing is assembled each morning (a three-hour process) with the day's fresh produce delivery. 252 Beverly Dr., Beverly Hills; 274-3474.

Hamburger Henry, Inc. About 50 items are featured here, too, including plenty of veggies, condiments, and squirrel food: seeds, nuts, and sprouts. There are also several different kinds of composed salads, including tuna, potato, macaroni, fruit, carrot, and raisin. A person could spend the afternoon sampling and nibbling until a person didn't even need dinner. 3001 Wilshire Blvd., Santa Monica; 828-3000.

The Lettuce Patch Now just about anybody can throw some Kraft Thousand Island on some lettuce and tomatoes and come up with a salad. But when it's the main course, well, you're talking about the difference between van Halen and van Gogh. The Lettuce Patch belongs in the latter category, with crisp, fresh veggies, superb homemade dressing, a wide range of salad accessories, and hot homemade bread. As a free bonus, you can carry your creation outside and enjoy the nearby sea air and view. 101 Santa Monica Pl., Santa Monica; 451-0152.

BEST TOSTADA

Sundance Cafe This is the real goods. The El Grande chicken tostada is about as grand a Mexican specialty as you can get in L.A. This $4.75 dish is stacked high with lettuce, tomatoes, and marinated, spicy chicken-breast meat. It is topped with creamy fresh guacamole, sour cream, cheese, and chips. The salsa at the Sundance, which is made with fresh red and green chili peppers, is a notch above other Mexican spots and the restaurant has a large and grand patio in which to enjoy the tostada with a view of the traffic of the busy Robertson decorator district. 350 N. Robertson Blvd., Beverly Hills; 659-1485.

BEST BURRITO SURPRISE

Campos Famous Burritos Getting dinner at Campos Mexican restaurant/take-out is like eating out of a grab bag. One never knows what one is going to go home with. This is because Campos is staffed almost entirely by congenial Mexicans who do not understand even one word of English. This makes things interesting, and rather fun, as one by one patrons return to the counter with the wrong order. You can make bets on how many surprised customers there'll be within a given period, and it's an adventure to guess what *your* surprise will be. There is a happy note, though; with the exception of the tacos that swim in a sea of grease, practically all of the food at Campos is so tasty that it doesn't matter what you get. 1014 Wilshire Blvd., Santa Monica; 395-6777 (and various other locations).

BEST BURRITOS

Burrito King Mexican-food aficionados know that true Mexican food is *not* by definition greasy, fatty, and bad for you. Yet there is some reverse snob appeal for greasy burritos, for the same reason people love Tommy's hamburgers—anything so perfect for cruising just can't be "good" food. Now, forget everything you've ever heard about burritos: they *can* be good food—tasty *and* nutritious *and* edible in a Mercedes as well as a Chebbie. That's how Burrito King makes them. Reasonably high-quality beef (not overcooked), yummo jalapeños (mild, without being bland), great beans—don't get too close to this place with empty pockets and an empty stomach. Their specialties are machaca and chorizo-egg burritos, and they also make cheap and scrumptious taquitos. Most burritos are around two dollars; hours are unpredictable, but they're often open past 2 A.M. Corner of Sunset Blvd. and Alvarado, Echo Park; 977-9078.

MOST SUREFIRE GOOD TIME AT A RESTAURANT

Oscar's Wine Bar There is something magical about Oscar's. A small restaurant, each of its three differently appointed rooms is conducive either to romance or a good time with a group. The service, from owner-hostess Michelle on down, is a dream; everyone is so friendly that you feel special as a result. The most everything-goes-wrong day can become a perfect evening at Oscar's. The menu is small, but a nice rotating selection of salads here makes it possible to eat lightly if you don't feel like trying one of the entrees (there are usually a couple of hot specials, a cold entree, steak tartare, and a cold buffet plate featuring delicious ham with your choice of a couple of salads). The desserts are invariably terrific, the house wine is Burgundy—the real thing, and the nice selection of French wines is now being complemented with a new selection of California wines. Not inexpensive, but a good time is absolutely guaranteed. 8210 Sunset Blvd., West Hollywood; 654-3457.

BEST BOARDWALK FAST FOOD

Del Cor Pizza Eating while walking on the street is an art not unlike walking a tight rope, requiring a magical combination of both grace and agility. Those who are accomplished at it glide from bank to army-navy store to pinball arcade while consuming a five-course dinner. Those who are not have high cleaning bills. The favorite entree of streeteaters is pizza by the slice, and nowhere is take-out pizza better than at Del Cor Pizza on the Ocean Front Walk in Venice. The house specialty is mushroom, pepper, Genoa salami, pepperoni, sausage, onion, and olives. Inch your way up to the front of the line and the clerk will shout to the cook, "Hey! For the man in the moustache—one slice of garbage!" (They also have whole pizzas that are excellent for streeteater conventions.) 1019 Ocean Front Walk, Venice.

Food Fantasy Featuring an assortment of Near Eastern and Greek specialties such as moussaka, falafel, pastitsio, and vegetable-filled filo pastries, Food Fantasy is a clean, greaseless alternative to the plethora of junk-food stands that line the boardwalk. Most everything is priced in the two- to three-dollar range. Food to eat there, as well as to go. Ocean Front Walk at Brooks Ave., Venice.

BEST FRENCH TOAST

The Yellow House We are speaking now of total decadence. Gastronomical lust. Original sin. This French toast transcends the paltry limits of mere food; it's an event. At the Yellow House, a small artsy-plantsy haunt at the outskirts of picturesque Rustic Canyon, you can sit at a polished wood table, sip herb tea, and space-out to a Bach Brandenburg as you wait for your order. Next to you, some jogger nibbles fruit and yogurt; above you, a hanging fern or two dangle peacefully. And then... *whammo!* The Gates of Hell open. Two enormous circles of honey-walnut-cinnamon swirl bread, each two to three inches thick, are suddenly plopped down in front of you. Fresh butter cascades off the doughy cliffs and hot syrup gleams from the glass pitcher on the side. "Enjoy it!" the waitress grins, sadistically. Twenty-four hours later you'll still feel as if you swallowed a plate of concrete, but trust us—the experience will have been worth it. This French toast rests eternal—on the hips and in memory. 147 W. Channel Rd., Santa Monica Canyon; 459-4401.

BEST AGING RESTAURANT

The Original Phillipe's L.A. is not in the habit of handing out landmarks to its oldest restaurants, but were it, the designation should go to Phillipe's, on the edge of Chinatown. Claiming to be the originator of the French dip sandwich, the boisterous restaurant has beaten the odds by remaining true to its origins. The floor is still covered with sawdust, the counters where orders are taken boast women who've worked there more than 30 years, and the coffee—here's one for Ripley's—is only a dime. Phillipe's specializes in sandwiches and serves them by the trayful. There's also a wider menu covering one wall, but it's the sandwiches and the double-dip standards that have kept a steady stream of customers coming since the first part of the century. People have fun when they eat at Phillipe's, and the room sometimes resembles a cafeteria at the United Nations in its ethnic mix. Prices are low, the service is quick, and the telephone booths are still wooden. If that's not enough, there's even plenty of free parking. 1001 N. Alameda, downtown; 628-3781.

BEST CAFETERIA

Clifton's Cafeteria is one of the classic L.A. dining experiences, a bizarre mixture of fantasy and drama. You'll have no trouble finding the joint: just listen for the screaming street Bible thumpers with their ringing condemnations of sex and their primitive sandwich boards proclaiming the end of the world. It's a tradition for them to congregate outside of Clifton's.

Inside, however, it's another world as you step into a huge room made to resemble (sort of) a forest. The poles holding up the ceiling have been disguised with bark to resemble giant redwood trees. There's a stuffed deer and a neon crescent moon over a Bavarian meditation room surrounded by plastic and dried shrubbery. You can choose from six levels of tables in this terraced room, although there seems to be an unwritten law here—the crazier or more deformed you are, the lower the level you occupy. For your dining entertainment, you can enjoy the waterfall and stream that cascade into the lobby, watch the locals, or look for Tom Waits. 648 S. Broadway, downtown; 627-1673.

MOST WORTHWHILE HOLLYWOOD SITE

Schwab's This is a tribute. Where else can you have a grilled cheese at your formica "marble top" table and contemplate the gold-vinyl booth benches and '50s sputnik chandelier while Shelley Winters, dressed in a cotton tent and courduroy slippers, gabs on the phone by the cash register? Yes, Schwab's is *the* traditional lunch hangout in L.A., and we just can't leave it by the wayside. This combination coffee shop, drugstore, and fountain is an enchanting blend of neosurreal tackiness, Polo Lounge importance, and genuine democracy, where the workers and the panhandlers of Sunset Boulevard mingle freely with actors and actresses both anonymous and famed. Everyone is treated equally; i.e., with brusque friendliness, as the waitresses scurry about with your soda or Shelley's pie à la mode. A truly atmospheric way to spend the noon hour. 8024 W. Sunset Blvd., West Hollywood; 656-1212.

BEST HOT DOG

Chic's Hot Dog Company of America It's in Beverly Hills, of course. Chic's hot dogs taste as if they come straight off a New York hot dog stand, which isn't surprising, since there's one right in the middle of the restaurant. They only serve all beef, and the dogs go for $1.50. Accompaniments include raw or sauteed onions, relish, mustard, and sauerkraut. For purists, chipped bottles of Yoo Hoo chocolate drink are available for 75 cents. But don't let Chic catch you putting mayonnaise on your dog, or you'll get a New York razz. Open seven days a week from 9:30 A.M. to 5 P.M. 318 N. Beverly, Beverly Hills; 271-2255.

The Wiener Factory The sign over the take-out window of The Wiener Factory spoofs, "We sold four hot dogs this year," but four dogs a minute would be more likely. This venerable, graffiti-decorated Valley institution, a few blocks, but light years away from a newer, more sanitized institution, the Sherman Oaks Galleria, serves an immense and loyal clientele. "What makes these hot dogs so great?" asked an uninitiated friend. Words like crunchy, juicy, savory, and genuine come to mind. They taste like hot dogs used to before they got chemicalized, and if there are really ground pig lips in them, somehow a person doesn't care. One day recently, a newcomer to this little restaurant-stand asked the next person in line, "Say, what's the thing to order here?" Everyone in line turned around and with one voice cried, "Spicy Polish dog with the works!" (The works include chili, onions, sauerkraut, cheese, relish, and hot mustard.) Now, with a testimonial like that, you don't need to look for Michelin stars. Woof! Rate that four woofs. 14917 Ventura Blvd., Sherman Oaks; 789-2676.

BEST WESTSIDE HANGOVER CURE

Lafayette Cafe For $2.25, you have two ways to face a bloodshot Sunday morning. The easy way out, of course, is to ease out of the pain with a Bloody Mary. Or you can head over to the Lafayette Cafe on Ocean Front Walk at Westminster in Venice and get an order of huevos rancheros: two tortillas, covered with Arturo's potent hot sauce made of tomatillos, cilantro, and jalapeños, with two eggs, either over easy or scrambled, plus a side of refried beans or tomatoes. A bottomless cup of coffee to help bring you around goes for 50¢. Your hangover doesn't have a chance against this medicine. Ocean Front Walk at Westminster, Venice.

BEST CHEAP BREAKFAST

Rae's As its popularity is still undisputed, we had no choice but to reiterate what has practically become common knowledge: Rae's has the best, the cheapest, and quite probably the biggest breakfasts around. For $1.99 you get a death-defying portion of eggs, bacon or sausage, and potatoes or hot cakes, along with choice of toast or Rae's own country biscuits doused in creamy gravy. Add to this the atmosphere of a genuine '50s diner, complete with turquoise and pink color scheme, and waitresses who know their business, and you've got a great place to start the morning (or end the night). A word of caution: get there early, i.e., before 8 A.M. Otherwise you'll join a line that spills out down the block. 2901 Pico Blvd., Santa Monica; 828-7937.

BEST ICE CREAM

All this fuss. Used to be a nice un-healthy Dixie cup did the trick. But the innocent days of choc-van-straw, or even B & R 31, are solidly past, succeeded by designer dips in 1,286 colors.

Cookies à la Mode   The phrase "all natural" is used with wild abandon, necessitating careful reading of those labels. Fortunately, the ice cream at Cookies à la Mode passes rigorous inspection. All ingredients are com-pletely fresh, contain no preservatives or sugar, and the honey-based ice cream and ices are made on the prem-ises. Especially titillating are the tan-gerine chocolate, caralua (carob and mocha), or any of the 36 other crea-tive flavors of the month. Corner of Pico and Lincoln blvds., Santa Mon-ica; 396-6812.

Via Dolce   is rapidly acquiring fame in L.A. as the literal crème de la crème of ice cream. Featuring exotic treats such as Chambord raspberry, crème de cacao, Bailey's Irish cream, and Cointreau orange, Via Dolce bills it-self as the "over 21" ice cream be-cause of its high alcoholic content and its elite appeal. According to the man-ager, Via Dolce's product is "20 per-cent butterfat; if not it's because it was replaced by alcohol." There are also such nonalcoholic winners as the white chocolate, which contains chips of Via Dolce's own candy, and the raspberry chocolate truffle. Not fran-chised; all ice cream made on prem-ises. 215 Rose Ave., Venice; 392-4921.

Gelato Classico and Gelati per Tutti Gelato, the treat of Rome and San Francisco, has finally gotten to L.A. This mysterious ice cream is of Italian origin, and its uniqueness lies in the fact that no air is injected into it, making it denser and richer. Plus, there's more fresh cream than ice cream. Because of its richness, the portions are smaller and you can get two or more flavors in your order as a happy result. At Gelato Classico, the dark chocolate with peanut butter is, well, classico, along with the vanilla bean, crema de limone, and arancia. At Gelati per Tutti, you can find dif-ferent flavors, such as Zambia, ama-retto, and espresso. Not cheap at $1.15 for a three-ounce portion, but that should last you for a *long* while. Gelato Classico, 445 N. Beverly Dr., Beverly Hills; 278-7619. Gelati per Tutti, 7653 Melrose Ave., Hollywood; 653-8970.

4.

GOODS AND SERVICES

BEST LIQUOR STORE

Robert Burns Liquor A clean, well-lighted place where you can plan a party, browse through a plentiful selection, and get answers from clerks who really know what they're talking about. The prices are reasonable. A Chateau Thieuley that goes for $12.00 a bottle at Chasen's or Sapgo, here sells for $3.25. Korbel Brut champagne is $7.95 and a French Moët et Chandon goes for $12.99. The store also features a changing list of specials. 328 South Doheny Dr., Beverly Hills; 274-0033.

BEST HARDWARE STORE

Gerald's Paint & Hardware Company There's something timeless about a well-used hardware store. Visions of Saturday afternoon shopping chores come to mind amidst all the screws, tools, and things you hope you'll never have to learn how to use. To the novice, a hardware store can be a mind-boggling mix of the mysterious and the mundane. Where to start looking for the elusive hook, or the unusual shade of chartruese, is something obviously best left to the clerks. That's where Gerald's Paint & Hardware Company comes in. They've got what has to be the most helpful sales staff of any store in the city. No question is too small, or too cheap, to be answered in detail. When it comes to tracking down just the right part, paint, or tool, Gerald's staff relishes the chore like a librarian on the trail of that vanished edition. The size of the store isn't gargantuan—that's best left to the chains—but the room is just right so as not to be intimidating, but still have the size to hold *everything* you ever wanted to know about hardware. And don't be afraid to ask. 7280 W. Manchester Ave., Westchester; 670-0652.

BEST CLEANERS

Magnolia Cleaners At how many cleaners can you find your shmattes swinging next to Shirley MacLaine's? Magnolia is "the cleaners of the stars," and not for nothing, either. They're genuinely the best. They do not ruin garments—they save them, and many a greasy, grimy nightmare has been restored in their loving hands. That's why Neiman Marcus sends its problems to Magnolia, and also why Magnolia is not exactly cheap. But if you've got a garment you really care about, pay them a visit. And who knows—you just might get to see "somebody's" silk undies drying on the line. 8410 Melrose Ave., West Hollywood; 653-0060.

BEST DIME STORE

Shatsky and Shapiro Otherwise known as Marlene Shatsky and Eddie Shapiro, an enduring team, they've successfully maintained a country store ambience in inner cityville, one that will metamorphosize you into a kid with an allowance burning in your pocket. Shatsky's (called thusly by doting habitues) is basically a hip version of a five and dime and then some. It has a little of just about everything, from household supplies to designer jeans, plus a well-stocked assortment of dire necessities. Holiday items (Mother's Day, Secretary's Day, etc.) are seasonably available at reasonable if not inexpensive prices and are selected with a droll eye. Halloween is a particular favorite, producing a deluge of costumes and trimmings. The clothing department is always neat, with an emphasis on un-usual accessories (especially socks). And Shapiro's passion for windup toys has resulted in a kinetic menagerie. 8936 Santa Monica Blvd., West Hollywood; 655-7808.

FRIENDLIEST SUPERMARKET

The Fireside It may be in one of the nation's highest rent districts, but it belongs on an oak-lined little avenue in Muncie, or maybe Abilene. The Fireside is one of those cozy, sociable markets from another time and place, with a staff of checkers who get to know you personally, an excellent butcher department where they have time for down-home chitchat, and an overall air of courtesy and cheer that would make Frank Capra proud. Why, there's even free coffee over in the corner, and a couple of picnic tables outside under a tree. Oh, once in awhile clouds may block the sunshine with a $1.39 avocado, but strangely enough, despite some higher-than-average prices, people seem to prefer shopping here to shopping at the Safeway down the street. Maybe that's because the Fireside has everything you want from a store, and a hell of a lot more. 1425 Montana Ave., Santa Monica; 451-5743.

BEST OLD—FASHIONED MALL

The Santa Monica Mall The multi-story mall has rewritten the book of shopping centers, but there was a time before real-estate prices went through the roof when any self-respecting shopping mall could stretch out for blocks. Which is exactly what Santa Monica Shopper's Mall does. For three blocks, to be exact, the stores bump up next to each other along a pleasing expanse of boxed trees and concrete. Strollers take their time wandering in and out of the stores — which range from typical discount houses to Spanish-language theaters to specialty shops — away from the hustle and bustle of its shiny cousin next door, glamorous Santa Monica Place. Canned Muzak provides a balmy soundtrack, and while it might appear that more people are out for a walk than a purchase, there's a friendly leisure in the air a world away from the "modern" mall experience. On Wednesdays, Arizona Avenue is blocked off to make way for a real farmer's market. See it while you can. Santa Monica Shopper's Mall, between Third and Fourth sts., from Broadway to Wilshire, Santa Monica.

BEST DRUGSTORE

The Rexall Drugstore in Dart Square can almost be equated with the Boys Market in the Marina as a place that combines useful and exotic goods and a lot of interesting characters hanging out. Even at 10 P.M., aisles occupy about 15 curious onlookers. Besides a great toy selection, the store boasts the unique quality of remaining open 365 days a year, with hours from 8:30 A.M. until 11 P.M. Rexall carries everything from electrical appliances to Gucci cologne, hardware to London-imported Mason-Pearson hairbrushes (ranging from $55 to $75). The only person we ever saw whose need wasn't fulfilled was the guy looking for an electronic fly zapper just before closing, but we bet if he'd placed an order, the store would have come up with one. Corner of Beverly Blvd. and La Cienega (across from the Beverly Center), Beverly Hills; 653-0880.

BEST CANDY SHOP

Bit of Sweetland Chocolate, chocolate everywhere, from bitterest dark to milkiest white. There is chocolate for baking, for dipping and dripping; chocolate powders in tins; chocolate extracts in bottles; chocolate rolled with a generous hand over orange peels, over nutmeats, marzipan, and other confectionery classics. And beyond chocolate, too! The shelves groan with flavorings, extracts, preserves, condiments, and various packaged items that are miracles of diversity. This is the place for your sugar fixes. The shop itself has an old-fashioned European flavor redolent of the idea that sweets are a part of the natural order and that the sugarless, post-Aquarian age is an impoverished way to live. 8560 W. Third St., West Hollywood; 275-5895.

MOST FUN FLORIST SHOP

Arturo's Flowers These folks celebrate every holiday from St. Patrick's Day to Halloween with juvenile-looking murals painted on their north wall. E.T. is currently featured, accompanied by several robots and buck-toothed aliens. On major holidays a costumed clerk disrupts traffic on La Brea. Inside, a perspiring woman plays the piano. You don't know whether to tip her, ignore her, or make a few requests. Free popcorn and soft drinks. Corner of La Brea and Fountain, Hollywood; 876-6482.

BEST PLACE TO TAKE A BATH

Healthworks For years gay men walked around in towels at bath houses and the only woman allowed inside was Bette Midler. Well, get ready for some divine madness, because L.A. now has a cosexual bath house. The Healthworks, featured in *Playboy* magazine's February 1983 "Year in Sex" review, has a clientele of roughly 40 percent gay men, 40 percent straight men, and 20 percent straight women, the sum of which yields more combinations and permutations than your high-school math teacher could shake a pointer at. Healthworks is a private club with the same reasonable membership fees for men and women, unlike similar organizations that charge exorbitant fees for men. 2114 Hyperion Blvd., Silverlake; 667-9905.

MOST THOUGHTFUL COPY SHOPS

Copy Spot and Copyland Okay, so maybe you've got your own personal desk-top copier. Good for you. The rest of us make do at the neighborhood copy shop, and when it closes on Friday or Saturday, we're SOL until Monday. Except if we live on the west side of town, where there are at least two Sunday saviors: Copy Spot, 712 Wilshire Blvd., Santa Monica (393-0693); open weekdays until 11 P.M., Saturday until 4:30 P.M., and Sunday noon–5 P.M. Copyland, 11717 Pico, West Los Angeles (479-3957); open weekdays until 7:30 P.M., Saturday 11 A.M.–6 P.M., and Sunday noon–4 P.M.

BEST OCCULT STORE

Ram Center Snuggled up unassumingly next to a store that sells cowboy duds is the Ram Center, the coolest place in town to purchase your alchemic accouterments. Run by amiable members of the Ramnian Church, the Ram Center supplies everything a wizard or novice would require for his or her ceremonies, from Special (Alleged) Uncrossing Oil to prepackaged black cat bones to tall glass-encased voodoo candles that have a list printed on the side—you fill in the names of those you want to curse. The long glass cases are filled with gorgeous pieces of unique jewelry in the shapes of skulls, fairies, eyes, bats, and astrological signs, and you can even purchase a bottle of dove's blood ink and some parchment for those . . . er . . . special notes you have to write. If the supernatural doesn't turn you on or you aren't interested in Keep Away Evil Spirits Scented Room Spray, try some of the Ram Center's essential oils. In scents like Black Orchid or Tuberose, they're divine and last for hours. There's also an entire selection of occult books: biographies of Marie La Veaux (the New Orleans voodoo Queen), numerology books, tarot cards, and the like, and the Ram's own catalog of custom-designed ceremonial robes. The Ram Center is definitely a must if you're unlucky in love, a budding sorcerer's apprentice, or just want some lovely perfume. 1642 N. Wilcox Ave., Hollywood; 462-7078.

BEST SHOP FOR USELESS ITEMS

Insanity A very Westwood paraphernalia shop that carries all those things you never had to have until you saw them. Featured in this bizarre bazaar are Earthquakes-in-a-Can, toilet T-shirts (*for* the toilet lid, not *with* a toilet on them), tennis balls with slits in them (you guessed it, change purses), and scores and scads of the most expendable items around, expressly made for the young collegiate with a full wallet and an empty head. But the most useless item at Insanity, or anywhere else, stands next to the cash register, patiently waiting for Mr. or Ms. Right. What could it be? Well, we'll give you a hint: it's seven feet tall, stuffed, and covered in black and white satin. Why, you're right—it's a Punk Palm Tree. At only $750, you'd better hurry, because this bargain won't last forever. 10904 Lindbrook Dr., Westwood; 208-7578.

BEST CIGAR STORE

The Cigar Warehouse There are tobacconists selling flavored cigars and fancy wrappings at fancy prices, but the Cigar Warehouse offers great variety (more than 100 brands), 15 percent to 20 percent discounts, and a 500-square-foot humidor where customers can browse, sniff, and ponder their selection. Brothers Larry and Jeffrey Wagner carry a full line of good-quality, top-name-brand cigars, discounted by the box, as well as "alternative" cigars purchased by the bundle from Honduras, Nicaragua, Dominican Republic, Jamaica, and Mexico. The best selling cigar here is "The Bravo," a house brand from Honduras. Also available are papers and tobaccos, 31 of which are blended in-house, just like Baskin Robbins. And—want to know your tobacco type? The Wagners and staff are available for consultation. 15141 Ventura Blvd., Sherman Oaks; 784-1391. 1632 Westwood Blvd., Westwood; 475-4325.

MOST INGENIOUS PARTY SERVICES

Tributes, Unlimited Shirley Siegel, entertainer, singer and party entrepreneur, writes and performs feature-length musical tributes for every occasion from birthdays and bar mitzvahs, to corporate and professional achievement awards. These elaborate presentations include full scale productions of "Your Life Set to Music," and "Oscar-gram" events, wherein the honoree is presented with a personally engraved Oscar replica.

Perhaps the most outstanding presentation to date was bestowed on a plastic surgeon by request of his patient, in commemoration of her breast lift. The ceremony took place, to his great surprise, right outside the operating room door following the woman's surgery, and the Oscar was engraved, "Best Performance, Leading Man—Body Design." Tributes, Unlimited is truly unlimited. 275-8407.

BEST REASON TO AVOID SHOPPING AT CHARMER'S MARKET

Chalet Gourmet Thank God someone is finally giving Charmer's Market a run for its money in the Santa Monica Bay area gourmet-food derby. The venerable, well-managed, friendly Chalet Gourmet, a Hollywood institution at the corner of Sunset and Fairfax (874-6301), has recently opened a Marina del Rey branch. The quality is every bit as high as Charmer's, but the prices aren't. Corner of Lincoln Blvd. and Mindanao Way; 306-5100.

BEST LANDSCAPED FLORIST

Flowers that Bloom in the Spring, Tra-La Owner Kristi Stevens missed Europe, where the flower shops sell not only blooms but enchantment. There, she sighed, you could buy a single rose or an exotic bouquet— while surrounded by the beauty of the flowers themselves, utilized to their utmost in the way of interior design. So, with the help of architect John Lautner (a protege of Frank Lloyd Wright), Stevens brought the Continent to L.A. as far as floral ingenuity goes. Her shop offers the most exotic imports imaginable, displayed in their natural beauty by means of an air wall keeping them cold in your midst, while a huge reflecting pool and fountain make you believe you're in a real garden instead of a real florist shop. You can get yourself a Colombian sterling silver rose (blue), flowers from Holland or Hawaii, and orchids from wherever they bloom, as well as more simple, familiar fare, and you can get a bouquet for as little as $1.25, or an arrangement of an orchid and other flowers, in a vase, for just $13.00. At these prices, you can afford to go to Brentwood. 11710 Barrington Ct., Brentwood; 471-1906.

BEST FLORAL DESIGN

Blossom's A rose is a rose is a rose ... until it gets to Blossom's, at which point it transcends the ordinary plant medium and enters the realm of high art. From this tiny floral enterprise come the most lavish and exotic arrangements imaginable, from Japanese lilies and other rare blooms to beautiful hand-blown vases and Zen-like design concepts. You can spend anywhere from $15 to $200, depending on your needs and dreams, but whatever the cost, your pleasure is virtually guaranteed. Blossom's creations belong in a gallery, not on a coffee table. Phone orders only; 666-2584 and 666-7271.

BEST SURPRISE

Stuffed People Sherwood Galleries in Santa Monica is peopled with stuffed critters from whimsical crabs and huggable worms to a life-size K-Mart–clothed cleaning woman wielding a mop as she confronts a little, less-than-life-size leering flasher. The toys aren't cheap; the smallest dragon runs around $40, and the macrame buffalo family—a beautiful wallhanging—is over $2,000. But you don't have to buy to enjoy. 279 Monica Pl., Santa Monica; 393-6181.

BEST LINGERIE

Playmates of Hollywood Frederick's of Hollywood is an institution; Trashy Lingerie caters to somewhat subdued tastes, but when it comes to good old-fashioned slinky, seductive, and sincerely sensuous scanties, Playmates of Hollywood beats the other two with a snap of a maribou-trimmed garter. The large windows in front, chock-full of delectable flimsies, fluorescent hotpants, and lacy merry widows, merely hint at the treasures inside. It's enough to make Gypsy Rose Lee foam at the mouth. Garter belts, bras, and panties in every shade of the rainbow, jungle prints, glittery Lurex blends, and, of course, the traditional black lace with red trim beckon from every shelf. There are belly dancer's costumes, brassieres designed to make those with the attributes of an ironing board resemble Mamie Van Doren, fishnet hose, fingerless lace gloves, chain-mail halters, and baby-doll nighties. And, and, and ... peek-aboo bathing suits, risque evening wear, how about rhinestone-studded stockings, or string bikinis with obscene statements embroidered on the crotch panels? What more could a girl want? Oh yes, there's a whole line of G-strings and pasties, in case you'd like to stage your own *The Night They Raided Minsky's*. Mae West couldn't have thought this place up in her wildest wet dream! And everything in the store is affordable. Any working (ahem!) girl can afford the booty. Steer your latest flame here when he or she offers to buy you a present. After all, if God had intended Eve to go about *au naturel*, why did she flee Eden in an electric-green gold-fringed fig leaf? 6438 Hollywood Blvd., Hollywood (PG); 464-7636.

BEST SEX SHOP

The Pleasure Chest A swanky supermarket for the epicure of erotica. Inside, dear ones, lies the country's largest collection of sensual merchandise, from lingerie to restraints, massage oils to enema kits, chastity belts to (mouth-watering?) edible panties. The ambience is actually elegant, intended to make you feel equally comfortable taking along Erica Jong or proving to Auntie Em that the Matterhorn is not the only joyride in Southern Cal. In case you purchase something that draws just a little embarrassment when you get home, The Pleasure Chest offers as remedy Guilt Away, available in a spray can. 7733 Santa Monica Blvd., West Hollywood; 654-2215.

BEST CARD SHOP

The Card Factory has long been the best place in the area to find the unusual in greeting cards. Sure, they've even succumbed to carrying the nauseating new-wave air-brush kitsch of Paper Moon Graphics, but they also had a wonderful selection of postcards long before it was trendy to collect — photograph cards from Man Ray, Avedon, and Horst, art reproductions, 3-D cards, and much more. Their greeting-card selection is unequaled, with everything from X-rated West Hollywood beefcake to delicate hand-cut wooden shavings adorning Mexican folk-art cards. There is also a great selection of writing paper, calendars, and letter seals. 8908 Santa Monica Blvd., West Hollywood; 652-0194. Beverly Center, 131 N. La Cienega, Beverly Hills; 652-0192.

BEST CARD SHOP ON THE BEACH

Homeworks is a little like one of those Russian babushka dolls — it's a store within a store within a store. Just when you think you've cased the tiny joint, something new and unexpected pops up, like a rack of clothes hidden behind the stuffed animals, or a shelf of kitchen utensils, or a squirting camera (remember those?). But one of the best features of the place is the card selection, specifically the postcard selection, even more specifically the Ronnie and Nancy postcard selection. At last your national angst can be indulged for a pittance, with such insurrectionist fantasies as "The First Lady," "Budget Cut," and "The National Bean." At 50 cents each, these just might be the only bargains left in Reagan Country. 2923 Main St., Santa Monica; 396-0101.

BEST NEEDLECRAFT SHOP

Nettie's Needlecraft, considered L.A.'s stitchery center par excellence by handicrafters the world over, contains a broad enough inventory to underwrite all fantasies. The yarn collection alone is peak experience stuff in its variety of color and texture. Countless are the preassembled kits, from knit booties for the kid sister's first born to needlepoint room-size rugs. If you don't know a cross-stitch from your buttonhole, there are also scheduled classes offering convivial instruction. The store is a swirl of activity, good cheer, and infinite variety, more than making up for the cramped quarters. If you can't find exactly what you want, Nettie can special order from an exhaustive list of suppliers—or it simply doesn't exist. 9742 Wilshire Blvd., Beverly Hills; 672-7700.

thereof. In their penguin line, for example, they have dozens of penguin dolls, decals, toys, T-shirts, and even a rolling penguin on a stick. The same is true for all the other animals, from alligators and peacocks to elephants and ants. 17200 Ventura Blvd., Encino; 981-9977.

BEST TOY STORES

Intellitoy About the only mind-blowing place in the new Beverly Center, so far, is a place called Intellitoy, featuring a wide selection of imported and domestic toys, computer games, and hobbies. It's a bit like the Fifth Avenue F.A.O. Schwartz, because they both sell expensive quality toys, but Intellitoy also stocks tons of stocking-stuffer-type knickknacks. Some choice items include The Friendly Stars That Glow, phosphorescent star-shaped decals for your ceiling that guarantee to "soothe, educate, and remove fear of the dark" ($2.50); wooden boomerangs that actually work ($2.00); Vampire Bat kites from Germany ($4.50); a hobby kit called The Mighty Molar (an eight times larger-than-life plastic model of a tooth that opens up to reveal the nerves and veins, for $9.00), and the entire line of beautifully constructed, British-made Pelham Puppets ($35.00). Look for the dancing skeleton with a special string that, when pulled, sends the head and bones scattering in all directions. 8500 Beverly Blvd., Los Angeles; 652-6414.

Critters Galore For anyone with a particular obsession for replicas and trinkets from the animal kingdom, Critters has got to be nirvana. The store is stuffed to the popping point with every kind of animal and spinoff

BEST WIDE SHOES

Chic Shoes specializes in stylish, contemporary shoes for the extra-wide, hard-to-fit foot. Open seven days a week, in two locations: 10746 Washington, Culver City (836-2568); 18768 Ventura Blvd., Tarzana (708-0855). The variety and friendly salesmen here are worth the trip to the Valley.

BEST CRAFTS SOURCES AND SUPPLIES

The Papermill is housed in a beautiful, columned space that was once owned by a coffee company, but is now part of a complex of art spaces in one of the pockets of the downtown art community. The Papermill provides fine, archival papers to artists, printmakers, calligraphers, and book artists. It stocks one of the last remaining shipments (in the original crates) from 1956 of a Whatman calligraphy paper that is no longer produced. The offices contain a permanent historical-technical display of paper making and changing displays of paper-related crafts. A good part of the office space is given over to changing exhibitions of more works on or of paper. As a bastion against the dwindling demand for quality paper in a media age, it is a touch of the old world in a modern techno society. 800 Traction Ave., downtown; 680-2469.

BEST CAR WASHES

What becomes a car wash most? Personalized attention and TLC, of course. Do you *realize* what those heavy brushes and blowers do to your car? Does it pain you to watch your precious import going down the line as anonymously as mail in a post office? Bang, splat! Bang, splat! You and your wheels deserve better. Here are three recommendations.

Sunset Carwash Because of the size of L.A., some residents spend more time with their cars than with their spouses. Hence, the high divorce rate and the development of close relationships between Angelenos and their autos. And when an owner wants to say to his car, "Hey, baby, you're somethin' special," why, he takes her on down to Sunset Carwash. Here, for just $4.50 (plus tip), *la voiture* gets star treatment: bath, shampoo, and individual attention to blemishes. The Sunset even looks classy, inside and out, and while they don't serve champagne while you wait, it feels as if they should. But you needn't be intimidated by all this ritziness if you're not on the affluent side; whether you're with a Jag or an Olds, the staff treats each couple the same. They understand that there's nothing quite like the moment when your

baby rolls off the line, as sleek and sexy as she can be, and the two of you ride off into the sunset together. 7955 Sunset Blvd. at Hayworth, Hollywood; 656-2777.

Classic Car Wash This is the Red Door of car care. No machinery will ever touch your car's tender flanks. All work is done by hand, from washing to chamois drying to tire dressing. Six dollars for the works. 2409 El Segundo Blvd., Hawthorne; 754-9528.

Handy J Car Wash Across from Stern's Barbeque, this establishment charges $4.95 for a hand wash, automatic rinse. 12681 Washington Blvd., Culver City; 398-6211.

MOST CREATIVE CAR RENTAL

Bundy Rent–a–Wreck David Schwartz is the guy standing next to the Pope (check out the picture in the office), and renting a car from him can be an event, like renting from Steve Martin. Schwartz and his "I'm a character" sense of pushy humor were already a success in the used-car business when he got the idea for a rental fleet of 650 used automobiles. Like found art, each car is in its honest-to-goodness original used and usually bedraggled state—but with the engines purring to the tune-up of scrupulous servicing. The cars are chosen with a sardonic eye for style, and include such gems as '58 Chevys, Ford Mustangs, Nash Ramblers, and vintage VWs. Convertibles, station wagons, pickups, and vans are available, along with one glorious '77 Cadillac limo with optional chauffeur. Schwartz and his partner have been franchising the Rent-A-Wreck concept, so you can now get one at more than 150 locations, from Alaska to Connecticut. The price is competitive, the requirements are as usual, but the Pico Boulevard joint is more fun than Hertz, a hive of *soigné* L.A. nobs who may be renting or just stopping by to hang out with David. 12333 W. Pico Blvd., West Los Angeles; 478-4393.

BEST LINEN STORE

Acme Linen Co. is a linen distributor with a retail outlet open to the public. The merchandise is current stock, *not* seconds. They carry all leading brands of linens, from Christian Dior to Cannon and Fieldcrest, and stock mattress covers, bedspreads, pillows, kitchen linens, etc. The prices are generally half those in the local department stores; Fieldcrest bath towels, for instance, were $7.50, with matching fingertip towels for $1.25. Best of all, the salesfolk, who have been there for years, will help you put together a set of linens. A word of advice: if you don't find exactly what you want on your first visit, try again; the stock changes. 229–239 E. Seventh St., downtown; 622-2269.

BEST PLUMBER

George Chambers, of Chambers Plumbing & Heating Plumber. The word itself draws weary sighs from anyone who's ever had a toilet go out. There goes next month's paycheck. Talking to a plumber is like consulting a doctor! You pretty much have to take their word for whatever's wrong. Still, if a plumber is absolutely necessary — why else call one — it's wisest to stick with the pros, and it'd be hard to imagine someone with more experience than George Chambers. He's got stories galore of Los Angeles when it wasn't much more than a series of unconnected suburbs, and can troubleshoot a situation over the phone, sometimes cutting out a house call. If Chambers does require a personal inspection, he's quick to eyeball the problem, give a flat estimate, and then *stick to it*. Depending on the availability of parts, he's even been known to knock down the price. Chambers takes pride in his work, and while he's not necessarily the cheapest, he's someone who gets the job done right the first time. With luck, you'll never have to see him again. Chambers Plumbing & Heating, 9623 Venice, Culver City; 838-2203.

BEST DANCEWEAR

Anne Simone, a dancewear shop just down the street from Jane Fonda's Workout, offers a lot of dancewear for your money. Goods are manufactured on the premises. A blend of 46 percent cotton, 46 percent Dacron, and 8 percent Lycra, the leotards are remarkably low priced at $15, with dyed-to-match tights at $16. Cotton dance pants are $22, and 100 percent nylon dance pants are $12. Basic as well as vivid colors are available. 3535 S. Robertson Blvd., Beverly Hills; 655-8658.

CLEVEREST BUSINESS ENTERPRISE

Hollywood on Location The folks from back East are coming out to visit again. They've already "done" the studio tours, and now they want to see the real thing. What to do? Call Hollywood on Location, a new service for people who like to watch the process of filmmaking. For $19 you get a self-guided tour of daily film and TV locations, as well as maps for locating the locations. This outfit promises five to ten productions a day, with names, stars, time, and exact shooting addresses, as well as tips on good spectator manners. The price covers as many people as you want to stuff into your car or van, and the tour takes as long as you want it to. As the brochure so subtly reminds you, "Your friends are going to 'eat their hearts out' when you tell them who you saw!" 8644 Wilshire Blvd., Beverly Hills; 659-9165.

THE BEST DOGGIE DO'S

The Bowser Boutique Without a doubt, the snootiest doggie do hangout around. When we made the mistake of calling it a pet shop, the owner nearly hung up. There was a long pause at the other end, followed by the frozen reply, "We are *not a pet* shop!" Well, *pardonnez nous*. The Bowser Boutique has everything from coats and hats (a complete line, in fact, of canine Chapeaux that includes Scottish tams and yarmulkes)

to pure gold-onyx-handled pooper scoopers. They also cater birthday parties for dogs, complete with party hats, "mutt" loaf entrees, and fire hydrant centerpieces ($15 per dog, $25 per person). 610 N. Robertson Blvd., West Hollywood; 659-0847.

Love on a Leash Owner Diane Bouchard specializes in custom-made outfits for dogs, among them bikinis, full-dress suits, and matching mother-and-puppy wear. Ms. Bouchard also performs psychic readings for her canine clients and caters birthday parties, too, where owners can either listen to her contact their dog's dear departed or simply "sit around telling dog stories" while their party-hatted progeny devour an Alpo cake ($15 per dog, six dog minimum). 875 Westbourne Ave., West Hollywood; 274-7057.

BEST PET CEMETERY

Pet Haven Evelyn Waugh satirized a place similar to Pet Haven in his immortal *The Loved One,* to the point of total absurdity. But the place does exist, and plenty of people take it seriously. Like the guy who spent the night in a sleeping bag on his cat's grave. Or the woman whose bronze and marble posthumous tribute to her Great Dane cost upwards of $10,000. In business since 1948, Pet Haven is the most popular pet resting ground in Southern California, with over 30,000 residents. The largest is Little Joe's horse from *Bonanza,* and the smallest is a goldfish. Celebrities such as Alan Ladd and Edward G. Robinson gave their dogs grand sendoffs here, and some of the more unusual inhabitants include two kangaroos, Wally, and Wallette, and Liz, a white rat. Owner Hal Hand and his aunt, Betty Halloway, are the lovely and sincere owners of this eternal Valhalla, and they will bury your pet, depending on its size, for anywhere from $88 to $450. Burials include a satin-lined casket, viewing room for payment of last respects, and a flower container. Cremation available on premises. 18300 S. Figueroa St., Gardena; 321-0191.

BEST BONSAI NURSERY

Fuji Bonsai Nursery Either you love 'em or you don't, these exquisite miniature trees that have been painstakingly shaped and cultivated by experts in this ancient Oriental art. Fuji Nursery in Sylmar offer by far the best and most reasonably priced selection in the area, from tiny, graceful juniper trees planted in rocks (about $20) to whole groves and forests. Some are over 100 years old. Incredibly, Shigeru Nagatoshi and his wife cultivate and take care of their vast collection all by themselves. It's better than an art gallery, well worth the trip to Sylmar just to admire them. Open Mon.–Sat., 8 A.M.–6 P.M.; Sun., 1–6 P.M. 13170 Glenoaks Blvd., Sylmar; 367-5372.

BEST GARDEN OF EDEN

Stewart Orchid Nursery With its 6,000 square feet of greenhouses and mossy pebbled pathways that give onto hallelujah displays of blooming orchids, Stewart Orchid Nursery, in operation since 1944, is considered one of the nation's leading growers. The delicate process of orchid breeding is open to public view, managed by a beehive of horticultural students and technicians who seem to take genuine delight in explaining each painstaking step, though they are wary of spies after top-secret hybridization and growing technology. ("Important" breeding plants pull in as much as $2,000.) The plants sell for as low as $9, and there's a fine selection of books, gardening tools, soils, and supplements, along with amiable advice to insure orchid-growing success. Well-drawn maps are available, and guided tours may be booked by calling ahead for reservations. For the armchair gardener, there is a full-color mail-order catalog that is second only to being there. 1212 Las Tunas Dr., San Gabriel; 285-7195.

A Guide to Bookstores

by Ann Edelman

Contrary to popular opinion, Angelenos do read. In fact, there seems to be a bookstore around every corner, and the literate browser can find a tome about practically anything. B. Dalton Bookseller and Waldenbooks now have stores all over town, providing well-stocked shelves of paperbacks and hardcovers, and the new kid on the block, Crown Books, known for its hardback discounts, is also multiplying. Here are the best of the rest, with the emphasis on stores that offer friendly personal service, unique atmosphere, and/or a "very special" specialty.

BEST BOOKSTORE MIX

Book Row, Hollywood, on the few short blocks between Argyle and Highland avenues, is known to publishers as far away as New York for its dozen bookstores that offer a variety of riches: books new and used, hardback and paperback, rare first editions, back-issue magazines, and movie memorabilia. Among the most intriguing are:

Gilbert's Mr. Gilbert, who opened his store in 1929, used to deliver books to the likes of Greta Garbo, Bette Davis, and Ronald Colman. Besides a wide selection of new and used books on general topics, Gil-bert's has one of the best collections in the city on astrology, metaphysics, and the occult. 6278 Hollywood Blvd.; 465-4185.

Marlow's Bookshop carries hardbacks and paperbacks, new and used, and review books at reduced prices, but the specialty is back-issue magazines. In his gigantic warehouse, owner Marlow Selco has more than 100 tons of magazines going back to the 1700s, with a stock so well organized that he can usually locate a magazine in a day. 6609 Hollywood Blvd.; 465-8295.

Larry Edmunds Book Shop, said to be Truffaut's favorite, is always crowded with film students and film buffs. Dealing exclusively in books about cinema and theater, it has without a doubt the world's largest collection of film memorabilia, including hundreds of thousands of stills, and rare and out-of-print books and posters. 6658 Hollywood Blvd.; 463-3273.

DENSEST AGGREGATION OF BOOKSTORES

Booksellers Row, Westwood Pick up a guide map at any one of the more than 20 bookstores between the UCLA bookstore to the north (the biggest and best student bookstore in the city) and Pico Boulevard to the south. It's possible for the serious bookworm to spend a fruitful day browsing among this cluster of bookstores that carry new, used, rare, and out-of-print books; foreign-language books; feminist literature; science fiction; art books and technical treatises. Allow yourself plenty of time. (Some of the stores in this area are listed elsewhere in this section.)

BEST NEIGHBORHOOD BOOKSTORES

Food For Thought is the only combination bookstore-cafe in the city. There's a good selection of hardbacks and paperbacks, a rack of overseas newspapers, and a wide range of magazines, including foreign publications and hard-to-find reviews and quarterlies. The adjoining cafe serves wine, beer, espresso, and food. Beverly Center (ground floor), 131 N. La Cienega Blvd., Beverly Hills; 559-2416.

Fowler Brothers, the oldest bookstore in California, has been a downtown tradition for 95 years. The founder's grandson now runs this favorite personal-service general bookstore. 717 W. Seventh St., downtown; 627-7846.

George Sand Books, a general bookstore with an excellent selection of poetry and fiction, specializes in books about film, theater, music, and dance. It's a favorite of authors, and almost every Sunday afternoon there are free literary events, such as poetry readings and autograph parties. 9011 Melrose Ave., West Hollywood; 858-1648.

BEST SPECIALTY BOOKSTORES

Artworks The only place in town that deals exclusively in books made by and about artists. Here are some beautiful, original, one-of-a-kind works ranging in price from very reasonable to expensive. 170 S. La Brea Ave., Hollywood; 934-2205.

Bodhi Tree *The* store to find books on spiritual topics, from yoga, western and eastern mysticism, and holistic health, to alchemy, astrology, and tarot. There are records and tapes, the air is fragrant with incense, and you can sip herb tea as you browse. 8585 Melrose Ave., West Hollywood; 659-1733.

A Change of Hobbit This fascinating bookstore that features a rather spectacular "special effects" decor has "catered to the cravings of S.F. and fantasy fiends since 1972." There is a truly comprehensive selection, very well organized, and much activity in terms of such bookish events as discussion groups with authors; Ray Bradbury is something of a regular here. 1853 Lincoln Blvd., Santa Monica; call GREAT-SF.

Children's Book & Music Center Teachers and conscientious parents come here to get the very best in books and records for children. Everything is carefully chosen, and everyone in the store in knowledgeable. There's a fine collection of records by Pete Seeger, Ella Jenkins, and all the folk-song greats, plus simple, fun rhythm instruments from all over the world. 2500 Santa Monica Blvd., Santa Monica; 829-0215.

Hennessey and Ingalls This is the best place in town (except for the museums) to find books on art and architecture. In addition to new titles, they carry rare books and catalogs, prints, and posters. 10814 W. Pico Blvd., West Los Angeles; 474-2541.

Scene of the Crime This place looks more like a Victorian living room than a bookstore, with its red-flocked wallpaper and fireplace flanked by velvet-upholstered armchairs. The store specializes exclusively in crime, with whodunits galore, plus a top-notch selection of serious books about crime, criminals, and puzzlements. Books both old and new, and out of print and imported. 13636 Ventura Blvd., Sherman Oaks; 981-2583.

Sisterhood Book Store is the place to go for books by, for, and about women. They carry a large and varied selection, including books on health and self-help, as well as nonsexist and non-racist children's books. 1351 Westwood Blvd., Westwood; 477-7300.

BEST PAPERBACKS

Papa Bach is a combination bookstore and community gathering place, and its long hours make it a browser's heaven. The stock is 95 percent paperback, with an excellent selection of literature of the left, American poetry, and women's and Third World studies. 11317 Santa Monica Blvd., West Los Angeles; 478-2374.

Small World Books, located right on the beach, has a truly comprehensive stock of paperbacks, including poetry, fiction, classics, and small-press books. Used books are sold in an annex at 216 Pier Avenue in Santa Monica. 1407 Ocean Front Walk, Venice; 399-2360.

BEST MUSEUM BOOKSTORES

Los Angeles County Museum of Art Bookshop One of the best places in the city to buy books about art, artists, art history, photography, and the decorative arts. Some of the books pertain to exhibitions that have been on display at the museum. Children's books are carefully chosen, with good texts and beautiful illustrations, and there are prints and posters for sale. 5905 Wilshire Blvd., midtown; 857-6144.

Los Angeles County Museum of Natural History Bookstore This deceptively tiny store is one of the best museum bookstores in the country. It has books geared to both layman and scientist, about insects, birds, mammals, and fish; archeology and anthropology; life sciences and natural history. They'll special order hard-to-find books, and the inexpensive posters are a real find. 900 Exposition Blvd., Exposition Park, downtown; 744-3434.

The Norton Simon Museum of Art Bookshop This spacious bookshop carries the largest and most comprehensive selection of art books in the city, very well organized and displayed. You can find anything here, and there's also a fine collection of prints and posters for sale. Orange Grove and Colorado blvds., Pasadena; 449-3730.

Page Museum Bookshop Here's a nice selection of books about prehistoric and extinct creatures, mammals and insects, gems and minerals, and other scientific subjects. Most of the books are inexpensive paperbacks, geared to laymen and children. 5801 Wilshire Blvd., midtown; 936-2230.

BEST USED BOOKSTORES

Acres of Books was dubbed the "best in California" by author Ray Bradbury. One can spend hours here browsing among its 13,000 square feet of dusty, musty, and endlessly fascinating used books, finding long-lost authors you never heard of, books from your childhood. Lots of bargains. 240 Long Beach Blvd., Long Beach; 437-6980.

Baroque Books Here one can find a meticulously chosen selection of modern first editions and literary titles at exceptionally reasonable prices. Also in stock are books on history, music, drama, and film, plus a small but choice selection of paperbacks. 1643 N. Las Palmas Ave., Hollywood; 466-1880.

Other Times A small store with an attractive choice of books on literature and mythology, theater, cinema, and music. The city's best selection of books about jazz. 10617 W. Pico Blvd., West Los Angeles; 475-2547.

THE BEST OF THE REST

Following is a somewhat miscellaneous list of bookstores that should not be left off any list: the best of the larger general bookstores, those that are off the beaten track, and establishments that deal in the more esoteric specialties.

Amerasia Bookstore Books about Asian cultures and the experiences of Asians in North America. 338 E. Second St., downtown; 680-2888.

Art Catalogs Museum publications of art, architecture, and photography; a huge selection of over 4,000 titles. 625 N. Almont Dr., near Beverly Hills; 274-0160.

Aviation Bookstore A complete selection of books about airplanes and aviation. 1640 Victory Blvd., Glendale; 240-1771.

Barry Levin Science Fiction and Fantasy Literature Rare, used, and new first editions. 2253 Westwood Blvd., Westwood; 474-5611.

Bernard H. Hamel Spanish books and records from Europe and Latin America. 2326 Westwood Blvd., Westwood; 475-0453.

Book City An enormous selection of secondhand books, miraculously organized so they can find you what you want. Good collection of Hollywood memorabilia. 6625 Hollywood Blvd., Hollywood; 848-4417.

Bread and Roses A full-line bookstore and resource center for women. Poetry readings and discussion groups. 13812 Ventura Blvd., Sherman Oaks; 986-5376.

Butler's Book Center An excellent general, personal-service bookstore by the Marina. 4722 Admiralty Way, Marina del Rey; 823-1605.

Centro Mexicano del Libro Books from Mexico, by Mexican authors, or about Mexican culture, most of them in Spanish. 5318 Wilshire Blvd., midtown; 938-5216.

Cherokee Book Shop Fine first editions, rare engravings and prints, children's literature, and books on the occult, housed in Hollywood Boulevard's most beautiful store. 6607 Hollywood Blvd., Hollywood; 463-5848.

La Cité des Livres French books, and best of all, a complete assortment of Michelin maps and guides, 2306 Westwood Blvd., Westwood; 475-0658.

Dangerous Visions An excellent choice of science fiction, plus modern literature. 13603 Ventura Blvd., Sherman Oaks; 986-6963.

H. G. Daniels This venerable store has a superb stock of art and architecture books, plus "how-to" books on graphics. 2543 W. Sixth St., downtown; 387-1211.

A Different Light L.A.'s largest and most complete selection of books by and about gays and lesbians. 4014 Santa Monica Blvd. (at Sunset), Silverlake; 668-0629.

Hunter's Books A fine selection of hardcovers; knowledgeable salespeople. Movie stars used to browse in the Rodeo Drive store in their bathrobes. The Westwood location offers an excellent array of sale books and is also universally appreciated for its weekend hours of 10 A.M. to midnight, making it a favorite Village hangout for literary nightowls. 463 N. Rodeo Dr., Beverly Hills; 274-7301; 1002 Westwood Blvd., Westwood; 208-3166.

J. Roth Bookseller Books on Jewish culture and the Jewish experience. 9427 W. Pico Blvd., midtown; 557-1848.

Kinokuniya Bookstore Books about Japan and its culture, in both English and Japanese. 110 S. Los Angeles St., downtown; 687-4447.

Mariners Unlimited Almost anything in the nautical-book field, including out-of-print books and magazines. 1522 W. Washington Blvd., Marina del Rey; 392-5705.

Midnight Special A general bookstore with an outstanding selection of books on politics and the social sciences, and one of the biggest collections of magazines in the city. Discussion groups and poetry readings. 1350 Santa Monica Mall, Santa Monica; 392-7412.

Opamp Technical Books Here's where you can find out all about computers, engineering, and electronics. 1033 N. Sycamore St., midtown; 464-4322.

Page One Pasadena's feminist bookstore, with books by, for, and about women. 453 E. Colorado Blvd., Pasadena; 792-9011.

Revolution Books stocks those that promote a revolutionary perspective on the world, including books about Mao, Marx, Lenin, and the Revolutionary U.S. Communist Party. 2597 W. Pico Blvd., downtown; 484-2907.

Samuel French, Inc.   Copies of plays, of course, but also a truly outstanding selection of books about the theater. 7623 Sunset Blvd., Hollywood; 876-0570.

Ships Store, Inc. Right by the Marina, this store sells, appropriately enough, books about sailing. 14025 Panay Way, Marina del Rey; 823-5574.

Technical Book Company Medical books galore, and also legal and other scientific books. 2056 Westwood Blvd., Westwood; 475-5711.

Thomas Bros. Maps, where you buy the famous Thomas maps, which are indispensable to anyone finding his way around Los Angeles. Also books on geography and travel. 603 W. Seventh St., downtown; 627-4018.

Unicorn Bookshop A general bookstore with an excellent stock of gay and lesbian literature. 8940 Santa Monica Blvd., West Hollywood; 652-6253.

Vedanta Bookshop Located adjacent to the Vedanta Temple, this peaceful retreat carries books about Eastern religions. 1946 Vedanta Pl., Hollywood; 465-7144.

Vroman's An excellent general bookstore, with a comprehensive selection of books and an attentive staff. 695 E. Colorado Blvd., Pasadena; 449-5320.

Zarathustra Bookshop Carefully selected books, specializing in the arts, literature, and philosophy. Beautifully illustrated children's books. 8614 Melrose Ave., West Hollywood; 659-9235.

From A to Zed: A Guide to Rare Record Stores

by Les Paul Robley and Mary Katherine Aldin

If there's a particular record album or single that has eluded your grasp over the years, the odds are you'll find it in one of these shops (though you might have to pay a price for it). The stores in L.A. County specializing in rare or hard-to-get music fall primarily into four categories: new, used, collector or nostalgia, and hard to find. Most collectible items are considered used anyway, and many hard-to-locate records can be found new. By the same token, a hard-to-find record doesn't necessarily make it a collector's item. Poor distribution of, say, a local punk band's 45 single, or an imported collection of folklore dances from Bulgaria would not qualify as rare, collectible status.

The following list has been compiled alphabetically and deals only with specialty shops in the latter three categories. Chain stores of current domestic selections of the Wherehouse and Music Plus type have been omitted.

A-1 Record Finders Strictly a mail-order service, A-1 probably has L.A.'s largest collection of domestic and foreign out-of-print soundtracks and Broadway cast albums (shelves of them literally tower above you inside the warehouse). Owner Brian Burney describes his business as a "free national-search service" that serves customers from all over the globe.

A-1 is getting away from the major label in-print products and concentrating on the large output of Australian, European, and Japanese soundtrack reissues. They also carry nearly 10,000 out-of-print classical records, as well as rock and popular music (no imports on the latter). Burney does handle 78s, and will rent records at 25 percent of cost. While he doesn't make trades, he will accept records for sale on a consignment basis for a commission of one-third the selling price. (He has an excellent grading system to help determine the condition of your record.) The phone number is aptly listed as REC–ORDS, which Burney admits could justify a story in itself on what he had to go through to get that sequence of digits. P.O. Box 75071, Los Angeles 90075.

American Pie Specializing in 45s and out-of-print rock LPs of the '50s and '60s, this store carries more than 50,000 singles. It also boasts a wide selection of greatest-hits packages (domestic and foreign) and all categories of in-print reissues. 12222 Venice Blvd., Mar Vista; 391-4088.

Aron's Records In the used LP category, this store is hard to beat. They accept used records in trade for new ones, and their stock of unusual used discs is in the tens of thousands. Used prices range from 29¢ to around $4.98, depending on condition and rarity, and the selection encompasses everything from reggae to opera. But used isn't all that Aron's does well; they also have a diversity of new albums that leans heavily to import jazz and rock, with lots of English and Japanese pressings. 7725 Melrose Ave., Los Angeles; 653-8170.

Bodhi Tree Though their main product is books, the Bodhi Tree also sells music cassettes—and out-of-

the-ordinary ones at that. Guided meditation music for beginners, Celtic harps, Gregorian chants, music for airports, songs of the soul, Tibetan bells, Zen waterfall music, healing music, and our favorite, "How I Raised Myself from the Dead: Resurrection." 8585 Melrose Ave., West Hollywood; 659-1733.

Classical Record Shop In business since 1965, "the first all-classical record store" sells strictly new domestic and foreign products. They will, however, keep out-of-print discs in stock until they are sold (most new record stores send these discs back to the record company, even if unopened). 412 S. Clark Dr., Beverly Hills; 275-7026.

The Continental Shop Despite being called Continental, this store sells everything for the devout Anglophile, and not just records. British classics, semiclassics, military marching music, royal wedding documentaries, Beatles, Monty Python, London cast albums, and BBC soundtracks are a few of the musical categories. What they have outside of Britain for the most part falls under folk and festival music. For all you *Das Boot* fans, they also have a sampling of German World War Two documentaries. Oh yes, when you go in, please don't ask for the latest Tubes single. They won't have it. 3400 Wilshire Blvd. (inside the Ambassador Hotel), Los Angeles; 383-2995.

Disc Connection Mainly a "discount house," this store rivals Aron's with its used and cutout bins, though Aron's prices are a tad lower. But they do have a better domestic and foreign soundtrack selection, with more than 10,000 rare titles. 1050 Gayley Ave., Westwood; 208-7211.

Discontinued Records Calling themselves a service rather than a competitive store, Discontinued claims that if you've exhausted all your resources in locating a particular piece of vinyl, try them. They carry over a half-million items of mainly domestic fare (all categories) and are primarily a mail-order-by-phone service like A-1. 444 S. Victory Blvd., Burbank; 849-4791.

Festival Records Festival showcases international music and folk-dance records from practically every country. And for all you Balkans, the house specialty is Balkan heritage music. In addition, they sell cassettes, cookbooks, folk-dance books, and language records. 2796 W. Pico Blvd., Los Angeles; 737-3500.

The Hollywood Record Flea Market A swap meet for hucksters and music enthusiasts, where one can find hard-to-get records and tapes of every category, plus posters, buttons, and T-shirts. The two-dollar admission price lets you watch rock-and-roll video shows that screen throughout the day. The market is held the first Saturday of every month at Hollywood Roosevelt Hotel, 11A.M.–8 P.M. 7000 Hollywood Blvd., Hollywood.

House of Records Also known as The Collector's Paradise, this store is run by a little lady named Jane Hill, whom other store owners refer to as the "grandmother of record shops." She originally opened a small business on Main Street in 1951, and now has customers from all over the world visiting her store. She sells all categories of 45s from the first year they began pressing them (1949) to the present. 2314 Pico Blvd., Santa Monica; 450-1222.

Knight Education Incorporated Unusual is the word to describe this store. It's called the "supermarket of self-help," and carries, among other things, tapes and records on thousands of educational subjects. How to belly dance, build self-esteem, relax and cope with stress, and learn hypnosis or ESP are just a few of the countless listening courses available. 2406 W. Seventh St., Los Angeles; 385-2293.

Moby Disc The Valley's answer to Aron's, Moby specializes in used discs, cutouts, and imports, with a complete selection of domestic rock and lots of 45s by independent local talent. Used items not guaranteed. 14410 Ventura Blvd., Sherman Oaks, 990-2970.

Mr. Records When you enter this store, you are besieged by rare and collectible memorabilia. Beatlemania is the main course here, and it's served to you on rare LPs, EPs, and 45s, from what some say is the largest Beatles selection in Southern California. You'll also find in-print and out-of-print imports of other rocks artists of that era. Over 50,000 collectible items. 2924 Wilshire Blvd., Santa Monica; 828-8846.

Music and Memories This store specializes in two things: nostalgia and Frank Sinatra. Dan Alvino is proud to say that he has the largest collection of Sinatra records in the city, so if you're young at heart and keen on Frankie, blaze a trail to this door. He also has a handsome rare soundtrack and show section, easy listening of the '50s, and a few 78s. 10850 Ventura Blvd., Studio City; 761-2126.

Music Man Murray A collector's shop, this store specializes in helping you find out-of-print records. With over 500,000 items in stock, they offer a comprehensive selection of rare soundtracks, jazz, opera, and rock on 78s, 45s, and LPs, and they also have those venerable antiques known as Edison cylinders. Finders service on request. 5516 Santa Monica Blvd., Hollywood; 466-4000.

Off The Record Sixties rock is the specialty here, with British artists, surf music, psychedelic sounds, and one-hit bands leading the way. Off The Record has the largest assortment of new catalog records next to Tower's, and they stock over 2,500 soundtracks. A healthy Beatles collection is shown off by several *Yesterday and Today* butcher LPs starting at around $175. They do sell used and cutouts, but no "junk records." All used material is carefully cleaned, graded, equipped with inner sleeves, and guaranteed. 2621 Wilshire Blvd., Santa Monica; 829-7379.

Oz Records Heavy metal, heavy metal, and heavy metal. In other words, nonviolent, clean punk. Plus imports and domestic LPs of all categories. And for those of you who like to inhale substances and dress up while listening, Oz offers an array of pipes and T-shirts along with the music. 4873 Topanga Canyon Blvd., Woodland Hills; 887-5662.

Phil Harris Records The only record shop listed that's on Hollywood Boulevard, Harris sells classical, soundtracks, vocalists, and other nostalgic articles, plus current rock on both LPs and cassettes. 6723 Hollywood Blvd., Hollywood; 469-1505.

Poo–bah Records One of the Big Five new-wave stores in town, Poo-bah boasts a very good reggae section, imported rock from England, and some esoteric contemporary classical à la Steve Reich. 1101 E. Walnut Ave., Pasadena; 449-3359.

Ray Avery's Rare Records Besides selling all categories of music, Ray has a large auction list where you can make your bids by phone or mail. He'll send you jazz, pop-country, or show-personality lists, depending on your musical preference. He carries a huge collection of 45s and 78s (about 250,000 in all), plus rare sheet music, 16-inch large-transcription radio shows, and jazz photos (some of which he shot himself). All auction material is graded by the new minus method. A separate side building of the store sells current rock. 417 E. Broadway Ave., Glendale; 245-0379.

The Record Collector Sanders Chase, violinist and proprietor of this shop, says his customers include everybody at Tower Classical, because when something is out of print, they send people to him. About his museumlike store, he jokes, "We're like a small Library of Congress, only we sell the records." Chase specializes in out-of-print classical records and music from jazz's golden era. He also has many instrumental boxed sets and popular music from the '30s and '40s. Ninety to 95 percent of his product is mint. 1158 N. Highland Ave., Hollywood; 467-2875.

The Record Connection The Record Connection is one of the few stores that rents records on an experimental basis. RC handles mostly '60s rock and domestic out-of-print soundtracks, but they also carry a modest selection of out-of-print classical. 8505 Santa Monica Blvd., Hollywood; 655-7811.

Rhino Records This is the place for the independent labels. Rhino's got a terrific stock of reggae, bluegrass, country, blues, rock, and jazz, on both domestic and import small labels, plus some cassettes (not many) and a good selection of new import 45s. 1720 Westwood Blvd., West Los Angeles; 474-8685.

Rockaway Records A good selection of rock, jazz, classical, soundtracks, picture discs, and, occasionally, some genuine collectibles (a Buddy Holly and the Crickets EP adorns one wall). Plus, the knowledgeable and helpful staff make this a good place to check out. 2548 N. Glendale Blvd., Los Angeles; 664-3232.

RSI stands for Records and Service International, and they consider themselves a cross between what Disc Continued and Wenzel's provide, being one of the best sources for rare 45s. RSI has an inventory of over 50,000 selections and also offers a mail-order service and an out-of-print 45 and LP finders service. 1033 N. Cole Ave., No. 6, Hollywood; 467-7983.

2nd Time Around A relatively new store that sprang up to give Aron's competition, 2nd Time sells used material of all kinds, with an emphasis on local new-wave groups. The rental fee is only a buck for ten days. 7809 Melrose Ave., Hollywood; 622-9376.

The Tape and Record Room Old and new music of all categories, with a special bent toward soundtracks and 45s. 201 E. Broadway, Long Beach; 432-5001.

Tower Records Tower's boast used to be that they had at least one copy of every record currently in print. We're not sure whether they still make that claim, but if not, they should—they've got so many records that who'll notice? At the Sunset Boulevard location, their classical selection got so unwieldy that they finally moved it out of the building and into its own separate store across the street, leaving a veritable supermarket of rock, pop, jazz (including many rare imports), reggae, blues, country, folk, a huge children's section, dance bands from the '20s and '30s, polka records... need we go on? The Westwood location is not quite as mammoth, but perhaps more interesting, with the music divided between three floors. And Tower's hours can't be beat: 9 A.M.–midnight, every day of the week. 8801 Sunset Blvd., Hollywood; 657-7300. 1028 Westwood Blvd., Westwood; 208-3061.

Vinyl Fetish Lots of hard-core punk in this shop, with 90 percent of everything being British imports and 45s. (By the way, did you know that English record companies are the only ones marketing truly innovative material for 45s these days, despite their bad economy?) Fetish is also proud of getting English material "quicker than anyone," like papers, magazines, posters, and T-shirts. 7305 Melrose Ave., Hollywood; 935-1300.

Zed Records *The* import store of Long Beach, Zed carries things that the major labels don't seem to want to release. They stock several independent labels from Los Angeles, New York, San Francisco, and Washington, D.C. to name a few, and showcase many British singles and reggae artists. 2234 E. Seventh St., Long Beach; 433-9914.

BEST RECORD STORE OUTSIDE L.A. PROPER (MAYBE ANYWHERE)

Wenzel's Music Ecstasy is a wonderful thing, especially in the satisfied customer. It's like the man said at Pink's when handed his two chili dogs, "Hey, babe, I'm as happy as a sissy in a boy's camp." *Right on.* When it comes to that goofy collection of people who hunt down vinyl platters like their life depended on it, the smart road leads to Downey, specifically to Wenzel's Music. Here's a place with a real sense of priority. In the front room there are the intelligent groupings of both new and old music, plus the section that carries hundreds of reissued 45s, each and every one a classic to somebody. Then, behind the symbolic wooden gate is the side room where collectors pour through the record racks looking for that elusive single or LP without which they just can't live. The squeals of delight coming from the room is proof that Wenzel's has got the goods. Then, in the anteroom behind the counter, the real treasure lies squirreled away. Ask for a single by, say, Screamin' Jay Hawkins, and a box suddenly materializes, spewing forth several of the singer's masterpieces. The store is always good for a day's adventure, and depending on the size of your pocketbook and appetite, a whole world is waiting in the bins and boxes. It's like playing "Stump the Band," asking for oldies and coming up a smiling winner almost every time. 13117 Lakewood Blvd., Downey; 634-2928.

Fashion Hunting, L.A. Style: An Insider's Guide

by Jude McGee

Most Easterners love L.A. for two reasons: the weather and the fact that because of the weather—and the generally tolerant atmosphere—virtually anything goes from a fashion standpoint. On any given day, in any given place, you'll see every type of outfit, from track shorts and undershirts to jersey and silk, huffing and puffing or slinking and sleeking down Rodeo Drive, the Venice Boardwalk, anywhere. But fashion and trends do abound in our fair and feverish city, and if you really want to do it up right, à la new wave, '50s chic, Depression Wear, or just plain extraordinary, you've got to know where to go. And now you will. The following is a guide to some of the most individual clothing and accessories shops in town—with an eye, of course, to irresistible bargains whenever possible.

BEST IN NEW LOOKS FOR WOMEN

Neo 80 Lisa Eliot designs and manufactures under the name Neomaniac, and her styles are among the most imitated in town. The first to tube-top miniskirts and make those comfy, sexy clothes that both reveal and stay put, Eliot's main fabrics are cotton knit and elastic, and the primary focus is casual and fancier dresswear. Whatever's the latest, you'll have it at the earliest if you shop here. 7356½ Melrose Ave., Hollywood; 852-9013.

AND MEN, TOO

Parachute Fashions for the modern hero, based on sound architectural principles, made with sturdy, natural fabrics, and guaranteed never to go out of style while always looking new . . . too good to be true? Not really. These stylish, well-cut, comfortable and elegant clothes, suitable for casual, business, or dress-up, are really unusual. Linen, cotton, wool, and leather, colors and fabrics according to the season, all are metamorphosed into unique suits, shirts, pants, etc., courtesy of a London Fashion Institute grad and a Canadian architect. (Threads for the ladies, too.) 8215 Melrose Ave., Hollywood; 651-0177.

BEST FOR THE NEW USED LOOK

Bloomingsales This resale shop carries clothing that really looks brand new. There are manufacturer's samples as well as fashionable silk blouses, elegant pants, business suits, scarves, belts, and handbags. Items are hand-picked and in perfect condition, and they'll also take perfect clothes on consignment. 149 S. Barrington Pl., Brentwood; 471-4416.

Flip This is one of the newest legends in town. Owner Alice Wolf thinks used finery is the only way to bring true fashion to women and men, because the tailoring and workmanship can't be beat. So she's building an empire of impeccably fashionable used clothes, ingeniously displayed within this huge, rock-and-roll emporium. All merchandise is clean and pressed, and Flip's had also begun to make things themselves, for the lean moments when there's not enough high-fashion-caliber stuff around. (Also in the same two-block strip of Melrose, and carrying great cheap fashions: Creme, L.A. Gear, and many more.) 7607 Melrose Ave., Hollywood; 651-0280.

BEST ARTY LOOK

Steps into Space Eight years ago, Lyn Adolphson opened her shop to sell space shoes, those molded-to-the-feet numbers that are the last word in comfort. She has leather shoes, and also cloth footwear, made on the spot to your artistic specifications. And this year Lyn added fashions, almost all of which are by local designers. Prices are quite reasonable and the interesting stock is always worth taking a look at. For example, there are clear plastic vests, with screened T-shirts in complementary patterns to be worn underneath; painted shoes and bowties; earrings made of tea-bags; lots of jewelry; and gorgeous capes and dresses resembling clown suits. Come to Steps if you don't want to look quite like everyone else. 7518 Melrose Ave., Hollywood; 852-0070.

BEST DESIGNERS SHOPS

Grau California designer Claudia Grau makes a versatile line that's intended to coordinate on every level of dressiness. This year she started a trend with her "Depression Wear," which featured layering of pants, tunics, long and short-sleeved woven T-shirts, skirts, scarves, and vests. Grau is constantly coming up with new ideas that are always adventurous and ahead of the trends, and she's happily quite affordable besides. 7520 Melrose Ave., Hollywood; 651-3349.

Holly's Harp Holly Harp is our own California top designer. She plunked herself down on the Strip 15 years ago and has developed a reputation of catering to stars and those who look like stars. Grace Slick and Janis Joplin came to her for a look that was glamorous yet still counter culture; they got it and now the Grammy Awards and other industry events all seem to have Holly's fashionable touch. She favors sexy cling with delicate detail featuring beads, florals, and laces; this year, for example, padded epaulets sported streams of beads or pearls dangling from the accentuated shoulders, with sleek jersey skimming the body. Holly also specializes in bridal wear and carries accessories and less-than-formal wear, too. 8605 Sunset Blvd., Hollywood; 657-2699.

Zoe Elke Lesso is one of the designers who make Melrose Avenue such a special fashion street. She whips up simple, well-tailored looks for the California woman, combining some of the exigencies of the workplace with the madder side of things. The result is a versatile line accenting tailored comfort. Lesso has recently opened a new store on Canon Drive in Beverly Hills, with accordingly more upscale designs. 7562 Melrose Ave., Hollywood; 653-1691.

CAMPIEST SPORTSWEAR

Camp Beverly Hills Even if you can't afford to live in Beverly Hills, you can afford to come to this camp, where there are all sorts of cheerful things designed for casual, useful wear. Pants and sweats, shorts and tops, all reasonably priced, are arranged in stacks by size and color. It's fun and easy to shop here, and one can enjoy pleasant surprises, such a the one-of-a-kind dresses made out of old army shirts. Above all, this place is famous for its Camp Beverly Hills logo, which you may have seen on sportswear around the country. 9640 Santa Monica Blvd., Beverly Hills; 274-8317.

BEST DISCOUNT SPORTSWEAR

Sacks SFO Discount sportswear for men and women, all first quality at tremendous savings (40 to 70 percent off prevailing retail) has been sold by David Sacks in Venice for the past six years, and now there's the new shop in Culver City as well. Sacks, who visits New York frequently, stocks sweaters, designer suits, and an amazing selection of silk shirts for both men and women, as well as pants, jeans, and leathers representing a younger look. This may well be the best all-round bargain place for clothes. 8 Horizon St., Venice; 399-8890. 9608 Venice Blvd., Culver City; 559-5448.

BEST DISCOUNT KIDDIE WEAR

Le Re Finery Patti Page partnered up with Ann Gordon to create an outlet for her finery (you'll never see Patti in the same gown twice). Her shop carries a large selection of beautiful, celebrity-worn designer clothes, but a particularly nice feature is the children's wear, all new and unworn, which comes from a fancy local boutique and is at least half of the regular price. Although you may not find all sizes at all times, Le Re's large selection and breathtaking bargains are worth the uncertainty. 2821 S. Robertson Blvd., West Los Angeles; 558-3776.

BEST DISCOUNT SWIMWEAR

Kirkpatrick Sales This place started discounting bathing suits in 1937 and they're still at it. In the summer, there are as many as 14,000 on display, from the most daring bikinis to competition wear, in every size and color. While Kirkpatrick doesn't normally carry the big-gun designers, their high quality imitations are good substitutes. You can also find men's tennis togs and shirts at tremendous discounts, along with maillots in a cot-

ton and Lycra blend for aerobics. With the amount of time we Californians spend either at the beach or working out to look good at the beach, we probably couldn't live without this store. 8592 Washington Blvd., Culver City; 870-3912.

BEST QUINTESSENTIAL CALIFORNIA STORE

Fred Segal This is really a conglomeration of boutiques carrying everything from luggage and shoes to bathing suits and featuring a fine sampling of the hippest, newest L.A. looks. You'll find pants and shirts, leathers and active wear, all gorgeous and in all price ranges, plus shoes for men and women, too. A big annual L.A. event is the once-a-year sale here, where prices start at 50 percent off and continue downward. Malibu even has three separate Fred Segals, for swim, sports, and active wear. 8106 Melrose Ave., Hollywood; 651-1800. 3835 Cross Creek Rd., Malibu; 456-2702.

BEST DESIGNER DISCOUNTS

The Outlet Store All of this season's—and last season's—St. Tropez West designs are on sale here, for $10, $20, or $30. The Outlet is a huge warehouse room with a big communal dressing room, and new merchandise from St.-Tropez West and other manufacturers arrives regularly. 1717 Figueroa St., downtown; 746-2347.

Designer's Break, Inc. It would be tough to find a more complete selection of designer silks for women. Owner Avi Hakakian has top names at prices that are almost impossible to believe for first-quality goods: silk blouses from $19 to $35, and this includes Valentino and Oscar de la Renta. In addition, there are business suits in wools and silks, sporty cottons and leather suits, T-shirts, skirts, and pants. The collection is on the dressier side, with Georgio Saint Angelo, Tadashi (the only discounter of this line in town), John Yang, Robert Haik, Oleg Cassini, and more, all available at below wholesale prices. A true bargain wonderland. 1200 S. Wall St., downtown; 748-0131.

BEST ROCK/NEW WAVE LOOKS

Let It Rock Well, the stock might be English, but the look is L.A. all the way. "Brothel creepers" for men and women, high-heeled boots, leather jackets covered with straps and zippers—in short, all the fashions that take you back to early Elvis and Little Richard can be found here. For three years, Let It Rock has been nurturing the rockabilly revival and keeping the flame of the '50s alive with new-only classic rock-and-roll clothes, imported from England. Vintage '50s suits for men and women (you can also buy the baggy pants separately) and tight jeans of every color fill this little boutique, which also carries lots of accessories, including lace fingerless gloves and Mary Quant hose. Did our parents ever think they'd live to see the day? 7310 Melrose Ave., Hollywood; 934-4416.

Tiger Rose Here's where you go to find rock-and-roll clothing that acknowledges no generation gap. Much of it is Japanese, new wave, and heavy metal inspired, and some good-humored items of the S & M persuasion include pastel leather bracelets and anklets and belts with several pounds of metal studs (in pink and white, for spring, of course). There are truly amusing imitation shiny leathers (made of heat-sealed nylon) as well. In short, here you'll find all you need to indulge your most livid and vivid rock-star fantasies. 5257 Melrose Ave., Hollywood; 469-8359.

BEST IN LEATHER

Seventy-Seven Hundred Leather clothing is made on the premises by Nigel Wearing, who uses only the best hides and skins and transforms them into exceedingly modern creations. The cut is ample and the fit is destined to remain intact, with such great care taken in the choice of skins. There's a large collection of jackets and vests in embossed hides, but these you can wear with a clear conscience, unlike the imprinted and more expensive endangered-species variety. Imaginative and well-tailored clothes for both men and women. 7700 Melrose Ave., Hollywood; 651-0261.

In Skin Call for an appointment to see the incredibly low-priced leathers in this garage showroom. All the latest styles, imported from Europe, are here, and many boutiques buy from In Skin. You can't beat the prices: men's leather jeans at $79.95, leather minis for $40.00. Plus, there's a selection of chamois shirts and bikinis, and dresses, jackets, vests, and shorts. A continual garage sale of top-quality new leather clothing. 701 El Medio, Pacific Palisades; 454-6953.

BEST ACCESSORIES

Emphasis This is the only exclusively accessories shop in town, and they specialize in the unusual. Men can find painted ties in leather and all manner of belts; for women there's a gigantic selection of earrings and other costume jewelry, as well as imaginative touches on ankle socks, hose, wide-brimmed hats, sunglasses, and purses. This shop regularly features California designers such as Michael Morrison, who makes leather scarves and studded bracelets and belts; Diane Payne, who works with crystal for earrings; and Jan Michael, who designs all sorts of things in plastic. All merchandise is up-to-the-minute and colorful, with new items arriving weekly. 7704½ Melrose Ave., Hollywood; 653-7174.

BEST HEADGEAR

Marc Valerio Designs If you ever wondered how Joan Collins of "Dynasty" managed to get her clutches on Blake while good wife Linda Evans sat home, here's the scoop: vamp Joan was wearing a Marc Valerio hat. The custom and ready-to-wear hats and fur accessories in this boutique are all created by hand, and Valerio's works are so flattering that you'll be wearing them to bed. A specialty of the house is wedding and bridal parties; where else, for instance, will you find a white horsehair cowgirl bridal hat with veil? Prices are exceedingly reasonable, and the quality is far superior to department-store wares. 9901 Santa Monica Blvd., Beverly Hills; 553-9177.

Brown's Hats For $40 or $50 you can have a nearly custom-made, handmade, beautifully fitted hat of a quality you'd gladly pay double for. Anthea Brown, one of the pioneers in the renaissance of Venice, opened her shop in 1975, and she sells her dramatic wide brims, straw Panama fedoras, berets, little veiled numbers right out of *Sophisticated Ladies,* and many of her other personal designer models to lots of stores as well. 68 N. Venice Blvd., Venice; 399-0181.

AND LET'S NOT FORGET THE FEET...

Privilege The California look—cheerful, bright-colored leather shoes, in mostly flat and low-heeled styles—is done up here by European manufacturers. But that doesn't matter. The colors and styles are perfect for L.A. Low leather boots with rubber soles, stenciled leather flats, and sandals in every color combo make for fun-to-buy, fun-to-wear footgear for the ladies. 9460 Brighton Way, Beverly Hills; 278-8116 (also in the Beverly Center).

Right Bank Clearance Center Set up like a modern loft, with coffee served and couches to lounge on, RBCC has racks and racks of the fanciest footwear around, at incredible discounts. There's a code card that you carry around with you, and shoes are arranged by size on huge racks, with their original prices tantalizingly intact. 450 N. Camden Dr., Beverly Hills; 273-3031.

5.

HOLISTIC HEALTH AND EXERCISE

by Carolyn Reuben

BEST HOLISTIC MASSAGE AND TREATMENT

Rich and Carin Clayton An unmatchable pair. They've kept folks of our acquaintance from getting sick for years on end and have helped dozens of injured people we know heal themselves faster and with enormous pain relief. Besides, everything they do feels good. The Claytons are state licensed practitioners of Touch for Health, polarity therapy, applied kinesiology, orthobionomy, and reflexology—all big words that add up to the fact that they seem to know more about the body and how the thighbone is connected to the hipbone, and what nerve centers influence what organs, and what lymph nodes do what, than just about anybody. They're also expert nutritional counselors, Carin in particular, and teach all the techniques in which they are licensed. Go to them to get in shape or to stay in shape, or just for the sheer pleasure of what they do. An added inducement is that they are among the nicest people on the planet. Call 876-0188.

BEST HOLISTIC FACIAL

Mariana Chicet inspects your skin with a magnifying glass, then brews up the most exquisitely pleasurable, personalized 1½-hour facial experience imaginable. Full body "facials" for women are also available. She uses only natural ingredients. And don't pass up the opportunity to purchase her skin-care products. The best! 8238 W. Third St., Los Angeles; 651-0979.

BEST HOLISTIC MEDICAL CLINICS

Saram Khalsa, M.D. and Joe Want Khalsa, M.D. are family practitioners in a swanky office next to Cedars-Sinai Medical Center, where they have hospital privileges they rarely use—not after treating their patients with herbs, homeopathy, acupuncture, kinesiology, and nutritional supplements. Saram has been known to give an IV of vitamin C for acute bronchitis. 8631 W. Third St., 11th floor, Los Angeles; 653-8687.

Shaw Health Clinics offer a potpourri of healing modalities, including dentistry, chiropractic, bodywork, reflexology, nutrition, optometry, cosmetology, and chelation (cleaning clogged arteries), as well as homeopathy and herbs, colonics and nutritionally oriented physicians. No appointment necessary. Open seven days. 5336 Fountain Ave., Los Angeles; 467-5200.

Baraka—a Holistic Center includes (take a deep breath) chiropractors, an acupuncturist, a gynecologist, preventive cardiologist, movement therapist, massage therapist, biofeedback technician, and general practitioner. Director is John-Roger, a spiritual teacher, but facilities are available to the general public without proselytizing. 2105 Wilshire Blvd., Santa Monica; 829-0453.

Dr. James Blechman, an M.D. specializing in holistic healing and diet therapy, operates a highly popular, distinctly patient-oriented practice with the help of trained acupuncturists/acupressurists, spiritual and rebirthing counselors, and even a holistic dentist. Blechman has had a high success rate with virtually every disease from cancer to allergies, but be forewarned: this is a practice that places a lot of emphasis on the patient's responsibility toward assisting in his own cure. And at present, Blechman is booked up months in advance. 8631 W. Third St., Los Angeles; 659-8670.

BEST NATUROPATH

Janet Zand, N.D. Trained in an English medical school, Zand is qualified in Great Britain to diagnose and treat disease, and even prescribe certain drugs. Although California doesn't recognize the naturopath as a legal health-care provider, Zand is a quite legal acupuncturist, herbalist, and nutritionist, with a caring manner that endears her to a wide spectrum of patients, from Watts to Beverly Hills. 1424 Lincoln Blvd., Santa Monica; 451-9789.

BEST SEXUALITY SEMINAR

Seminars on Sexuality, organized by Rona Lee Cohen, R.N., assistant clinical professor at UCLA and certified sex educator, offers courses in expanding your sexuality for women and couples, as well as special workshops for men and mixed singles. Educational, joyful, and life enriching. 8845 W. Olympic Blvd., Beverly Hills; 556-8357.

BEST CLASS ON CHINESE HERBS

Oriental Healing Arts Institute (OHAI), founded by a Taiwanese pharmacist, researcher, and prolific author named Dr. Hon-yen Hsu, offers a ten-week class geared to health professionals. OHAI is also the best source for books on Chinese herbs; Hsu and the herb class instructor, Matt van Benschoten, C.A. (certified acupuncturist), have translated ancient classics as well as compiled modern herbals for specific ailments (*Treating Yourself With Chinese Herbs; For Women Only*) and general problems. 8820 S. Sepulveda Blvd., Suite 218, Los Angeles; 645-9672.

BEST CANCER COUNSELING

Center for the Healing–Arts Clinic Nonhospital self-regulatory workshops and psychological services for those with life-threatening illness and their families. Visualization, meditation, stress reduction, bodywork, and journal or art therapy are included. 11801 Missouri Ave., Los Angeles; 477-3981.

BEST LIBRARY FOR ALTERNATIVE CANCER TREATMENTS

Cancer Control Society Library, open to the public by appointment. The society publishes *The Cancer Control Journal*, sponsors a yearly conference, and offers referrals to practitioners using metabolic, cellular, laetrile, and other alternative therapies. 2043 N. Berendo St., Los Angeles; 663-7801.

BEST CHRONIC PAIN THERAPY

Genevieve Meyer, Ph.D. leads groups and gives individual counseling. Her groups, for those aged 55 or older, are free through the Senior Health and Peer Counseling Center, Santa Monica. There is a fee for private consultations. Meyer teaches people to release the "pain-tension-pain cycle" through guided imagery, relaxation, and meditation. She works with those who've been told "nothing further can be done" and guides them out of daily pain into autogenics and conscious control of their nervous system. 2107 Montana Ave., Santa Monica; 395-5401.

BEST AURA READING

Rosalyn Bruyere has been inducted into Indian tribes as a shaman, as well as having been certified as the first scientifically authenticated aura reader in history (after research in UCLA's Department of Kinesiology). Bruyere sees variations in your aura up to six months before you feel any physical manifestations of a health problem. She calls her talent "selective seeing" and helps restore health by repairing the aura, transmitting energy through her hands. The Healing Light Center, 138 N. Maryland Ave., Glendale; 244-8607.

BEST SOURCE OF HEALTH BOOKS

Bodhi Tree Bookstore, opened in 1970, reflects the eclectic interests of its owners, Stan Madson and Phil Thompson. Good source of books on radionics, homeopathy, iridology, yoga, alternate therapies, massage, and cooking. 8585 Melrose Ave., West Hollywood; 659-1733.

BEST FEMINIST HEALTH CENTER

Feminist Women's Health Center offers abortion services, prenatal care, alternative birth experience, artificial insemination, and birth control (including the cervical cap). 6411 Hollywood Blvd., Hollywood; 469-4844.

BEST MASSAGE SCHOOL

Massage School of Santa Monica offers evening classes in Swedish massage theory and technique. State approved. 1151 Fifth St., Santa Monica; 393-7461.

BEST MOVEMENT THERAPIST

Anna L. Wager, M.A. offers sensitive, astute psychotherapy using movement and dance, as well as talk. Call 785-9099 for an appointment.

BEST MACROBIOTIC STORE AND KITCHEN

Grain Country, run by the Los Angeles East West Center for Macrobiotic Studies, is a source of macrobiotic books, foods, equipment, and information. 7827 Melrose Ave., Los Angeles; 852-9083.

The East West Center also offers the East West Family Kitchen, with macrobiotic meals (no sugar, meat, dairy, or refined products) around the corner from Grain County. (The center holds courses in macrobiotic cooking and philosophy as well.) 706 Orange Grove, Los Angeles; 852-9587.

BEST MACROBIOTIC HEALING COUNSELOR— EDUCATOR

Cecil Levin, M.A. is the only Westerner to be certified in using food as medicine by both Lima Ohsawa, widow of the macrobiotic movement's founder George Ohsawa (who taught Levin cooking in Japan), and the macrobiotic movement's current leader, Michio Kushi. Levin teaches cooking for cancer and other degenerative illnesses and gives private consultations for anyone interested in using food as a healing tool. 1864 Pandora Ave., West Los Angeles; 474-2708.

BEST EAST—WEST SELF—CARE SYNTHESIS

Touch for Health is a self-care system combining acupressure treatments with the instantaneous feedback of muscle testing. Using the system, the lay person can figure out what needs to be done, do it, and see, instantly, if what he or she did was effective. Call or write the Touch For Health Foundation, 1174 Lake Ave., Pasadena; 794-1181.

BEST PREVENTIVE CARDIOLOGIST

Joe E. Goldstrich, M.D. loves it when a patient who is heavily on drugs and stuck in his or her illness comes to him. Goldstrich's forte is guiding one in life-style changes that reduce and eventually eliminate the need for medication. This former medical director of the Pritikin Longevity Center is the doctor you've been waiting for to care for your favorite hypertensive aunt. Goldstrich can be contacted at 454-7514.

BEST NON—SURGICAL FACELIFT EXERCISES

Bonnie McWhinney, Ph.D. guides individuals and groups in myofacial exercises to tone and strengthen facial muscles and smooth wrinkles naturally. Through these exercises, the face can be reprogrammed for "choiceful expression," eliminating unconscious negative expressions that eventually become manifested by deep lines. Bringing consciousness to the face is one of McWhinney's most satisfying goals. Contact her at 399-1009.

BEST NON—BRACES ORTHODONTIA

The Crozat Seventy years ago a New Orleans dentist named George Crozat perfected a teeth-straightening device that fits behind the teeth below the gum line. The Crozat, as it was named, allows nature to move teeth naturally; it's invisible to anyone looking at you, and by capturing the forces generated by chewing food, transmits enough force to the jaw to actually widen your dental arch. Few dentists are trained in fitting Crozats, but the best in L.A. is Victor Diamond, D.D.S., 9201 W. Sunset Blvd., Los Angeles; 273-3650.

BEST HOMEOPATHIC PHARMACIES

Standard Homeopathic Pharmacy; Santa Monica Drug Homeopathy is a system of remedies for physical ailments, derived from natural animal, vegetable, and mineral sources. Basic to the system is the concept that like cures like, or, an extremely dilute potion of a substance that causes a certain reaction will cure a disease in which that same reaction occurs. This theory is something like the basis of innoculation, except in homeopathy, the greater the dilution the more powerful the remedy. Homeopathy is popular in England; even Queen Elizabeth has seen a homeopathic physician. In Los Angeles, you can discuss homeopathy at Standard Homeopathic Pharmacy, 436 W. Eighth St.

(at Olive), downtown (627-1555); or at Santa Monica Drug, 1513 Fourth St., Santa Monica (395-1131).

BEST ANIMAL ACUPUNCTURIST

Sheldon Altman, D.V.M. is one of the handful of vets incorporating acupuncture with needles and electric current into his regular medical practice. Pet owners and their pets love him, plus he's open on Sunday. 2723 W. Olive Ave., Burbank; 845-7246.

BEST GET—OFF—YOUR— DIET PROGRAM

Lighten Up! is not about losing weight, but rather about losing the struggle to lose weight. And if you can understand that, you'll probably understand why people who take the Lighten Up! workshop often lose weight anyway. 2265 Westwood Blvd., No. 395, Westwood; 824-5332.

BEST NEW AGE CENTER

The Center for the Healing Arts "provides a safe community for people who choose to enrich the quality of their lives." Originally founded to give support and offer alternative healing techniques to victims of severe illness, the center has expanded greatly during its ten-year existence. Four programs are offered: Wellspring Dialogues and Workshops; Healing Arts Workshop, presenting alternative methods of healing, from meditation to movement to acupressure; Transformational Support and Training Groups, for nurses, physicians, and others; and a clinic that offers individual psychotherapy, plus various support groups for those with life-threatening illnesses. 11081 Missouri Ave., West Los Angeles; 477-3981.

BEST PLACE TO HAVE A BABY

Natural Childbirth Institute (NACHIS) Obstetrician and gynecologist Victor Berman and his wife Salee, nurse and certified midwife, founded the Natural Childbirth Institute as a friendlier alternative to the antiseptic hospital experience. NACHIS (Yiddish for "joy") is an appropriate acronym for the institute. Founded in 1974, NACHIS was the first medically attended out-of-hospital birth center in California, and has been a prototype for birth centers across the country. Births take place at the center with no anesthesia, in a warm, familiar room; siblings, relatives, and friends are welcome to attend. (There's a full complement of safety equipment, but in the rare case of complications, a backup hospital is only eight blocks away.) Bonding between baby and parents takes place immediately, and all often go home after two or three hours. Ask those who've done it; the happy consensus is that NACHIS really delivers. 10862 Washington Blvd., Culver City; 559-6270.

BEST PLACE TO LEARN HOW TO HAVE A BABY

The Los Angeles Childbirth Center One of the few places in the city to offer alternative birth services, including prenatal care, childbirth, nutritional and parenting education, and home birth attended by a midwife. It's a package arrangement, with fees based on ability to pay. The center also offers gynecological services for all women, plus assistance in family planning. Cervical caps available. 757 Pier Ave., Venice; 392-3931.

BEST ALEXANDER AND FELDENKRAIS PRACTITIONER

Judith Stransky guides individuals in the Alexander Technique, a combination of mental directions and a teacher's guiding hands that reeducates the body to do daily activities free of pain, stress, tension, and poor posture. One seems to float through one's day. With groups, she teaches the gentle and ingenious movement-exercises developed by Russian-Israeli physicist and judo master Moshe Feldenkrais. These, too, use mind as well as body to influence one's self image, posture, and well-being. 2869 S. Robertson Blvd., Los Angeles; 836-0778, 215-0734.

BEST INFO ON BRAIN RESEARCH

The Brain/Mind Bulletin, published every three weeks by Marilyn Ferguson (Aquarian Conspiracy) and edited by Noel McInnis, is the source for the newest research on the theory and practical application of brain-mind-health relationships ($20 per year). P.O. Box 42211, 4717 N. Fiqueroa, Los Angeles 90042; 223-2500.

A Short Guide to the Six Basic Fitness Systems

by Mary Beth Crain and Mike Fatula

WHAT TO LOOK FOR IN A FITNESS SYSTEM

Once upon a time, keeping fit was a fairly simple operation. You did a few pushups, a few jumping jacks, a few laps, or a few strokes and then went out for a sundae. Then along came The Gym, and fitness suddenly became more complex. Machines that looked as though they came straight out of a Vincent Price movie arrived on the scene, along with fancy names for jumping up and down, like "aerobics," and fancy substitutes for the good old bicycle, like the "Exercycle" and "Lifecycle."

The '80s fitness scene has evolved into a departmentalized science, especially in Los Angeles, where prospective health buffs can choose from among a wide variety of systems guaranteed to provide them with eternal sleekness and endurance. But what do you look for when you're shopping for the "right" program?

For the answer to this question, the *Weekly* interviewed two of the top fitness experts in L.A.: Patrick Netter, the owner of High Tech Fitness, who has served as an on-the-air consultant to, among others, consumer crusader

David Horowitz, and Henry Siegel, owner of the Voight Fitness Center, a professional dancer, who, with his wife Karen, has trained top entertainment personalities and is currently working as a consultant to the 1984 Olympics.

Siegel: In terms of specific problems, certain weight-lifting or equipment systems are fantastic. For someone who has back difficulty, for instance, the Gravity Boots and the Gravity Guiding System is the best thing that's come along. But an exercise system that somehow encompasses random movements and complete muscle workout will be most helpful for people just doing everyday activities, from carrying groceries to climbing stairs.

If you want to join a health club, the most important thing is to look *beyond* the facility and into the service itself. The attrition rate at health clubs is extremely high because of overcrowding and poor service. Instructors who are young, inexperienced, and paid four dollars an hour are not likely to give you optimum effort. You'll want a gym where classes are limited, and where there are people showing you how to actually use the equipment.

Also, you'll want a facility that will teach you exercise skills that you can do on your own. You have to *understand* exercise technique; it's not enough simply to show up for a class, or jump up and down for an hour. Speaking of jumping up and down, look for a facility that has a shock-absorbent floor. Most health clubs put carpeting on concrete, and the result is everything from shin splints to back problems. At Voight, we have a floating hardwood floor, and we use high-density, polyethi-foam mats, which are very thin but very dense.

Above all, try not to get suckered in on unfair pricing schemes that leave you with a year's membership at an inferior establishment. If a program isn't put together with consistency and continuity in terms of class instruction, it just isn't worth it.

Netter: In shopping for an exercise system, you'll want to consider things like timesaving devices, if you have a tight schedule, or whether you're more comfortable and less self-conscious working out at home. For some people, the camaraderie of the health club is where it's at, and that's fine. But many people are looking toward the home gym because it saves time, driving, and they can get a complete, compact workout system for less than the price of a gym membership.

If you are going to a gym, look for a place that's not crowded, has class limitations and a relatively soft, shock-absorbing floor, like Voight. If you're into home instruction, there are people who can come in and give you and your friends classes. But look for someone to whom you can relate, who has experience and knowledge about different types of systems and the ability to work both with and without equipment.

In terms of actual equipment, beware of schlock merchandise, because there's a lot of it. The rebound tramp, for instance, is very popular, but don't buy the round one, which causes your feet to turn inward, or one that doesn't have shock absorber legs. And stay away from "weight-loss suits" and all of that trash; they're useless and dangerous. There's only one way to lose weight: decreased caloric intake with increased caloric burn, i.e., diet and exercise. Period. Remember, in looking for serious fitness equipment, don't go to places like Big 5; those outfits are great for soccer balls or baseball mitts, but they don't know much about fitness. You're dealing with your health, and you want to talk to someone who's qualified.

AEROBICS

Aerobics in Motion This facility is an aerobic exercise studio that offers choreographed exercise routines that integrate jazz-dance-based movements into exercises. This not only makes the workout more interesting, but also improves coordination and balance. According to Aerobics in Motion, an aerobic exercise system is preferable to other exercise systems because it provides a combination of cardiovascular strengthening while toning and shaping the body. As alternative or additional activities, swimming and bicycling are recommended as two of the best ways to exercise, as each, again, will provide endurance as well as toning. Note: watch for the television series, "Aerobics in Motion," on PBS Channel 28. Masonic Lodge, 2244 Westwood Blvd., Westwood; 558-1155 (call for other locations).

The Jane Fonda Workout This is one place that's had its share of super-hype, but deservedly so. The Fonda Workout is the Marine Corps of ladies' aerobics and its philosophy is that if you aren't engaged in nonstop movement and your muscles don't feel as if they're burning off the bone, you've just wasted an hour. But as practically everyone who's been there can attest, the classes are exhilarating, the energy is high, and the instructors are dedicated. According to the Fonda Workout, the best kind of exercise system is that which combines a constant level of cardiovascular activity with firming and toning, and their classes demand an output of exertion not encountered at very many other places. 369 S. Robertson, Beverly Hills; 652-9464.

Move to Music Move to Music offers aerobics, stretch, and prenatal- and postnatal-care classes. They consider aerobics preferable because the full one-hour workout includes stretch and limbering, providing tone, flexibility, stamina, and balance. As alternative or additional activities, Move to Music recommends dance and body movement. 3007 Washington Blvd., Marina del Rey; 821-9352.

Richard Simmons Anatomy Asylums Remember your high-school gym teacher? You know, the one with the bulging muscles and the scar on his cheek who bellowed, "Okay, Fatso, 100 pushups just 'cause I don't like your looks!" Well, suppose your gym teacher had been a hyperkinetic koala bear who chanted, "Thighs, thighs, go away! Give them all to Doris Day!" Maybe you wouldn't have made the football team, but you would have lost those pounds and enjoyed every minute of it. It's with this same infectious humor and enthusiasm that Richard Simmons and his merry band cuddle the inches off you at the Anatomy Asylums. There are ten in L.A. and many more nationwide, and the instructors are all trained by Ritchie himself. The asylums offer exercise classes with a combination of stretching, isometrics, yoga, muscle-toning movements, and cardiovascular aerobics—and gym teachers you can love. 9306 Santa Monica Blvd., Beverly Hills; 550-8879 (call for other locations).

DANCE/AEROBICS

Main St. Dance Studio A combination dance-exercise studio that emphasizes aerobics, muscle toning, firming, and flexibility. Main St. Dance Studio offers all levels of classes with a variety of music. Dance workouts are geared toward the acquisition of grace and expression through movement. 2215 Main St., Ocean Park; 399-9313.

Voight Fitness Center Offering pay-by-the-class, high-quality instruction in dance and aerobics, Voight is run along the lines of a dance academy, with graduated but strenuous classes that are geared to both the professional dancer and actress and the average person. Voight feels that dance/aerobics is the most complete type of fitness system because it enables the individual to acquire the non-specific, everyday-beneficial skills of movement, agility, endurance, and grace. 980 N. La Cienega Blvd., West Hollywood; 854-0741.

Dance Ergetics This facility combines the professional dancework of places like Voight or Main St. with the monitored aerobics of the Beverly Hills Workout. Dance routines are specially choreographed and regularly updated, with a graduated rhythm within the class, which starts slow and works up to fast cardiovascular activity, slowing down once more with a stretch and relaxation routine. Instructors are trained in kinesiology, anatomy, and physiology, and pulse rates are taken regularly. Dance Ergetics feels that this type of individually oriented dance/aerobics system is both the safest and most beneficial way to exercise; other recommended activities are swimming, bicycling, and yoga/stretch. Alternating locations; 885-6787.

GYMNASTICS

Carreiro Physical Fitness, Inc. Highly recommended by fitness experts, Carreiro's emphasizes gymnastics as the best means of achieving strength and endurance as well a balance and flexibility. All levels, from rock-bottom beginner to the professional, are instructed in floor, ring, and trapeze bar exercises, and all ages are welcome. Carreiro's feels that gymnastics is a superior exercise system because it requires you to use only your body and thus to develop your center of balance, which creates both a physical and mental equilibrium. 722 N. La Cienega Blvd., West Hollywood; 625-3060.

WEIGHTS

The Sports Connection The Sports Connection offers instruction in a wide variety of systems, including aerobics, yoga, stretch, and body building. Their weight rooms are some of the best around, with a complete line of Nautilus equipment, separate facilities for both men and women (although the women may use the men's equipment), and guided instruction programs for the individual. According to them, the Nautilus system is preferable to Universal weights because Nautilus emphasizes variable resistance throughout, so that the entire muscle is both toned and strengthened, while Universal emphasizes constant tension, no variety, and is geared to the build up of bulk by working only the middle part of the muscle. The Sports Connection does not consider any one exercise system preferable to another, but does feel that a combination of stretching, aerobics, and weights provides the optimum degree of fitness. Four locations in Ocean Park, Encino, and Beverly Hills; call 450-4464 for the one nearest you.

World Gym is owned by Joe Gold, the former owner of Gold's Gym and the big daddy of body building. Joe designs his own equipment and collects "the best of everything else." His gym blends top-quality free weights and machines, a combination that "exercises your muscles from the right angles." Joe is no longer associated with Gold's Gyms and he's licensed five World Gyms nationwide. The Santa Monica World Gym provides both indoor and outdoor facilities, so members can exercise under the sun. Consultations are not provided because members are serious enough to know that they're doing. Workout facilities are for both men and women; a women's locker room is available, but no women's showers. 2210 Main St., Santa Monica; 399-9888.

Gold's Gym now licenses 80 facilities around the globe, with the original recipe in Venice, California. California sports 12 of the 80, with L.A. having 4. The Venice gym has a reputation from way back as the birthplace of the muscle, and it offers the tops in free weights and machines. There is an initial consultation with one-year memberships, but again, this gym is for the serious who can take it from there. Several contests are sponsored annually and Gold's markets an extensive line of workout attire. Workout facilities for both men and women; a women's locker room with showers is available. 360 Hampton Dr., Venice; 392-3005.

BEST TRAINER

Mike Sable Weight-lifting instruction and individualized programming? You simply don't get it at most gyms and health clubs. So, for the personal touch, many Angelenos seek the professional services of private consultants and trainers. And one of the best is Mike "The Zipper" Sable, so named for the part of his competition-posing routine where he "opens up" his thigh muscles to the audience as if he were unzipping a zipper. Mike holds numerous titles, including Mr. America and Mr. World, and he trains men and women around the United States and Europe. But The Zipper offers something more to the world of body building: a gain in muscular size without a gain in body fat. Long the Catch-22 of body building, getting big often meant growing grotesque, and the drastic weight gains and starvation diets gave the sport an unhealthy reputation among outsiders. Mike combines a background in kinesiology and nutrition with years of body building and athletic experience. The result? You look healthy and feel healthy, too. Contact Sable at 427-7727.

YOGA

The Center for Yoga Offering instruction in hatha-yoga, the center recommends yoga as a fitness system because it is totally balanced, providing the cardiovascular benefits of aerobics with the tension-releasing, limbering, and toning of stretch. In addition, yoga balances upper-body flexibility with lower-body mobility, cleanses and purifies the body through proper breathing technique, and encourages sensitivity and respect for the body as a healing instrument. While the center feels that any type of fitness program is beneficial, they recommend that yoga be included in the daily routine because of its benefits to the emotional as well as physical aspects of fitness. 230½ N. Larchmont Blvd., Los Angeles; 464-1276.

Kollar Center The Kollar Center emphasizes elimination of health problems and preventive health care through physical and emotional fitness. As a holistic facility, the center offers workshops, seminars, and classes in everything from rebirthing and shiatzu to yoga and aerobics. The center considers the optimum fitness system to be one that integrates bodily flexibility and endurance with spiritual harmony; in this regard, they consider yoga one of the best programs. 881 Alma Real, Pacific Palisades; 459-7834.

Sivananda Yoga Community On Sunset Boulevard, where everyone likes good cocaine but no one wants caffeine in their cola, the Sivananda Yoga Center sticks out like a green thumb on the Strip, but the students prefer to say it offers "a balance of energies in the area." Classes teach proper exercise through Sivananda hatha-yoga posturing, breathing, relaxation, vegetarian diet, and positive thinking through mediation. The first class is free; thereafter there are member and nonmember fees. The center also offers resident programs, teacher-training courses, and a children's camp. Hip Sunset Boulevard types may check their designer jeans at the door. 8157 Sunset Blvd., Hollywood; 650-9452.

HIGH TECH HOME GYM SYSTEMS

High Tech Fitness According to High Tech, the major trend of the '80s has shifted from weights and health club membership to an increased emphasis on aerobics and home fitness. High Tech offers a variety of exercise equipment, including the Amerec Precision Rowing machine, which combines aerobics with muscle toning, the Space-Saver Gym, which is a type of home weight-lifting system that does over 50 things, and the Rebound Trampoline, or soft jogger, which they consider to be the "single best way to aerobic exercise," as the user is running and jumping on a shock-absorbing surface instead of concrete. Also unique to High Tech is the Gravity Guiding System, which enables the user to hang upside down in inverted positions in order to increase circulation to the discs. High Tech feels that almost any individual exercise program is excellent; however, they consider theirs superior because it combines all of them along with spinal and back care. 617 N. La Cienega Blvd., West Hollywood; 854-7744.

6.

THE BEST OF GAY L.A.

by Steve Holley and Ken Dickmann

Though probably not touted by the Chamber of Commerce as one of our city's major draws, Los Angeles does have a sizable and dynamic gay population. Taking the fairly standard estimate that gay people account for 10 percent of the population, a conservative estimate would reveal that approximately 300,000 gay citizens reside in Los Angeles. That figure doesn't take into consideration the fact that L.A. happens to be a veritable gay mecca, drawing refugees from the less tolerant communities across the country. Thus our city may be home to more than its 10 percent "quota" (a conclusion you may have drawn yourself on occasion while traversing Hollywood and West Hollywood on that great gay way, Santa Monica Boulevard).

But be aware there is a great deal more to the Los Angeles gay community than what meets the eye on Santa Monica Boulevard. With its emergence as a progressive, international center of urban gay culture, gay Los Angeles boasts a number of "Bests."

BEST GAY SOCIAL SERVICE ORGANIZATION

Gay and Lesbian Community Services Center The center is exactly that: a center for solving problems and meeting the needs of gay applicants for housing, jobs, medical treatment, counseling, legal aid, and much more. If they can't provide what you are looking for in the gay world, their extensive directory (ext. 222) can probably refer you. The center remains the largest social services agency of its kind in the world. 1213 N. Highland. Ave., Hollywood 464-7400.

BEST SOURCES FOR GAY RESEARCH AND INFORMATION

Gay and Lesbian Community Services Center The center maintains the city's most extensive directory of organizations, information, and referrals (ext. 222). Lesbian Central (ext. 231); Gay Latino Unidos (ext. 281); Educational Outreach (ext. 492); and Society for Senior and Gay Lesbian Citizens. 1213 N. Highland Ave., Hollywood; 464-7400.

The National Gay Archives A private collection of gay-related literature and publications maintained by curator Jim Kepner, invaluable for reference and research work. 1654 N. Hudson, Hollywood; 463-5450.

BEST GAY RADIO PROGRAM

IMRU Broadcast on the second, third, fourth, and fifth Sunday of each month at 8:30 P.M. on KPFK (90.7 FM), as an hour-long magazine-style radio show addressing gay and lesbian topics through features, interviews, listener call-ins, and weekly calendar of events.

BEST GAY COUNSELING SERVICES

The Case Center for Human Behavior The first openly gay counseling service in the city. Directed by Jack Hamilton, this private, nonprofit center offers individual and group therapy, as well as special workshops and seminars. Low-cost therapy with emphasis on long-term therapy. 489 S. Robertson Blvd., Beverly Hills; 275-0175.

The Gay and Lesbian Community Services Center Accepts clients regardless of their ability to pay. Operating on a sliding-scale fee schedule. Offers peer counseling and supervised psychotherapy and provides crisis intervention. 1213 N. Highland Ave., Hollywood; 464-7400.

BEST NEIGHBORHOOD BAR

The One One day it was empty, the next day is was packed and it's remained that way every since. Now it's L.A.'s most popular bar, providing current taped music from disco to jazz to new wave, with some show biz thrown in. Overhead fans, plants, and wood decor house a varied crowd of all ages, with hardly a clone in sight. As Melrose Avenue epitomizes the L.A. of the '80s, this neighborhood bar is a step in the right direction for gays. 7302 Melrose Ave., Hollywood; 434-2025.

BEST WESTERN BAR

The Rawhide This was the first gay C & W bar and it has remained generally the most popular. Complete with a wood-paneled and beamed interior, Rawhide is one of the largest and coolest bars around and continues to have live bands seven nights a week, with occasional appearances of C & W headliners. A good crowd of cowboys and cowgirls dancing, tapping their toes, and drinking Lone Star with shots. And the boys all look prettier at closing time. Burbank Blvd. at Vineland, North Hollywood; 760-9798.

BEST LEVI'S BARS

The Spike It has its ups and downs during the seasons, but then one night you'll walk in and bam! Men, men, men, nothing but men in Levi's, leather, bare chested, shooting pool, and looking for you. Basically a friendly crowd dominated by some of the best (and loudest) music in town and hunky leather bartenders. The party goes on into after-hours on Saturday, but chances are you'll be gone with Mr. Right by then. 7746 Santa Monica Blvd. (at Genessee), Hollywood; 656-9343.

Detour Several years back in the era of tambourines, whistles, poppers, and all that, the guys at the Detour were routinely having such a good time partying that the guys at the ABC just decided the bar had to be shut down. Rebounding in the '80s, the Detour is still festive, though not quite as frantic, and this popular macho cruise bar in Silverlake still has its moments and its men. It also has more pairs of Levi 501s in it than a Levi-Strauss warehouse. Disco party music keeps the place loose and lusty, facilitating what these guys are without a doubt here for: cruising. Leave your tambourine on the bedpost. 1087 Manzanita, Silverlake; 664-1189.

BEST LEATHER BAR

The Pits When the Road Warrior wants to soak up some suds, he stops here. The interior of The Pits, L.A.'s prime-cut leather bar, is like a man's underarm—dark and sweaty. Owner Charles Ellis gutted out the glitter of what used to be the Club Can Can and slapped the walls with black paint and murals of men on motorcycles. He says, "The greatest compliment anyone could pay me is to walk in, look around, and say 'this place is the pits.' " The Pits laughs in the face of high-tech pretty-fern gay bars of the '80s and takes you back to the low tech of the '50s, when a gay bar was a bar and you could have a conversation because the background music was in the background. And The Pits attracts what we in Los Angeles call "hot." They're bikers. They're musclemen from L.A.'s top gyms who slink in and out of the darkness, shirtless or in torn tank tops. They're serious leathermen for whom leather is a life-style, not a trend. The mood is best expressed by the bar's logo: The Pits. Motorcycle spoken here. 6202 Santa Monica Blvd., Hollywood; 462-9509.

BEST MOTORCYCLE BAR

Griffs The central rendezvous for bikers. The club meets here, the Sunday afternoon beer busts are very popular, and the amount of machinery in the parking lot exceeds that of any other place. Unfortunately, most of the Knights in Black Leather here are somewhat older than we'd ideally prefer. 5574 Melrose Ave. (at Gower), Hollywood; 464-5576.

LEAST PRETENTIOUS GAY RESTAURANT

The Golden Bull You'd hardly know you were just a block away from the ocean here inside this little brown stucco restaurant, it's just so very . . . Fort Worth or Des Moines. A middle America steakhouse with one twist: the place is teeming with gays of all descriptions and ages. And its dim lighting, roomy booths, and swank decor are from the '50s, as are the prices: a nine-ounce sirloin for $7.25. Best of all, they don't serve quiche. 170 W. Channel Rd., Santa Monica; 454-2078.

BEST AFTERNOON BARS

Mother Lode On prime gay turf in West Hollywood, the Mother Lode is the best one place L.A. gay men love to dish, yet it's consistently the busiest gay bar in town from afternoon until closing time. It just seems that nobody ever picks up any of those young, attractive, clean-cut, trendy boys who epitomize the stereotypical West Hollywood look. Could the challenge be the attraction? 8944 Santa Monica Blvd., Hollywood; 659-9700.

The Gold Coast A friendly drinking-man's bar, this place features windows on the nonstop street hustle at this busy gay intersection, making it a popular afternoon stopover. An oasis for this part of Santa Monica Boulevard, the Gold Coast, done up in a quasi–Barbary Coast motif, attracts a looser, Levi's-clad clientele, including some colorful neighborhood characters and street folks. 8228 Santa Monica Blvd., West Hollywood; 656-4879.

BEST GAY GYMS

Bodycenter This attractive gym was responsible for bringing Nautilus to L.A. nearly six years ago. The club features personalized supervision by trained instructors on the two super-lines of Nautilus equipment for streamlined and unintimidating workouts for the beginner or average guy not obsessed with spending hours at a gym. This air-conditioned facility on two levels includes: Universal equipment, Olympic, free weights, weight-loss and weight-gain programs and aerobics instruction, good energizing music, and a Jacuzzi and dry sauna. 8711 W. Third St., Hollywood; 278-5613.

The Body Builder If you're serious about working out and sweating a lot while doing it, this gym, considered the best equipped in the city, is the place for it. Owner Jim Mielko and staff supervise your workout, are always available for questions, and will be the first to increase your weights and change your program as they check your progress in getting a beautiful body. Sauna, showers, and towels are available, as well as athletic clothing such as workout shirts, shorts, and jocks, and a complete Nutrition Center with vitamins and supplements. Universal, free weights, cables, and pulleys in an immaculately kept two-story, 6,500-square-foot pumping and hunky environment. 2516 Hyperion, Silverlake; 668-0802.

L.A. Body and Health Club Not exclusively gay, it attracts, according to owner Richard Gurney, a mix of gay, straight, and bisexual men. Formerly Easton's Gym, it was renovated three years ago. Includes barbells, Olympic circuits, and custom cable equipment in a three-level workout area; shower-locker area and steam room, health-food bar, nutrition center, and aerobics space with a roof-top sun deck. 8053 Beverly Blvd., West Hollywood; 651-3636.

Jim Morris Club If the Beverly Center were a gym, it would be called Jim Morris's. His club not only offers the top-of-the-line equipment for serious body building, but once your muscles are pumped you can get them stretched (aerobics classes), steamed (steam room and sauna), fed (health-food restaurant), and tanned (outdoor pool, indoor and outdoor Jacuzzi, tanning machines, sun decks). Jim also plans to offer consultations with various professionals such as a doctor (for nutritional advice) and a chiropractor, and there may even be a barbershop opened on the premises. Morris creates individual workout programs and he's Hollywood's premiere designer of chic muscles. The club's members include the best-built, best-looking men anywhere, and down on Santa Monica Boulevard there's nothing quite as complimentary as hearing a passerby murmur, "He's got a Jim Morris body." 8560 Santa Monica Blvd., West Hollywood; 659-6630.

BEST GAY GIFT SHOP

Severe A number of gay gift shops have become so glitzed out and cutesy that it's a refreshing relief to come upon Severe, an original shop of eclectic, handcrafted leather items, assorted industrial-tech doodads, and just plain neat, inexpensive gifts. Owner John Appleton uses half of the tiny shop as a workspace where he creates one-of-a-kind belts, with industrial-hardware workings. In addition, he carries selected ashtrays, roachclips, industrial housewares, T-shirts, etc., all displayed in a mostly black, silver, and red high-tech space. 1107 Hayworth (off Santa Monica Blvd.), Hollywood; 650-1647.

BEST GAY PHARMACY

Marvin's Pharmacy In the heart of that very gay lane of Santa Monica Boulevard from Robertson to San Vicente, Marvin's attracts a West Hollywood and Beverly Hills clientele. Featuring friendly assistance and free delivery, the pharmacy carries your usual drugstore stock, as well as many specialty items, including every line of cosmetics. 8932 Santa Monica Blvd., West Hollywood; 659-7455.

BEST GAY BOOKSTORES

A Different Light Owner Norman Laurila prides himself on having the most complete gay bookstore in Southern California. This oasis for gay literature, whether magazines, hardbound or paperback books, or research materials, has just expanded its quarters and increased its selections. Though not a gallery, Laurila also features monthly exhibits of the works of gay and lesbian artists among the literature. Cards and posters are also available, and a 3,000-title mail-order catalog listing the store's stock can be requested. Gertrude Stein would have had her salons here. 4014 Santa Monica Blvd. (at Sunset), Silverlake; 668-0629.

Unicorn Bookstore West Hollywood's community bookstore, the Unicorn is a comfortable, attractive shop that offers a well-stocked selection of all types of popular hardbound and paperback books, including an extensive inventory of gay and lesbian literature, books of gay and lesbian poetry, and gay publications. The store also carries an extensive selection of general interest, specialized, and erotic magazines. The West Hollywood Ticket Agency, located in the back of the store, handles tickets for theater and concert events around town. 8940 Santa Monica Blvd., West Hollywood; 652-6253.

BEST GAY FESTIVAL

Gay Pride Parade and Festival   Every
June the gay community knocks down
the closet door with a spectacular
parade and festival celebrating gay
pride. Third largest in the city, the parade commemorates the 1969 Stonewall Riots in New York, when gays
and lesbians fought city police in the
streets after New York's Finest ha-
rassed customers at the Stonewall bar.
Many credit the riot with launching
the gay liberation movement in this
country, and 15 years later that day is
honored with a peaceful and joyous
nationwide celebration. The local
media often cover the parade by fo-
cusing on the more flamboyant
groups, and you may be surprised to
learn that there are gay religious organizations, track clubs, choruses,
bands, bowling leagues, judges, doc-
tors, scientists, etc. The Los Angeles
County Sheriff's Department monitors
the event. Call Christopher Street
West, 656-6553, for more information.

7.

THE BEST OF LESBIAN L.A.

by Sharon McDonald

They're stuntwomen and stock-brokers, producers and politicians, comediennes and counselors. In this creative city, lesbians can be found acting in sit-coms and administrating governmental departments, attending film premieres in limos and jumping out of airplanes. L.A. lesbians are diverse, active women whose only shared characteristics may be an orientation toward success and a preference for the company of other diverse, active women.

As in most places, much of the lesbian population is submerged within the mainstream, but not without a trace. Ever since Anita Bryant's attack on gays catalyzed the biggest burst of growth in gay activism in history, lesbian life in L.A. has been much easier to find. Instead of yesterday's dark little word-of-mouth bars, we now have spacious, classy dance palaces that advertise openly. It may still take a bit of tracking down, but L.A.'s lesbian world is well worth the search.

BEST POINTS OF DEPARTURE

The Lesbian News This newsletter will tell you virtually every event of interest to lesbians during the current month. The hard part is finding a copy. They're distributed free in numerous gay-frequented locations, but they get snapped up within the first few days of each month. Call 704-7825 to find out a location near you that might have some left.

Lesbian Central While you're on the phone, give a call to Lesbian Central, the women's office at the Gay and Lesbian Community Services Center. This is a social services agency that provides multiple services to gays, from employment placement to counseling to STD (Sexually Transmitted Diseases) testing. Lesbian Central can tell you lots of places to go and people to see. One of the places to go could well be Lesbian Central itself. It sponsors social events and discussion groups of various kinds, has a library, occasional art shows, and a friendly staff. 464-7400, ext. 231.

L.A. Women's Exchange You say you're *still* on the phone? Then dial the Women's Exchange to get a taped message about meetings and social events of interest to "Los Angeles women," which can often and easily mean lesbians. 256-5304.

Community Yellow Pages Now *this* is a telephone book. Devoted to putting gay folks in touch with other gay folks, CYP is set up just like the real thing, with white pages listing individuals and yellow pages with gay-owned business ads. If you've never browsed through an all-gay telephone book before—several cities have them—you may be surprised by the number and variety of businesses willing to advertise in a gay book. And speaking of "gay," in this case it isn't synonymous with male crotch shots. CYP is the brainchild of longtime lesbian activist Jeanne Cordova, who held the line on sexually explicit advertising to produce a, dare we say it, tasteful book. CYP is available at community bookstores, or by calling 939-1200.

Women's Yellow Pages Again, "women" does not always mean "lesbian," although there is an overlap that's not too difficult to figure out when you look at the ads here. This beautifully produced book also has white and yellow pages, and follows a policy of refusing advertising that is deemed sexist or homophobic. Call 398-5761 for information on getting a copy.

Women's Music Distribution Company At the risk of being repetitious, this company distributes women's (and lesbian) music to mainstream record stores and women's and gay outlets. These folks always know what women's musical events are coming up soon. 956-6624.

Now that you have a basic idea of what's available for lesbians here, let's get specific. Perhaps you're a little shy about the bar scene, but you'd like to go someplace where you could meet other lesbians. Here are some regular lesbian events that can serve as thinly disguised cruising grounds, while also serving their stated purpose of education.

BEST NONBAR PLACES TO WATCH THE WOMEN

Lesbian and Gay Academic Union Women's Program This monthly meeting is for women only, and features a different woman speaker each time. It'll cost you four dollars to attend and mingle with the turnout, which can range from a few dozen to a hundred. 656-0258.

Southern California Women for Understanding (SCWU) This is a lesbian organization that sponsors a variety of educational and social events, from lectures to softball games to moonlight ocean cruises. To see what's on the calendar and to request a copy of their bimonthly newsletter, call 388-2446.

BEST PLACE TO CATCH UP WITH LESBIAN CULTURE

The Woman's Building It hardly seems possible that a decade has gone by, but the Woman's Building is ten this year. Since its inception, it has become a repository of lesbian, feminist, and women's art and culture, as well as a school for aspiring artists, writers, graphic designers, printers, and others. Often on the verge of financial collapse, the building has nevertheless remained afloat and kept the door open to those coming to attend classes, art shows, readings, dances, lectures, and plays. An astonishing amount of creative work has occurred within these walls. 1727 N. Spring St., downtown; 221-6161.

BEST PLACE FOR A LESBIAN TO BUY FRUIT—FLAVORED EDIBLE PANTIES

Herotica Goddess knows, there are a lot of sex-toy shops in this town, but here's one that actually knows the difference between a lesbian and the heterosexual male fantasy of a lesbian. Herotica carries a wide range of sex toys and lingerie, from the silly to the sensual, but all the merchandise is scrutinized for safety before being stocked. Dildoes, for example, must not have any type of hard core or be made of any material that might cause injury. Woman owned and operated, Herotica is a place you can try on some of that lingerie, sniff the body oils and creams, and ask questions comfortably. They have gone to considerable trouble to put you at ease, including their classy and attractive interior and exterior designs that prove that stores dealing in erotic merchandise don't need to look cheesy and sleazy. 8722 Santa Monica Blvd., West Hollywood; 854-1038.

BEST PLACE TO EXPLORE YOUR ROOTS

National Gay Archives This magnificent library is the lifework of founder Jim Kepner, who has been collecting lesbian and gay literature for longer than some weary lesbians have been alive. The collection holds books, pamphlets, magazines and periodicals, photos, posters, tapes, buttons—you name it. Books by and about lesbians have been separated into a distinct section, so you don't have to plow through hundreds of gay-male volumes to find those feisty foremothers. Stroll through the stacks; you'll be amazed at what's there, and will probably have a hard time dragging yourself away at closing time. 1654 N. Hudson Ave., Hollywood; 463-5450.

BEST PLACES TO BE A DANCING FOOL

The Flamingo Once a popular gay-male bar called The Jungle, The Flamingo is now a popular lesbian bar with a decent-size dance floor and a DJ on the weekends. A very cruisy bar, Flamingo also has a place to get away from the music and talk to that woman you've just met: a large outdoor patio area furnished with tables, chairs, and lots of ledges. 3626 Sunset Blvd., Silverlake; 666-3736.

Catch One Black gays have made Catch One the number one black gay dance spot in the city. This is an enormous, and we mean enormous, club whose dance floor can hold 900 happy bodies moving to some great music. Both men and women go there; few whites. 4067 W. Pico Blvd. (at Crenshaw), Los Angeles; 734-8849.

Clones Whether you're there to dance or watch the dancers, Clones is one hot place to be. It's one of the new breed of clubs that rents space from an existing establishment on specific nights of the week only. A women-only membership club, Clones solicits and gets an attractive, affluent crowd. Not the place to wear your jeans and T-shirt; break out the sequins or French cuffs. For current information on times and locations, call 66-CLONE.

Peanuts Lots of room here to dance, dance, dance, with a hip, young crowd that's primarily lesbian, but includes some gay men and some heterosexual singles and couples. 7969 Santa Monica Blvd., West Hollywood; 654-0280.

8.

COMMUNITY SERVICES AND HOTLINES

by Alice Fisher

From legal aid to the address of the Pope—everybody's got questions and needs that can be answered through that vast network known as community services. But in a city the size of L.A., finding the specific person or organization to help you out can be an overwhelming task. If you're clever at decoding the telephone directory, for instance, you might be lucky enough to find, listed under "Los Angeles, County of—Human Services," the INFO Line, an around-the-clock bilingual information service. But if you don't have the telepathic powers necessary to fathom the phone system's circumvented listing process, or if you don't know what INFO Line stands for, your best bet is to visit or contact your public library, where either extensive files or a phone referral service can connect you with virtually any community service you're seeking.

Libraries are becoming known as "community information centers" because they provide continual updated information about their communities' resources in an effort to assist residents in everyday living and problem solving. Libraries have always done this informally, of course, but in recent years, because of changing societal needs and the unprecedented proliferation of social agencies, librarians have begun systematically indexing their communities to make this information readily accessible, in a central location, to the public.

Through the library you can find out where to apply for help with elderly relatives, developmentally disabled children or delinquent youngsters, the blind and deaf, the alcoholics and drug abusers, legal and medical problems, and many other difficulties. You can also find out about a host of resources for just simple but necessary information. For instance: where to go to get your cat spayed inexpensively; where to get a copy of your birth certificate; how to stop unwanted junk mail; and so on.

Much of the resource and agency information at local libraries comes from the County Department of Public Social Services' Community Resource Information Bank (CRIB) program, which supplies computer-generated directories, or CRIB books, for all the community agencies in all the areas of Los Angeles County, as well as for special groups, such as "older adults." The library also has comprehensive collections of area telephone directories, as well as out-of-state and foreign phone books.

The Santa Monica Public Library (SMPL) has one of the county's most complete community services access systems. In addition to the CRIB books and numerous books on everything from women's services to jobs and employment programs, we have a Reference Folder File with more than 350 files (constantly being updated) on everything and anything in L.A. To give you an example of the diversity of subjects on which we have information, here are some of the headings: Loans, Nuclear Power Plants, Piano Tuning, Olives, Survival Skills, L.A. and San Francisco Coming Events, Ski Info, Medical Support Groups, Stucco, Ronald Reagan. In other words, if you have a problem or question that you think is too obscure to be solved, chances are you're wrong. At SMPL, we've answered questions on everything from getting rid of backyard bee swarms to places to go to pick apples, oranges, and cherries. Remember, too, that if the Santa Monica Library, or another large library, is inconveniently far away, the library nearest you can provide assistance through phone referral to the reference desk with the necessary resources.

When it comes to everyday problem solving, Los Angeles can seem too big a place to handle. But the library can help cut it down to size. The next time you've got a question on where to go or who to call, start with us. We'll get you pointed in the right direction.

COMMUNITY– REFERRAL HELP LINES

CALL (The Community Access Library Line) is a comprehensive, multilingual information and referral program providing assistance through a toll-free number available to persons who reside in the 213, 714, and 805 area codes. By dialing 1-800-372-6641, residents can obtain information and referrals on a wide variety of topics and can be directed to the appropriate public or private agencies for needed services.

A key feature of the CALL program is its three-way telephone conferencing system. This enables the information specialists to connect callers directly to those agencies or organizations that can provide the proper assistance. It also allows the specialists to remain on the line to act as facilitators or interpreters.

CALL is a service for everyone; however, the Spanish-speaking, Afro-American, Chinese, Japanese, American Indian, and handicapped communities have been specifically targeted for service. The hearing impaired are served via a telecommunications device for the deaf (TTD).

INFO Line—213-686-0950   A 24-hour bilingual information and referral service.

The Sundown Line—2' 3-974-1234
Also known as the Public Social Services Department's After-Hours Information and Referral, this is an emergency number with hours of 5 P.M.–8 A.M. weekdays, and 24 hours weekends and holidays.

HOTLINES AND EMERGENCY LINES

The Help Line—213-482-8000 Provides information, referrals, crisis intervention, and counseling 24 hours a day, seven days a week. The Help Line in Pasadena (449-4500) provides contact with the eight other Help Lines in the area and the 100 lines nationwide.

Santa Monica/Westside Hotline—213-394-3577 (39-HELPS) A volunteer hotline servicing Malibu to Culver City. "Listeners" provide help, both with "active" listening and by creating a supportive and encouraging climate in which the caller feels safe to explore his or her problem. Active 24 hours a day, seven days a week.

Torrance/South Bay Hotline—213-541-2525 Referral and counseling, all crises; 24 hours a day, seven days a week.

Suicide Prevention Center—213-381-5111, 213-386-5111 Counseling and referrals to appropriate therapists or clinics; 24 hours a day, seven days a week.

Nar-Anon Families—213-547-5800 Self-help group for family and friends of drug addicts; 24 hours a day, seven days a week.

Alcoholics Anonymous — 213-387-8316 (L.A.), 213-988-3001 (S.F. Valley)

Al-Anon—213-387-3158 Referral of families of alcoholics to Al-Anon and Alateen; Mon.–Fri., 9 A.M.–5 P.M..

PCP Hotline–213-295-3231 Provides basic information, methods to "come down" from PCP experience, and referral for further help; Mon.–Fri., 8 A.M.–6 P.M.

Youth Contact (Drug Help)—213-988-8050 Counseling and referral of drug users for further help; Mon.–Fri., 9 A.M.–5 P.M.

Child Abuse Hotline—213-989-3157 Free shelter care provided; 24 hours a day, seven days a week.

Child Abuse Hotline—Ask Operator for Zenith 2-1234 Handles public complaints of child abuse; makes protective service report to the district, and, if necessary, to law enforcement officers. Also referral and crisis counseling.

National Runaway Switchboard—1-800-621-4000 Completely confidential referral and information service for runaway youths. Also provides message and conferencing-messages service. Active 24 hours a day, seven days a week.

ON A CHEERIER NOTE:

The Butterball "Turkey Talkline"—1-800-323-4848 A save-the-bird service for Thanksgiving and Christmas cooks, operating November 2 through December 31. Swift and Company home economists will answer all questions on buying, thawing, stuffing, roasting, etc. (We just *had* to put this one in!)

9.

THE BEST OF THE WORST

WORST WALK AFTER 6:30 P.M.

Radio Walk Take Franklin Avenue east into Silverlake over the Shakespeare steeple bridge, up the hill and watch for the street sign across from 3863 Franklin that marks Radio Walk. There's something about this two-block length of seemingly purposeless steep concrete stairs that is appealing, especially at night, when most of your long descent is in pitch darkness, with overgrown foliage and trees providing the perfect location for senseless murder.

L.A.'S RUDEST WAITRESS — A TRIBUTE

There are many of them out there, we know, pens poised like daggers over quivering order pads, eyes glis-tening with contempt, feet tapping with impatience. But one in particular will never be forgotten. Her name is Carol and she was last seen at Ship's Coffee Shop in Westwood, dishing out more than just food. A patron is to Carol what a workout bag is to Larry Holmes; she thrusts and heaves at you with lightning consistency. "Can't you read?" for instance, is just Carol's way of saying "hello." Other memorable punches include:

To the guy who asked what kind of pie was available: "Apple, cherry, blueberry, and banana—just like it ways on the menu, *stupid!*"

And to the woman who asked for directions: "Do I look like a road map?"

P.S. Since the writing of this, it's come to our attention that Carol is "no longer with" Ship's. Well, maybe she's graduated to the Comedy Store. Or Canter's.

THE WORST CLASSIC RESTAURANTS

Old restaurants are like old people. Some are charming, some cranky; some are clean, some dribble soup. But somewhere in the cosmos there is the unwritten and heretofore unchallenged rule that once a person or a restaurant has survived a certain number of decades, they are immediately accorded the title of *institution* and are thereafter exempt from criticism. Well, we demur. We think it's time to issue long overdue report cards to three vastly overrated classic L.A. eateries.

Canter's has been broadcasting deli and pastry since 1922. Take out the "since" and substitute "from" and you might have an explanation for the whipped cream cake, which is dry, or, on occasion, moldy, and the waitresses, who are perennially in the throes of menopause. 419 N. Fairfax Ave., Los Angeles.

The Apple Pan has been serving its famous Hickory Burgers and apple pie "since 1947." Big deal. The burgers are greasy, the hickory sauce no longer a thrill, and the apple pie à la mode is certainly not worth $2.20. The best thing in the house is the view of the roaches, perched admiringly over the open grill. 10801 W. Pico Blvd., Westwood.

C.C. Brown's apparently covered the market on the most sensational hot fudge to light up your life and clog up your intestines in 1906. Seventy-odd years later, this magic recipe is still functioning, but you need a magnifying glass to find your sundae and a Swiss bank account to cover your bill. The service is also nonexistent, so be sure to bring a sleeping bag. 7007 Hollywood Blvd., Hollywood.

WORST MOVIE AUDIENCE

The World Theater Have you always wanted to watch a movie in a nursery? How about in a Greyhound bus station? Well lucky you, the World Theater, replete with screaming babies and snoring winos, offers both! Entire extended families from little junior to great grandpa flock to the World on weekend nights to see three movies for $2.50; that's 84¢ a movie. Basically, the audience is predominantly that section of the Los Angeles populace who can afford Jordache jeans but not babysitters. And if you become bored with the films, there's plenty to occupy your time. You can join in one of the numerous discussion groups around, share a homemade chicken dinner with a neighbor, or place bets on the children running races in the aisles. Should your activities separate you from your date, rest easy. It is considered quite chic to stand up on your seat and yell, "Hey, Betty Weimer, where are you?" So, if you regret missing the Romans feeding the Christians to the lions or if you just need a place to sleep for the night, try a movie at the World. Hollywood Blvd. at Gower, Hollywood.

WORST LAUNDROMAT

The Washamatic at 43rd Avenue and Figueroa Street Laundromats are rooms of gloom, and only out of dire necessity should anyone pay a visit. Most of these washing emporiums attract people at their worst: dressed in the dregs of their wardrobes, everyone seems to be in a mental funk. The machines whirl away, the dryers heat the room to the stifling point, and the children do their best to turn the joint into a raucous romper room. Bad, huh? Imagine a laundromat where only a third of the washing machines are ever without weeks-old dirty water gracing their innards, the dryers go 'round and 'round but without heat, and the dazed customers resemble the holding tank of county jail. There are probably dozens of laundromats like this, but none worse than this. The only repairman who ever enters the place is there strictly to collect the coins, and the yellowish light throws off a cancer wardlike effect for the confused customers. Even the graffiti covering all the walls is illegible. The one redeeming feature is the taco truck parked outside. If you can't leave with clean clothes, at least you can always eat.

MOST EXPENSIVE IMAGINARY MEAL

Michael's The chic, tailored presentation that is part and parcel of the nouvelle cuisine rage of the last five years reaches absurd lengths at Michael's, where it is not pleasant to mistake your entree for garnish—especially when the bill of upwards of $100 for a dinner for two arrives near the infamous plate. We don't mind paying for quality, mind you, but this price is just a bit excessive for outright culinary illusion. On the other hand, we could be polite and say that if you're on a 40-calorie-a-day diet, Michael's is bliss. 1147 Third St., Santa Monica.

THE UNTIDY BOWL AWARD

The Hollywood Bowl This is the place that our local music critic recently dubbed "The Cahuenga Pass Picnic Club." This is where the music lovers gather to dine al fresco with a musical accompaniment. Concertgoers here are so attuned to music that they often tune up along with the orchestra, using instruments like paper sacks, plastic bags, crinkly foil, pop tops, wine corks, ice chests, and Kentucky Colonel boxes. Besides the tune-along, these folks practice the hum-along, clap-along, and incessant talk-along. You can absolutely count on one of the following diversions during any melodic passage:
1. Wine bottles rolling down cement stairs—thonka, thonka, crash.
2. Bored children running up and

down those same stairs.

3. Premature applause.

4. Applause for any loud or fast music. Also yipping, howling, and cries of "All *right*!"

5. Stampedes to the exit any time after intermission.

Someone has even reported that in the middle of Ravel's *Daphnis et Chloé*, a sports fan clutching a transistor radio yelled, "A home run with bases loaded! We won!"

What's next for bowl culture? Personal TVs and portable video games?

MOST DISAPPOINTING CLEAVAGE

Elvira Interruptus of the Dark. Everybody worshipped Vampira, some still do, and it was past time for a ghoul-host revival. Even the cleavage is cool, a little sex with your terror. But that's the problem: the theme music is scary, the atmosphere tolerable, but then she opens her mouth and begins her standup routine.

RUDEST CLERK

This dishonorable mention goes straight to the voluptuous blonde ticket agent at PSA Airlines who scolded a blind man because he couldn't read the TV screen. When the man inquired about his gate number, Miss PSA pointed to the overhead monitor. "Can't you read?"

"No," the man replied. "I'm blind."

"Well, that's not *my* problem."

WORST MINIATURE GOLF

Castle Park Miniature Golf For those with happy memories of Putt-Putt golf, a word to the wise: the Castle Park course in Redondo Beach is about as much fun as playing in rush-hour traffic. First, the greens are designed with the patient in mind, and are usually packed way beyond the pleasure point. If your idea of jollies is waiting in line with stoned teenagers, crying kids, and sundry social rejects, this place is the perfect training ground. The holes apparently were created by a frustrated amusement park designer, with balls disappearing everywhere in windmills and lighthouses. The trick, of course, is they never show up again. The "greens" themselves are a charming mix of concrete and carpet, with enough potholes to keep a street repair crew busy for a week. Miniature golf should be kept simple: a few loop-de-loops, an over-the-water hole or two, and, horrors, maybe even a straightaway shot here and there. At Castle Park none of this seems to matter when you notice that the huge clubhouse is a screaming madhouse of video-game addicts. 2410 Compton Blvd., Redondo Beach.

WORST ARCHITECTURE

The **Brotman Medical Complex** in Culver City, on beautiful Venice Boulevard, renders the descriptive powers of the English language inadequate. The entire north wall of this ten-story building is a glass and brick facade with an occasional colored cube—a sleazy tribute to Mondrian. At night, lit from within, the wall looks like an enlargement of a dirty screen door. The hospital, located just behind, on Delmas Terrace, seems to have sprouted from the same mind that brought us Osko's Disco on La Cienega. It's highlighted by a multistoried "bay" window containing glass panes in the shape of kitchen cabinet doors. The main building, laid out in the shape of an ×, appears to have been cut out with pinking shears. The whole thing is so cheap looking, you definitely wouldn't want to be anywhere near it when a strong wind blows. Actually, it looks like the prefab castle a nouveau riche oil sheik might build on Mt. Olympus (another dubious architectural achievement off Laurel Canyon) if he had to house 200 relatives.

WORST SCULPTURE IN THE WORLD

The Wilshire House's Chicken Claw On the northwest corner of Wilshire and Westholme sits the already legendary chicken claw sculpture, a 25-foot-tall clay-looking monstrosity announcing the grand entrance to another supposedly posh Wilshire corridor high-rise condominium project called The Wilshire House. The developer's wife is reportedly a society art collector and actually commissioned the artist for this special project. The results have to be seen to be believed.

WORST BANK SCULPTURE

Wells Fargo Looming in the dark and sterile plaza outside the Wells Fargo Bank are four shiny aluminum "things." Somewhere between 12 and 80 feet tall, they resemble pieces of gigantic kindergarten play equipment. A monstrous sandpail, a set of rectangular blocks, a great cone, and a tent-shaped, well, *thing*. Upon inquiry, the bank's receptionist informed us with great pride that this was the grand opening of the Wells Fargo Sculpture Museum. Soon to be included is the original Wells Fargo coach. Norton Simon, move over. Fifth St. and Figueroa (across from the Bonaventure Hotel), downtown.

WORST BANK ART, OR L.A.'S ANSWER TO MOMA

First Los Angeles Bank Situated in posh Arco Plaza, the First Los Angeles Bank is a happy monument to questionable taste in modern art. They're very proud of their collection, most of which looks like the results of a pie-throwing contest. Colors splash and spurt along the walls like uncontrollable children on the beach. Particularly eye-catching is a huge canvas with a pink X splattered across it. The really sobering thing is not the mere existence of such a monster piece, but the fact that someone's desk actually faces it, day in and day out. Arco Plaza, downtown.

WORST METHOD FOR INTERRUPTING MOVIES FOR COMMERCIALS

KABC is a butcher. They indiscriminately hack to pieces every movie they've ever shown. Until the press got wind of it, they were going to show *Lawrence of Arabia,* originally 222 minutes long, in a two-hour time slot. They are insane! *Bye Bye Birdie* is always shown in a 90-minute time slot; the movie runs 111 minutes in original form. Their worst crime is the incredibly annoying commercial breaks. These geeks don't care if someone happens to be in the middle of a sentence, or you've just witnessed a downbeat or depressing dialogue. They have only one tune to lead you into or out of a commercial break and that is *the most obnoxious blaring racket* you have ever heard.

WORST TV SCHEDULING PRACTICES

Channel 13 Whoever schedules movies for KCOP must be a real sadistic mother. They have a great library of horror classics (*The Creeping Terror, Whatever Happened to Baby Jane?, Hush, Hush Sweet Charlotte,* and the immortal *Twisted Brain* amongst 'em), but insist on showing the same four or five movies week after week, month after month. *Dear, Dead Delilah* has been on 20 times this year; no lie, check your back issues. One night their tired print is literally going to dissolve on the air from overuse. Among the worn out are *Point Of Terror, Decoy For Terror, Plan Nine, Big Foot,* and *Dementia 13.*

Index